RECONSTRUCTING
PUBLIC
PHILOSOPHY

RECONSTRUCTING PUBLIC PHILOSOPHY

WILLIAM M. SULLIVAN

UNIVERSITY OF CALIFORNIA PRESS

Berkeley   Los Angeles   London

University of California Press
Berkeley and Los Angeles, California
University of California Press, Ltd.
London, England
© 1982 by The Regents of the University of California
Printed in the United States of America
1   2   3   4   5   6   7   8   9

Library of Congress Cataloging in Publication Data

Sullivan, William M.
   Reconstructing public philosophy.

   Includes index.
   1. Political science—United States.   2. Liberalism—United States.   I. Title.
JA84.U5S92   320.5′1′0973   81-16418
ISBN 0-520-04488-6   AACR2

To my mother, and in memory of my father

Contents

Foreword

Even though academic philosophers talk mainly to each other (as do scholars in most disciplines), William Sullivan suggests that philosophical presuppositions and arguments play an important part in our public life. In this book he examines some of the best writing on public policy and on the moral and political grounds for public policy and discovers that it reflects the prevailing liberal individualism which is such an important strand of American culture generally. In displaying the weaknesses in the writings he discusses, he is engaging simultaneously in philosophical criticism and cultural criticism. In short, he is interested not only in the arguments put forward by some of our most sophisticated liberal theorists but also in their writings as a lens through which to view aspects of our society and culture. The result is a book that moves easily between philosophy and sociology, and illuminates both our present social condition and our ability to think about it.

Though recognizing the centrality of liberal individualism at the moment, Sullivan points out that it is far from the only tradition upon which Americans can draw. He calls our attention to the tradition of civic republicanism, with its classical roots and its important contributions at earlier points in our own history as a republic. In this connection his work has a recognizable continuity with that of Hannah Arendt. From another angle it is interesting to think of *Reconstructing Public Philosophy* as complementary to Alisdair MacIntyre's recent *After Virtue* (University of Notre Dame Press, 1981). MacIntyre, another philosopher who moves easily in the realm of sociology, is concerned primarily with moral philosophy, but, as Aristotle taught us, ethics and politics are part of a single whole. Just as MacIntyre's volume has important implications for social thought, so Sullivan deals with problems of morality and virtue. Sullivan is, on the whole, more explicit about what the public and political implications of the classical tradition are for today; both authors, however, emphasize that the philosopher writes from within a specific social context and must always attend to the social and historical sources of his thought.

Reconstructing Public Philosophy has a close connection to a research project in which Sullivan and I are both currently engaged, a project that is in some ways a logical next step from this book. It is a study of "The Moral Basis of Social Commitment in America" and includes interviews with citizens in several parts of the United States in an effort to understand what public involvement means to them and why some of them remain so aloof from it. We are discovering among ordinary citizens fundamental conceptions of the individual and society, latent "public philosophies," that are continuous with the self-conscious and explicit traditions considered in this book. We have found that those to whom we have been talking have welcomed the chance to exchange views and clarify ideas with our interviewers.

If, as Sullivan argues, radical individualism has just about played itself out as a philosophical option and as a principle for the organization of social life, as Hegel, Tocqueville, and other social philosophers long ago predicted it would, then we Americans are greatly in need of somewhere to turn. In this situation *Reconstructing Public Philosophy* has much to offer.

Sullivan is incisive in his criticism but generous in spirit to those he criticizes, frequently finding in them the germs of more fruitful alternatives. But it is for its positive contribution, its firm delineation of what a revived public philosophy might look like, that this book is most to be valued. Sullivan has given us a profoundly hopeful book. At the moment in which we live, that is no small thing.

Robert N. Bellah

Preface

This book began to take shape in the late 1970s as the shocks of the 1960s—Vietnam and its aftermath—were giving rise to a new concern with the American political heritage. Some responses to the Bicentennial of the Revolution were marked by the kind of disillusionment with the Cold War consensus that had been evident in the previous decade, but this disillusionment now sought direction by turning to elements of the American tradition nearly forgotten in the post-war era. For many, the warring Enlightenment faiths of liberal individualism, bureaucratic expertise, and a mechanistic Marxism seemed less a range of options than symptoms of the exhaustion of political imagination. This book attempts to explore another American vision, one not so much new as offering hope for renewal.

A living culture is a conversation in many voices, often conflicting, about a common way of life and destiny. As a society, the United States has sustained, and has been sustained by, a dramatic argument over the meaning of its self-identification as a free land. Our political culture, particularly our characteristic language of public life, has remained since its beginnings plurivocal. Beside the accents of the Enlightenment philosophy of liberal individualism, which casual observers have sometimes taken to be *the* spirit of American laws, there has continued a counterpoint of civic ideals that speak of the public realm as at least a potential commonwealth. In opposition to liberal individualism, civic republicanism has envisioned the end of politics as the realization of a public good that is more than the sum of individual wants and desires. It speaks for political life as a project to achieve such ends as security and justice, as leading to the enjoyment by citizens of this achievement, that is to say, as leading to public happiness.

The argument of the book can be stated simply. To realize the nation's central value of popular self-rule, a renewed democratic political life of active citizenship and enlightened discussion is needed, and that in turn requires an expanded political culture, a public philosophy.

Philosophic liberalism, the set of beliefs common to the Liberal and Conservative tendencies of post-New Deal American politics, is deeply anti-public in its fundamental premises. Conceiving of human beings as exclusively and unchangeably self-regarding, liberal philosophy has viewed human association as a kind of necessary evil and politics as an arena in which the clashes of individual and group interest can be more or less civilly accommodated. As a philosophy of government and social life, liberalism exalts both the supremacy of private self-interest and the development of institutional means for pursuing those interests. In its extreme forms, this philosophy denies meaning and value to even the notion of common purpose, or politics in its classic sense.

The dominance of liberal individualism in American public life is reflected in our institutional arrangements and in the language we use for discussing matters of public import. Because of this inheritance Americans have had to struggle to develop what slender common understandings they could in order to maintain an imperfect union and sustain vital public undertakings. The typically American way of accommodating conflicting interests has been the liberal strategy of separating the different, of drawing military, legal, or cultural boundaries and trusting to various kinds of open frontiers—and, occasionally, force—to prevent fatal clashes.

Yet no nation could remain a self-governing, communicating whole if it were only a precarious assemblage of mutually suspicious segments. Whatever may have been the case in the early years of the republic, in our own time there is a clear lack of fit between the segmental individualism rooted in liberal culture and the overwhelming fact of interdependency that has for some time characterized nearly every aspect of our national society. Recognition of the incongruity between our dominant liberal political culture

and our social, international, and environmental situation was
fended off in the post-war era by the relative success of a govern-
ment-managed strategy for corporate economic growth, but even
in those palmier days social critics such as Walter Lippmann saw
that a society dominated by liberal premises had few resources for
dealing with the stresses bound to attend the inevitable dissatisfaction with those arrangements. However, as a philosophic liberal,
Lippmann could find no "public philosophy" that might command loyalties and orient action except for an invocation of presumed principles of reason known only by the few. What Lippmann's deeply pessimistic—he would have said, realistic—conception recognized is that liberal individualism cannot provide a
convincing conception of a common good. That realization,
sharpened by our experience of the relative ease and success of
nationalistic propaganda in mobilizing and compelling an apparent public consensus, suggests that our present situation holds
great potential for tragedy.

If the period of American world dominance is receding and the
economic boom of the post-war years is past, then desire for social
stability, even barring military adventurism, could push the United
States toward an imposed "public purpose" concordant with the
interests of our dominant social groups, organized under the rubric
of "prosperity," national interest, or security. Philosophic liberalism, for all its rhetoric of freedom, provides few resources for
avoiding such an outcome. It is ultimately these very practical
reasons which give urgency to the conceptual and philosophic
task of formulating a genuine public philosophy that can provide
a reasoned basis for a new ethic of equity and cooperation.

Given the specificities of American institutional and cultural
tradition, our best hope for renewing public philosophy may lie
in reassessing and recovering our civic republican heritage. In this
book I try to provide reasons for thinking that the ethical vision
underlying that tradition, so long under the shadow of liberal
individualism, is still available to us and, indeed, is operative in
the interstices of liberal culture, even though it remains conceptually fragmentary and undeveloped. This task demands an approach philosophically different from the model of inquiry typical
of Enlightenment science. I have attempted to begin recasting in
contemporary idiom a tradition of practical reason that reaches
back to Aristotle and receives a suggestive echo in the work of John

Dewey. Standing within our present situation, I seek to understand the incoherence of contemporary public language by reconstructing a partially lost and suppressed form of speech and practice. It is an interpretive effort that cannot help but be, however, imperfectly, philosophical and historical at once. It is an attempt, and an invitation, to understand ourselves better by reinvigorating an important tradition within American public discourse.

This book has been a more collaborative effort than its authorship indicates. The project was seeded indirectly by a fellowship from the National Endowment for the Humanities in 1976/77. It came to completion several years later while I was investigating reasoning about public matters through interviews with numerous fellow citizens. That project was also supported by the NEH and by the Ford and Rockefeller foundations. I am grateful for the opportunities such support provided.

The book grew from many conversations and I am grateful to a number of friends and colleagues for having read all or parts of the manuscript, as well as for having provided criticism and encouragement. I owe Robert N. Bellah special thanks for his generosity as both colleague and friend. I have benefited immensely from a long and continuing conversation with him about the concerns of the book. I want to express my thanks to Richard Madsen, Michael Maccoby, Dennis McGrath, Robert Neville, and Ralph Potter, as well as to David Rabaut, Paul Rabinow, Edward Schwartz, Ann Swidler, Steven Tipton, Gwendolyn Wright Rabinow, and, in a special way, John Van Cott and Maureen Sullivan.

The manuscript could never have been completed without the extraordinary typing and editorial abilities of Laola Hironaka and the gracious assistance of Eugenie T. Bruck. Finally, I want to thank Grant Barnes, Executive Editor, and Sheila Levine of the University of California Press. None of the book's faults, but many of its virtues, are due to their able and judicious editorial support.

Introduction

:: I

The passion that made America, wrote Robinson Jeffers, was
the love of freedom. The republic was born not to prosperity but
to a kind of virtue which the poet thought ultimately incompatible
with luxury. Jeffers was knowingly restating a long tradition of
republican wisdom that sees a self-governing community, one
whose public life embodies and in turn enhances the moral qualities of its members' lives, as a great yet precarious human achievement. Jeffers's own pessimism about America's future prospects
led him to the ironic counsel: "Keep the tradition, conserve the
forms, the observances, keep the spot sore. Be great, carve deep
your heelmarks."[1] That doom of the American republic to which
Jeffers was alluding is the tragic fate of republics, retold by the
same republican tradition: the weakening of the intensity of concern for the public weal under the impact of pursuit of self-
interest and particular advantage. The result is a national life
"heavily thickening into empire," in which "protest, only a bub-
ble in the molten mass, pops and sighs out, and the mass hardens."

The pessimism Jeffers expressed about the vitality of citizenship and the future of self-governing institutions in America has
been relatively rare in American history. Certainly in this century
the belief that economic abundance and republican vitality go

1. Robinson Jeffers, "Shine, Republic" (1934) and "Shine, Perishing Republic"
(1925), in *Robinson Jeffers: Selected Poems* (New York: Random House/Vintage,
1965), pp. 9, 7.

hand-in-hand has been widespread. And this majority view has gained considerable credibility from the nation's history, which has been, relative to many other lands, a happy one. American society has been able to absorb large numbers of diverse groups and to manage significant social and political conflict with considerable success, even taking into account the great breakdown of the Civil War. The nation has been able to fulfill for many its promise, not just of material cornucopia, but of a society that accords self-respect and dignity to its citizens. Though the dream of American democracy has been deformed by racism and prejudice of various stripes, these attitudes have been regarded at least as national scandals and have rendered uneasy the public conscience. Yet by using value-laden terms of the republican heritage, casting America's developed market economy and status as a world power as dangerous tendencies toward luxury and empire, Jeffers's language brings into relief the ambiguity of the American dream.

The celebrated pluralism of the twentieth-century United States has been possible largely due to the availability of land and, above all, due to the development of a highly productive market economy. The political arrangements of the federal constitution played a real part in this process, but very often the political institutions of law and administration have operated to facilitate market economic growth. The protection and advancement of civil rights, particularly of the rights of economically and socially disfavored groups, has been the other major task of national government, and this task has often clashed with the goals of economic development of the capitalist market system. So long as the growth of that system seemed assured and so long as that growth provided the prospect of material betterment as the reward of individual economic effort, there seemed to many little reason to question that democratic self-government would flow naturally from a focus on competitive individual economic achievement. The dominant weight of public opinion in this century, even among reformers, has been laid on that framework.

Of course, by no means all Americans believed that self-governance and the equal dignity of citizens would result in any natural way from the operations of a competitive economic order. Particularly after the great concentrations of economic power in the Gilded Age, movements made up of citizens disadvantaged in the

increasingly unequal economic market rallied to the causes of
Populism and Socialism, which aimed to bring economic life within the direct control of self-governing, popular institutions. However, it proved possible to accommodate many of the demands of
those movements within the framework of a national economy
directed by large economic concentrations. The Progressives
sought to manage these economic developments and their concomitant social dislocations politically, by means of enlightened
public administration and regulation. Later, reforms begun by the
New Deal continued this trend, using public administration to
check and coordinate private economic institutions. New Deal
Liberalism also focused on aiding disadvantaged groups to enter
the private economy while directly caring for those unable to compete in the market. But changes in the structure of the American
economy and major alterations in the international situation have
undermined the basis of these reforms by slowing economic growth
in ways that have upset the old hope that growth must benefit all,
even if in differing degrees.

During the decade just past, a series of military, political, and
economic shocks, as well as awareness of ecological limitations,
ended the optimistic vision of continuous economic and social
progress for American society. The energy crisis and slower growth
have meant that the gains of some have increasingly come to mean
the losses of others. This situation has created doubt about the
future. Various groups are struggling to increase their relative
advantage in a suddenly more constricted arena at a time when
Americans have grown increasingly skeptical about their leaders
and public institutions. Skepticism in turn has bred a narrow and
often mean-spirited concentration on immediate self-interest that
portends a social and political stalemate.[2]

It is now clear that any future improvement in the status of the
less advantaged, and even the maintenance of social decency, will
require conscious political resolution. Achievement of effective
social equity can no longer be entrusted to market forces unguided

2. These trends have recently been perceptively examined from different con-
ceptual and political points of view by the sociologist Morris Janowitz and the
economist Lester C. Thurow. See Morris Janowitz, *The Last Half Century: Societal
Change and Politics in America* (Chicago: University of Chicago Press, 1979) and
Lester C. Thurow, *The Zero-Sum Society: Distribution and the Possibilities for
Economic Change* (New York: Basic Books, 1980).

by a political commitment to the general welfare. The troubling question is what aspects of our national life and traditions we can draw upon to meet these challenges of the late twentieth century while maintaining and revitalizing our commitment to an active, democratic self-governance.

The difficulty of the situation makes the reasons for Jeffers's pessimism less remote than they probably seemed to many when he wrote. The ambiguity of America's greatness has always been the coexistence of an economic life of private self-interest with a public commitment to justice and the common welfare. The contradiction between the inducements to acquisitive competition provided by the open frontier, on the one hand, and the moral bases of a cooperative public order, on the other, gave rise to both anxiety and militant criticism as early as the Puritan settlement of New England.[3] However, to many European and some American observers, the nation's ethos has appeared so monochromatically individualistic and obsessed by the pursuit of wealth that the resiliency and openness of the society seemed fated to follow the fortunes of a dynamic capitalism. For such social analysts, America's lack of a feudal past has both fostered the capitalist spirit of individual enterprise and eliminated the cultural bases for a collective approach to resolving social problems.[4] From that perspective the closing of the frontier of cheap energy and resources is likely to mean either social disintegration or authoritarian rule; hence the urgency of the search for a social and cultural basis for a new sense of citizenship and the common good in contemporary America.

:: II

Certainly the individualism of American culture is deeply rooted and pronounced, especially compared to European societies. Indeed, American individualism was "discovered" and entered into popular understanding on both sides of the Atlantic largely through the work of a European observer, Alexis de Tocqueville,

3. See Wilson Carey McWilliams, *The Idea of Fraternity in America* (Berkeley: University of California Press, 1973), pp. 640ff.

4. Louis Hartz argued this thesis in his highly influential work *The Liberal Tradition in America: An Interpretation of American Political Thought since the Revolution* (New York: Harcourt, Brace, World, 1955).

whose characterization of American civilization has continued to frame discussion for a century and a half. Yet Tocqueville's highly nuanced interpretation of the nation he visited during the Jacksonian 1830s reveals a picture more complex than simply an anarchic society of self-interested individuals. Tocqueville was heavily influenced by the tradition of republican political thought, particularly as it had been elaborated by the Baron de Montesquieu and Jean Jacques Rousseau during the previous century.[5] From that tradition Tocqueville drew his insight that a political regime is closely related to the nature of the society in which it exists and to the character of its members. His premise was that success in maintaining a democratic republic is tied to the maintenance of its moral basis, which he saw as the "mores" or "habits of the heart" shaping the dispositions of individuals in action.

Tocqueville judged the United States of the 1830s as a successful experiment in republican self-rule. It had resisted the entropic pull toward anarchy and despotism which had fatally hobbled his native France both under the Old Regime and during its lurch through successive revolutions and reactions. He sought the reasons for America's relative success in the particular pattern of American mores. At their best, Tocqueville argued, American conditions combine a normative tradition of public concern, rooted in both religious life and local political activity, with personal interests to produce the public-spiritedness which institutions of collective self-governance require.

The free institutions of the United States and the political rights enjoyed there provide a thousand continual reminders to every citizen that he lives in society. At every moment they bring his mind back to this idea, that it is the duty as well as the interest of men to be useful to their fellows. Having no particular reason to hate others, since he is neither their slave nor their master, the American's heart easily inclines toward benevolence. At first it is of necessity that men attend to the public interest, afterward by choice. What had been calculation becomes instinct. By dint of working for the good of his fellow citizens, he in the end acquires the habit and taste for serving them.[6]

5. The best overall presentation of the modern republican tradition to date is J.G.A. Pocock's *The Machiavellian Moment: Florentine Political Thought and the Atlantic Republican Tradition* (Princeton, New Jersey: Princeton University Press, 1975).

6. Alexis de Tocqueville, *Democracy in America*, translated by George Lawrence (Garden City, New York: Doubleday Anchor, 1969), pp. 512-13.

In this way the institutions of local government gave otherwise self-interested and private persons a practical education in citizenship.

The relative equality Tocqueville observed in Jacksonian America was based on the economic independence characteristic of a society of farmers and artisans, in which the face-to-face community of the small town provided the social context for democratic self-rule. In Tocqueville's America the basic unit of both economic and political life was the local community. It was to the relatively egalitarian and autonomous mores of local life that Tocqueville traced the foundation of citizenship and individual dignity in America. There the individual acquisitiveness stirred by commerce was controlled and counterbalanced by the religious ethic of stewardship and a civic culture of initiative and communal responsibility nurtured through custom and personal ties. As a student of Montesquieu and especially of Rousseau, Tocqueville was highly sensitive to the tense and contradictory relationship between "commerce" and the republican spirit, between the citizen and the bourgeois, private man. Indeed, his great anxiety was that the tense and precarious balance between these two poles in America would gradually shift in the direction of an exclusive concern for individual advancement.

The inevitable result of an unrestrained pursuit of private betterment, Tocqueville thought, would be the sapping of the civic ethos and, with that, the atrophy of democratic institutions. But the final consequence of such a development would itself be ironic —not greater freedom for all, but acquiescence in a despotism that could provide the conditions for private well-being which the isolated citizens could no longer provide for themselves. In fact, Tocqueville noted with apprehension two forms of organization in the United States of his day which he judged seriously to threaten civic culture. One was the slave society of the South; the other was the new industrial factories. These latter Tocqueville feared would give rise to a petty despotism of owners and managers, exercised on concentrated masses of poor and dependent workers. The traumatic civil war that destroyed the slave society had also greatly furthered the growth of the industrial and commercial structures which undermined the pattern of town democracy.

Still, Tocqueville anticipated not a sudden and violent change but a gradual and almost unnoticed spread of despotic control. He envisioned a despotism which "does not break men's will, but softens, bends, and guides it, so that it hinders, restrains, enervates, stifles and stultifies" by keeping the pursuits of individuals purely private ones. This atomizing of society he thought could be accomplished "more easily than is generally supposed, with some of the external forms of freedom," so that it has "a possibility of getting itself established even under the shadow of the sovereignty of the people."[7] Tocqueville felt compelled to warn not of the danger of a despotic conspiracy but of the entropic course of political drift in a society in which the spirit of capitalism developed unchecked and uncivilized by political understanding. Like Jeffers, Tocqueville restated a warning derived from meditation on the fate of commercial republics.

While that grim rhetoric of impending despotism has an upsetting ring of truth to it and leaves no room for easy complacency, it is not yet a description of American reality. The intent of Tocqueville's reflections was both admonition and pedagogy: to point out what can and must be done to counter the trends he described as possibilities. He realized, as more naive lamenters of the individualist ethos often have not, that the mores of individualism, which accustom persons to living with no concern beyond their own welfare, are themselves social, collective developments.[8] In modern societies increasingly organized and coordinated by market processes, this development of individualistic and acquisitive mores has not required conscious public consensus, although those practices have often been championed with self-conscious plan and effort. However, the practices of citizenship and self-government, precisely because they run counter to the commercial ethos, do require conscious, collective cultivation to flourish under modern conditions. Indeed, attempts to strengthen resistance to the commercializing process have formed opposition movements ranging from populism and socialism to more moderate reform efforts.

But Tocqueville was not Marx. He did not seek, and does not seem to have imagined under modern conditions, a social organization of production based upon an ethic of participation and responsibility that could substantially replace the market. Rather, he feared the administrative apparatus of the state as merely intensifying the tendency toward the breakdown of communal organization already occurring under the impact of commerce. He sought

7. Ibid., pp. 692-93.   8. See ibid., pp. 690ff.

to counter that trend in ways that could draw upon the bedrock of strongly developed moral practices in everyday life. America might be successful in preserving a self-governing society because in America administrative centralization was so little developed and met considerable resistance from the kind of popular republicanism he described. Tocqueville's warnings about an "industrial feudalism" coming from the factory system should be seen in this context.[9] The great danger of capitalist society was its tendency to generate conflict and defensive isolation, so that it prepared the political basis for centralizing administration which could maintain private benefits, at least for some, at the price of genuine participation and self-determination.

Today, amid the crisis of American institutions, there are still strong intimations that our society has not succumbed to passivity. Criticism of the bureaucratic structures of corporate capitalism and a government policy primed to corporate priorities has again become strong. While many citizens have confirmed Tocqueville's fears by reacting in narrow-sighted and even mean-spirited ways to contemporary problems, others are raising questions that suggest an ethos of mutual concern rather than egotistic individualism. There is a renewed interest in restructuring economic and social institutions that is propelled by a new vitality in movements of citizen participation, of the disadvantaged as well as the more affluent. There is also a spread of interest in ecological ways of thinking, which stress interdependence, nurture, and responsibility rather than competition and control. These developments suggest a continuity in the bedrock of mores that could support a reconstruction of a consensual understanding of politics.

Any society seeking to organize itself for self-government requires a widespread diffusion of habits and skills of active citizenship such as Tocqueville described. This is particularly true for a territorially large and socially diverse nation like the United States. The distinctive feature of republican political life is its dependence not only on participation in public institutional forms but also on

9. Tocqueville's analysis of the French difficulty in replacing the despotism of the Old Regime with a consensual order of public participation emphasized not the political economy but the atomization of French society under the old system, which destroyed the social basis for post-revolutionary solidarity. See *The Old Regime and the French Revolution*, translated by Stuart Gilbert (Garden City, New York: Doubleday Anchor, 1955), esp. pp. 117-19, 137.

the more diffuse quality of public communication and understanding. That burden cannot be carried alone by the administrative organization of the state, staffed by professional functionaries, without undermining the very nature of self-government. Traditional republican teaching affirmed that great wealth and extreme poverty and intensely adversarial relationships among social groups were all dangerous. In the context of a commercial society, economic dislocation and unpredictable shifts in relationship among social groups generate in the individual a sense of isolation and powerlessness. To combat those tendencies sympathetic critics such as Tocqueville reaffirmed the importance of active civic associations and political organizations as forums in which an understanding of the meaning of citizenship could be developed on a face-to-face basis.

Associations were to provide regular opportunities for opinion to be intelligently and publicly shaped and for learning and passing on the subtle habits of public initiative and responsibility. And despite both the development of the mass media and the tremendous encroachments of large bureaucratic organizations upon decisions that affect the lives of citizens, Americans are still publicly active. However, in the face of the continued weakening of political parties, the decline of organized labor, and the breakup of established coalitions, the effectiveness of political organization is closely linked to the development and maintenance of a widely shared sense of political meaning and direction. That general understanding needs to find expression in a public philosophy.

American politics has suffered from the lack of a continuously developed and coherent public political discourse adequate to the complexities of social and political life. This lack contributes importantly to our present problems. At its best, a public philosophy could provide expression for the meaning and worth of the political commitments embodied in republican institutions and mores. The social task of a public philosophy is critical in a highly differentiated society in which common consensus is always in some measure the achievement of an active process of discussion and persuasion among involved citizens. At its deepest level, a public philosophy is a tradition of interpreting and delineating the common understandings of what the political association is about and what it aims to achieve. In a democratic political tradition such as the American one, this requires developing anew the

understanding that dignity, mutual concern, and a sense of responsibility shared by all members of the society are essential to a
morally worthwhile life. The narrowing of political vision into
the perspective of self-interest alone has hampered this process and
aided the growth of anti-democratic concentrations of economic
power.

A public philosophy, however, must be closely tied to the mores,
the practical understandings of everyday life. If it is to maintain its
authenticity and power to infuse the public acts of individuals
with significance, it can neither be an intellectually detached theory
about politics nor a mere set of slogans. Finally, a public philosophy is both a cause and an effect of awakened discussion of those
things most important and at issue in the life of the nation. What
is ultimately at issue is the radical question of what is a worthwhile life. A republican public philosophy begins with the realization that this is necessarily a public concern, precisely because
human life is interdependent, requiring mutual trust even for
individual survival. However, while this is true for any human
society, a public life develops only when a society realizes that
reciprocity and mutual aid are worthy of cultivation both as good
in themselves and as providing the basis of the individual self.

Seen in this way, a republican public philosophy is a rare and
delicate achievement. The various local and particular communities within the larger American society have each had their own
practical understandings of life. These have received conscious
expression in particular skills and styles of living, in shared moral
sentiments and ideals of character. These are the "little traditions"
in which everyday life is mostly lived. Tocqueville searched among
them in Jacksonian America for the roots of the attitude toward
association, participation, and mutual respect about which the
consciously wrought tradition of republican politics spoke. Part
of what a public philosophy must do is to give more general
expression to these often taken-for-granted understandings, translating into a common language shared moral sentiments which
previously may not have been understood as identical. But at its
best it does more than that: it provides a continuing tradition of
understanding about what it means to be not just a responsible
member of this or that local community or religious tradition or
political group, but a participant in forms of life that are the
common concern of many diverse communities. These are the

forms of republican association, institutions of self-government
that impart practical skills and moral understandings embodied
in reflective citizenship—for example, concern for the welfare and
dignity of citizens who do not share more specific traditions, and a
concern for the common good. This latter concern is the special
focus of republican politics, since the practical task of government
must be to coordinate, adjust, and, if necessary, alter social and
economic differentiations in the interests of equity and the dignity
of all.

In American experience the revolutionary founding remains
the paradigm case of development of an effective public philosophy. There leaders of the movement of resistance to Britain succeeded in integrating the resources of the republican tradition
with popular political and religious aspirations to create a coherent and effective understanding of the revolution as an experiment
in political responsibility. The public intellectuals such as Jefferson, Adams, Paine, and Madison spanned social class, region, and
religion. Because they were able to draw upon common moral
understandings, they were finally successful. But in the process of
struggle and political development they also forged new understandings of citizenship and government which they were able to
render intelligible through the language of revolutionary republicanism.[10] Republicanism gave patriots a public discourse whose
moral conceptions had strong resonances with the biblical religious tradition so important in eighteenth-century America.

The patriots' conception of politics was strongly shaped by
their struggle against what they saw as the despotic policies of the
British Crown. They traced those policies to a moral condition
embodied in institutions that encouraged the untrammeled pursuit of greed and power. For the American republicans, denying
the moral dignity of citizens—a necessary aspect of despotism—
promoted a universal and lawless self-interest in which each pri-

10. This complex process is examined, with a concentration on the development
of republican conceptions of politics, by Gordon S. Wood in *The Creation of the
American Republic: 1776-1787* (Chapel Hill: University of North Carolina Press,
1969).
   For an illuminating case study of the process by which high cultural tradition
and popular understandings were woven together by revolutionary leaders, see Rhys
Isaac, "Preachers and Patriots," in Alfred F. Young, ed., *The American Revolution:
Explorations in the History of American Radicalism* (De Kalb: Northern Illinois
University Press, 1976), pp. 125-50.

vate person aimed at petty tyranny. Republicans threw the epithet "corruption" on this degrading consequence of a political regime bent on empire. Thus a chief concern of revolutionary public philosophy was to avoid at all costs the possibility of despotism and its forerunner, the encouragement of exclusive self-interest. They sought to promote civic virtue through an active public life built up through an egalitarian spirit of self-restraint and mutual aid.

Yet the revolutionary experience proved disillusioning to earnest republicans. There was the persistence of slavery. In a commercial society the active initiative of citizens was continually threatened by the pull of private enrichment through the market. Many republicans searched for institutional means to prevent these tendencies from undermining public commitment. Others such as Madison, Hamilton, and the Federalists, fearful of the instability of republican governments, explicitly urged abandoning the language of civic virtue. They concentrated instead upon creating mechanisms to keep tyranny at bay without requiring common goals or institutions of intense popular participation. These developments had a fateful impact on political life and political discourse in America. The Federalist constitution of 1787 and the language of political mechanics it advanced together institutionalized the notion that politics is a business of balancing interests, leaving the actual formation of interests outside politics proper, in the realm of contractual relations guided by the market. Thus a consistent development of a republican public philosophy was greatly complicated by the establishment of institutions that embodied substantially different political purposes.

Indeed, the novelty of the conception of politics embodied in the Federalist constitution was its assertion that the end of government was not the achievement of a particular moral quality of civic life but, rather, the guarantee of individual security. This was the now familiar idea of philosophical liberalism. Where the civic republicans had emphasized conscious responsibility for the destiny of the political community, the Federalists emphasized the constitution as a framework which could protect the workings of commercially competitive civil society.[11] Republicans valued a

11. These changes in the understanding of republican politics had momentous and not always positive effects for the future of the nation. See Wood's discussion in *Creation of the American Republic*; also Benjamin Barber, "The Compromised

constitution and formally coded laws as ways to institutionalize the equality of citizens. But for the tradition, the meaning of equality was above all else an equality of desire in which citizens foreswore the pursuit of tyranny, of personal aggrandizement at the expense of one's fellows. By contrast, the liberal view took legal equality as a means to enforce fairness in the competition for gain in civil society and as a bulwark against arbitrary rule. The liberal conception drew a firm distinction between public and private realms, thereby gaining autonomy for religious and intellectual as well as economic pursuits. But this reduced the public realm to formal institutions in which the conflicts among the "interests" of civil society were umpired and negotiated, draining public life of intrinsic morality and significance.

The philosophical basis of these developments was the liberal conception of life as essentially a business of individual self-interest, a notion highly compatible with a fundamentally economic and strategic view of human action. It is thus not surprising that popular acceptance of the liberal understanding would truncate development of a public philosophy in America. The dominance of liberal thinking in the nineteenth century meant that the traditional republican search for the social conditions of republican citizenship was unable to find an independent language for its own development. In the programs of the Jeffersonian republicans large parts of the tradition remained vital, but already in the 1830s Tocqueville found the language of individual self-interest ubiquitous, though guided by the civic practice of community democracy into forms of association that outstripped liberal explanation.[12] In part, this was because of the unusually close relationship between biblical religion and civic life in the United States, so that republican themes have often been carried by religious language and practice.[13] However, without an intellectually continuous and coherent development, the republican culture of citizenship has lived from one movement of revitalization to another, as a kind of political underground, often reinvented and partially lost.[14]

Republic," in Robert H. Horwitz, ed., *Moral Foundations of the American Republic* (Charlottesville: University of Virginia Press, 1976), pp. 19-38.

12. See Tocqueville, *Democracy*, vol. II, part II, Ch. 5.

13. Tocqueville returned to this point many times. See also Robert N. Bellah, *The Broken Covenant: American Civil Religion in Time of Trial* (New York: Seabury, 1975).

14. Lawrence Goodwyn has provided a detailed and convincing examination of

Still, while there has been no intellectually continuous republican tradition of importance in American politics, there has been a heavy indirect influence of republican civic culture. In some cases this has been explicitly combined with liberal ideas in public discourse and understanding of politics. But civic republicanism has exerted a more lasting influence less directly, by protecting against the disintegrative tendencies of commercial society. Culturally, republicanism has supplied a crucial context of assumptions about human solidarity absent in liberal thinking. If there is genuine hope for American democracy, it lies in developing a widespread commitment to dignity and justice and making that commitment politically effective. In large measure that is tied to the possibility of our making contact with tacit republican practices and reconstructing a public discourse that can reunite economics, power, and morality.

:: III

There are several ways in which this task of reappropriating American republicanism could be carried out. One is to locate living forms of republican civic practice and understanding so as to rearticulate the meaning of equality and justice for contemporary conditions. That effort would assess and assemble cultural resources in theory and practice. Another approach, particularly appropriate in the present situation, is to begin with the present crisis of confidence and legitimacy that is both cause and effect of the American inability actively to shape economic and social change through public consensus and negotiation. The weakness of our accustomed forms of public discourse is revealed in the poverty of responses to our situation coming from the tradition of philosophical liberalism. Liberal thinkers such as Daniel Bell in sociology, John Rawls and Robert Nozick in moral and political philosophy and Lawrence Kohlberg in moral psychology and education are important figures in contemporary debate. Precisely because in their work the forms and assumptions of liberal discourse are given great clarity, it is especially there that its inade-

---

the greatest revival of the tradition in the late nineteenth century in *Democratic Promise: The Populist Movement in America* (New York: Oxford University Press, 1976).

quacies appear.[15] In comparison, the insights of critics of liberalism who speak both from inside and outside it, such as economists Fred Hirsch and Robert Heilbroner, are especially fruitful.

The inadequacies of liberal political discourse chiefly revolve around its inability convincingly to connect an assertion of the intrinsic dignity of the human self with its own premises about the nature of the world and the capacities of human reason. The immediate problem for liberal political philosophy, which appears in different ways in the work of all the thinkers mentioned, is the need to develop and justify an enduring consensus about the entitlements and responsibilities of citizenship. They attempt to do this while proceeding on the premise that politics is the management of the relations among unrelated individuals seeking essentially private goals. This difficulty reveals the center of philosophic liberalism as a highly utopian teaching masquerading as common sense. That is the notion that social solidarity, reciprocity, and mutual aid can and should result exclusively from contractual relationships of self-interest or individual moral decisions. In moments such as the present, when social solidarity and public commitment are under heavy strain, the intellectual search for the bases of moral consensus becomes critical for a democratic society. But the efforts of liberal thinkers to find such bases lead to a rediscovery of social and moral bonds which are poorly grasped in liberal categories.

However, the dominance of liberal discourse also colors perception of what is missing from that account of political life, so that the missing dimensions appear as negative images of dominant liberal categories. Liberalism understands social relations as contracts entered into by individuals seeking personal security and gain. It tends to see other kinds of social relationships not easily described as contract, such as family, friendship, and religious association, as a wholly different category of "emotional" as opposed to "rational" ties: thus the famous opposition of contractual organization (*Gesellschaft*, in Ferdinand Tönnies' famous terminology) to emotional community (*Gemeinschaft*), according to which noncontractual solidarity is necessarily irrational and ineffable. This categorization led to the simplistic view of history,

---

15. This argument is set forth in detail in Chapters One through Four.

popularized by Enlightenment liberals, as "progress" from irrational community to the contractual organization of society by rational individuals, and that view has been deeply influential in American thinking since the nation's founding. Given those resources, it is easy to see why liberalism can find no way out of the present difficulty except more "progress"—even when that seems to entail a further breakdown of social solidarity, a major cause of the present impasse. Hence the gloom of much liberal thinking in contemporary America.

The individualist ethos of liberalism, embodied in an expansive capitalism and a largely utilitarian conception of both state and society, seems, ironically, no longer to offer the hope for universal betterment and emancipation with which it began. This failure leads, as it has recurrently led in the twentieth century, to analyses which suggest that our problem is that there has been "too much freedom," that is, too much security and plenty, and that this has unleashed greed, particularly on the part of the less well-off. The answer proposed is usually that we modify, or even postpone or abandon, the aim at dignity for all, and focus instead on control and "order." But rooted in liberal assumptions as it is, this kind of analysis has few convincing moral arguments—except the fear and greed of the more fortunate classes.[16]

On the Left, which has never been as coherently organized or as powerful in America as in Europe, there is a recognition that in practice the individual ethos undercuts the moral aim of self-respect and self-determination. But often, as in most Marxist arguments, there is still a strong commitment to the Enlightenment idea of progress as a continuing extension of instrumental control over social relations. The effect of this logic has been a system of total social control which threatens the human values it ostensibly aims to achieve.[17] The Left wishes to propose community of some sort as the alternative to liberal individualism and as an answer to the contemporary malaise of American society, but this aim, while

16. For a good discussion of this development, particularly among former liberal intellectuals, see Peter Steinfels, *The Neo-Conservatives: The Men Who Are Changing America's Politics* (New York: Simon and Schuster, 1979).

17. The most penetrating analyses of these issues have been developed by the Marxist thinkers of the Frankfurt School. See especially Max Horkheimer and Theodor Adorno, *The Dialectic of Enlightenment*, translated by John Cumming (New York: Seabury Press, 1975).

it is in the general sense correct, is often proposed in a tradition and in language that share many of the aspects of liberalism which have led to the problems being addressed.

Some recognition of the profound difficulties engendered by the liberal ethos has touched off a search for articulations and, in some cases, whole new understandings of the values and meanings of both public and private life. These trends, often unfairly identified together as the "new consciousness," have developed from the cultural experiments of the 1960s. They emphasize the importance of intense subjective experience, in some cases explicitly tying this to social organization and criticism, in other cases not. They have given rise to intense controversy among thinkers dissatisfied with the liberal philosophical categories of nationality and the individual.[18] But whatever their merit, most formulations of the new consciousness share that lack of an historical awareness which characterized so many of their intellectual ancestors of the New Left of the 1960s.[19] This lack deepens the problem of gaining sufficient perspective on liberal assumptions and practices to make it possible to criticize them. The emphasis on subjectivity in particular is as much continuous with the mainstream of liberal culture as discontinuous and critical of it.[20]

For these reasons the recent "rediscovery" that the critical period of the American founding was strongly shaped by the tradition of civic republicanism is potentially of great importance. Debates about the past, particularly about such a crucial period as the nation's founding, are always at least implicitly debates about the nature of the society at present and about its possibilities for the

18. For a negative assessment, see Christopher Lasch, *The Culture of Narcissism: American Life in an Age of Diminishing Expectations* (New York: W.W. Norton, 1979). On the other hand, Michael Harrington invokes the "new consciousness" as a cultural resource for a Left politics in America: see *Decade of Decision: The Crisis of the American System* (New York: Simon and Schuster, 1980), pp. 313-27.

19. Which is not to deny that these movements may not develop an historical understanding nor that the New Left has created a certain morally significant sense of history among the members of the generation influenced by it and the "youth culture" of the 1960s. Sociologists Richard Flacks and Jack Whalen have provided helpful interpretations of these matters in an unpublished paper, "The Isla Vista 'Bank Burners' Ten Years Later: Notes on the Fate of Student Activists."

20. Steven Tipton provides a perceptive discussion of the continuities and discontinuities in the lives of participants in these developments in his *Getting Saved from the Sixties* (Berkeley: University of California Press, 1982).

future. It is the search for greater clarity about those aspects of social life not well described by liberalism which has enabled the republican tradition to emerge as an historically distinct strand of meaning in American culture. And that search is propelled by a sense not only of conceptual inadequacy in the liberal view but of a lack of understanding about the important qualities of human action which are struggling to find articulation. That intuitive sense is finally a moral one concerning what constitutes a society and a polity worthy of respect. The rediscovery of republicanism as an American tradition makes possible new conceptual analyses as an aspect of the historical reinterpretation.[21] That rediscovery is an important part of the larger contemporary struggle to achieve self-understanding and to gain a more adequate moral sense of our collective life and destiny.

Reconstructing the conceptual distinction between the liberal and civic republican conceptions of politics is important as a way of grasping the careers of both in American political culture. In particular, the distinction sheds light on the ambiguities inherent in the dominant American form of liberalism. Recovery and elaboration of republican understanding may provide both the most radical alternative to liberalism we have, and a way of salvaging from the wreckage of liberal theory liberalism's own chief moral assertion about human dignity.

The central ambiguity of liberal philosophy arises from the contradiction between its moral intent of protecting the dignity of the individual and the categories of thought it has employed to elaborate and establish that idea. This conceptual dichotomy can be summarized in the divergence between the strand of liberal thinking that emphasizes individual moral autonomy and its other, utilitarian strand. There is pathos in the historical development of liberalism in that the individualistic, utilitarian form of liberal thinking was developed in the seventeenth and eighteenth centuries as a means for emancipating individuals from subjection to arbitrary civil and religious power. But the consequence of that development has been the constriction of rationality to its purely instrumental form of power to control. At the same time this conception of reason has seemed to undermine the possibility of speaking rationally about the ends or purposes of power.

21. This development is discussed in detail in Chapter Six.

The basic notions of liberal philosophy far antedate the seventeenth century, but it was the English thinkers of that period, Thomas Hobbes and John Locke, who gave the new system of ideas a structure which has remained essentially intact ever since. Liberal philosophy includes three interrelated parts, each more encompassing and fundamental than the other: a theory of politics and society, a theory of human nature, and a particular conception of the nature of reason which can be summed up in the idea of science in its modern sense. The primary human reality is the individual, conceived independently of social relationships; this idea is expressed in the notion of a "state of nature" logically prior to society.

Individuals are conceived as driven by their passions—above all, fear of harm and desire for comfort—so that social relations are external to the personality and are entered into by the individual to advance his own interests as these are determined by his passions. The only ultimate source of value in society is individual preference and will. This conception of human nature strongly conflicted with the traditional social understanding of man inherited by republican thinkers. The effect was to dissolve values into power, specifically, power to augment and foster the individual's passion-driven will.

With this vision goes a correlative notion of knowledge as the reduction of complex wholes to simple elements. In this, liberalism is closely tied to the modern scientific view of knowledge as the power to analyze and recombine elements for the sake of control. In its social application, reason thus becomes instrumental, a means to satisfy individually conceived desires, and politics in its modern sense of power struggle is the logical result. Thus social relationships of whatever kind are ultimately conceived of as both artifice and an order of power. In its most benign extrapolation this leads to the prospect of a social engineering to harmonize needs and wants. That vision in fact guided the development of modern economics as the closest approximation of the liberal ideal of a social science with practical application.

However, in its full development this system of ideas is recognizable in the twentieth-century form of the perfectly controlled technological society as well as in the idylls of a self-balancing exchange system. Indeed, although liberalism arose as a weapon of emancipation, the demonic potential of a system of thought that tried to protect the individual by stripping social relationships and nature of any intrinsic significance at moments even rouses the anxieties of its progenitors. Hobbes explicitly drew the implication from his new anthropology that only a tightly organized and centralized state apparatus could guarantee the security of a society of self-interested egoists. And John Locke seems to have thought that his optimistic idea that such creatures could be civilized by judicious social engineering made sense only on the tacit assumption that this program could be contained and directed by the traditional Christian idea of a moral law. "If man were independent," Locke wrote, "he could have no law but his own will, no end but himself. He would be a god to himself and the satisfaction of his own will the sole measure and end of all his actions."[22]

Protecting the security of persons thus became a project of defending them against the effects of individual and collective egoism, the foundations of the liberal system. That project reached its highest conceptual development in Immanuel Kant's attempt to find a rational defense for the Christian dignity of the individual in a way that would be consistent with liberal premises. To do so, Kant had to invoke a distinct realm of reasoning governed by nonutilitarian rules. In that he set a pattern which has defined and troubled liberal moral thought for two centuries.[23]

The peculiarity of the development of liberalism in America gives a unique texture to American liberal political thought. Because liberal ideas of politics became significant during the same revolutionary struggle against an identified despotism that also brought civic republicanism to the fore, liberalism in America had to absorb into its outlook a number of republican concerns.[24] In addition, the unique religious climate of America meant that biblical religious language and organizations played an early role which reinforced rather than opposed the emerging political cul-

22. John Locke, *Ethica* (Locke Mss., Bodleian Library C-28, p. 141), quoted by John Dunn, *The Political Thought of John Locke* (Cambridge, England: Cambridge University Press, 1969), p. 1.

23. These themes form the burden of the discussion in Chapters Four and Five.

24. Thomas Jefferson seems one of the founding generation whose ideas on social and political institutions were heavily influenced by the efforts of Scottish Enlightenment philosophers to advance republican principles through modes of thought borrowed from the new liberalism. See Gary Wills, *Inventing America: Jefferson's Declaration of Independence* (New York: Random House, 1978).

ture, so that American liberalism, unlike European forms, has not usually been hostile to religious teaching and practice. Still, religious language on the national political level has frequently served as a substitute for explicit republican language, diluting republicanism's coherence as an alternative to liberalism.[25]

Compared to the instrumental cast of liberal thought, with its affinity for mechanical metaphors of social life, the republican tradition has seen politics as essentially the application of prudence, an understanding that relies on a sense of practical reason missing from the liberal ideal of rationality. Civic republican thought derives from the political philosophy of classical antiquity, was developed by the medieval Christian concern for individual dignity and universal participation, and received new impetus through the Renaissance and developments surrounding the new states of early modern Europe. As a tradition, it differs strongly from liberalism in its emphasis on the value of politics as moral cultivation of responsible selves.

Civic republicanism denies the liberal notion that individuality exists outside of or prior to social relationships. Instead, the republican tradition has taught that there is an ineluctably participatory aspect to political understanding that develops only through the moral maturation of mutual responsibility. Genuine political understanding, while it can be heightened by conscious reflection, is thus tied to specific experiences of political practice. Civic republicanism does not share the liberal idea that individuals are atoms of will essentially uninfluenced by their web of interrelationships, or the concomitant notion that all values are finally manifestations of the power to control. On the contrary, freedom is ultimately the ability to realize a responsible selfhood, which is necessarily a cooperative project. For republicanism, there are qualities of social relations, such as mutual concern and respect, that transcend utility and that can be learned only in practice. One reason republicanism has proved tenacious in a liberal America is this very embodied quality of its knowledge, although it requires explication to realize its own development.[26]

25. The relation of biblical religious themes, including eschatological, prophetic thinking, to the republican tradition has been long-term and complex: see Pocock, *Machiavellian Moment*, pp. 42-55. For the specifically American dynamic, see McWilliams, *Fraternity*, and Bellah, *Broken Covenant*.

26. These themes are developed at length in Chapters Five, Six, and Seven.

The most valuable message of the republican tradition follows directly from this understanding. It is that the protection of human dignity depends upon the moral quality of social relationships and that this is finally a public and political concern. Civic life is essential for individual security and integrity, but the ascendancy of liberalism has made it difficult to conceive those critical practices of mutual concern upon which liberal moral autonomy depends. The civic republican understanding of citizenship as shared initiative and responsibility among persons committed to mutual care provides the basis for a more mature public philosophy. But today that insight needs to be brought into explicit connection with large-scale governmental and economic institutions seeking to develop an effective citizenship in the areas of life controlled by those organizations.

ONE

The Contemporary Crisis
of Liberal Society

:: I

As the United States enters the 1980s the optimism in fashion during the 1950s and 1960s already seems an echo of a distant time, a theme to be traded upon in a politics of nostalgia but not a basis for serious decisions about our future.[1] The era of American world dominance following victory in World War II was perhaps the high-water mark of a kind of liberal "consensus" about the strengths of the "American way of life" celebrated by many intellectuals of that time. The basic assumption of that post-war consensus was a vision of a society centered on individual economic achievement in a competitive market, to be fostered by enlightened government policy. Social tensions were to be resolved through continuing increase in abundance, with the aid of scientific and technological advances.

The ideology of the Cold War presented the world as an arena of mortal combat between conflicting social systems identified with moral values. As leader and model of the Free World, the United States carried a trust to show that free enterprise could realize the aspirations of mankind in ways that outstrip the abilities of Communist nations. The "vital center" of American opinion was formed around the agreement that economic growth,

1. Michael Harrington has provided an incisive examination of these differences and an argument about the underlying reasons for the change in *Decade of Decision: The Crisis of the American System* (New York: Simon and Schuster, 1980).

quantified as the Gross National Product, defined the social good and the national interest. It was an age of self-confident social and economic management, management during which dissent, though never absent, failed to change the dominant context of debate in any radical way.

That meant that government stimulation of the market to generate an increase in the supply of goods, services, and jobs was the agreed-upon means to ensure social and political well-being. The political designations that came out of the New Deal era likewise defined attitudes toward economic growth. Liberals shared a belief in the need for government to play an active role in extending the benefits of growth to all sectors of the population, particularly through public education and aid to those who were for various reasons unable to compete effectively in the marketplace. Conservatives also favored growth but were wary of the expansion of centralized government in various regulatory and interventionist roles, as well as being uneasy about the upsets the government's interventions might cause in the existing order of political and social power and the stability of local ways of life.

The goal of social policy enacted by the federal government was in one crucial respect identical for liberals and conservatives: they saw the American Dream as individual advancement in a competitive economy. Consistently the post-war consensus defined problems and conceived policies in instrumental terms. There was a common assumption that citizens' fundamental motivations were economically self-interested and, further, that a policy which took this into account was likely to be successful because of the natural and self-sustaining character of economic motivation. Freedom was likewise understood in a private sense, as security of person and possessions. The tasks of government were to secure this private liberty and to promote orderly growth by regulating economic desires. Even liberals arguing for welfare-state policies justified the redistribution of wealth on the grounds that the disadvantaged, too, were consumers and thus potential markets for more growth. Distributive justice did not fit well into this picture. It smacked of collectivism. If there was a general good or, in the phrase of those times, a national purpose, it lay in maintaining private liberty and achieving equality of economic opportunity. Indeed, American foreign-policy strategists prescribed "take-offs" into economic growth as the cure for international ills and the antidote to Communism.

The old labels no longer describe the current political situation. The old Democratic coalition appears in disarray. Some supporters of the former New Deal consensus have emerged as so-called neo-Conservatives who, while not repudiating the welfare state altogether, judge government social interventions as mostly failures and see stability, not growth, as the major goal of social policy.[2] Others have rejected the whole conception of New Deal social policy—the extension of the economic benefits of growth—retreating to arguments for a conversion to laissez-faire in economy and society.[3] Others, on the Left, speak of a new economic democracy or social governance of the economy.[4] This shift of labels and policies stems from the evident exhaustion of the former growth strategy. Very importantly, the slowing of growth has precipitated a new search for explanations, calling into question the efficacy of the instrumental approach to policy. By scrutinizing the foundations of the old consensus politics, the new questioning has begun to change dramatically the focus of concern and to alter the ways in which we see American society.

The present crisis of government is a general crisis of the liberal capitalist form of society. The word *liberal* here refers in particular to the philosophy of government that has dominated political discourse in modern America, but it also suggests a general cast of mind found throughout the society and typical of much of American culture. Liberalism is thus both a philosophical teaching usually identified with the European Enlightenment thinkers of the seventeenth and eighteenth centuries and also a popular set of attitudes at work in day-to-day life. As a philosophy, liberalism includes three parts: a theory of politics and society, a theory of

2. The epithet *neo-conservative* has been applied to the intellectual current represented by Irving Kristol's editorship of *Public Interest* and the group of intellectuals and political figures associated with that journal. For an overview and critique of that position, see Peter Steinfels, *The Neo-Conservatives: The Men Who Are Changing America's Politics* (New York: Simon and Schuster, 1979). Also see Michael Walzer's review of Steinfels in *The New York Review of Books* XXVI, 15 (Oct. 11, 1979), pp. 5-8.

3. This tendency is most explicit in the politics of the Libertarian movement and Party. Murray Rothbard and philosopher Robert Nozick, whose work is discussed in Chapter Two, are representative figures of this kind of "back to basics," which is in most respects a return to classic liberalism.

4. A new kind of socialist or left-wing populist vision has begun to develop in the United States since the 1970s. For an example of its approach see Barry Commoner's discussion of "social governance" of the economy in his *The Politics of Energy* (New York: Knopf, 1979).

human nature, and a conception of science and the nature of reason. Liberalism views politics as a structure of institutions designed to protect civil society, which it sees as a realm of contracts among individuals. These contractual relationships are entered into because they are necessary or useful for individuals as means to pursue their private ends. Both the compulsory realm of government and the voluntary, contractual realm of social institutions including the family, church, and business are instruments to be utilized by individuals to advance their own needs and desires.

Thus the moral and political outlook of liberalism is instrumental in its view of political and social life. It identifies value with what is useful to the individual. Human beings are conceived of as self-interested individuals driven by their passions to fulfill their needs by means of rational calculation and planning. This view of human nature is in turn supported by the notion that reason is a tool for analysis, taking apart the elements of a situation or entity so as to reorganize it for greater usefulness. The logical goal of liberal rationality is a scientific social engineering that will be able to bring about a perfect adjustment of needs and wants. Economics has thus represented the nearest approximation to the liberal ideal of a social science with applications for social engineering.

In practical life, liberalism has been embodied in a public philosophy that has conceived of government as a balancing of private interests, the social basis for which is the operation of the market economy. The great mission of government, and in particular the law, has been understood as the defense of individual security of person and possessions, a liberty to be extended with equal care to all citizens. It was this public philosophy that after World War II ruled American political discussion virtually without challenge. But today, as this utilitarian and instrumental spirit weakens in the face of apparently intractable obstacles, philosophic liberalism is forced to play a role it is ill-suited to play. It must answer not simply problems of management but root questions about the moral justification of the whole economic and social order.

As a public philosophy liberalism has from its early formulations in the seventeenth century deliberately restricted its aim and aspirations toward promoting the human good to a manageable, calculative level. Promoting freedom, that is, security and prosperity through economic calculation, promised to provide a safer basis for public peace and order than the dangerous passions of aristocratic honor, religious enthusiasm, or civic virtue. Yet the pursuit of prosperity, the augmentation of what is one's own, not only dampens the dangerous ardor for glory; it also threatens to slacken the sinews of self-restraint and moral virtue. As Alexis de Tocqueville noted, liberal societies need restraints upon self-interest precisely as they succeed in becoming prosperous, if they are to maintain the public concern and respect for fellow citizens upon which their cohesion depends.[5] Yet modern American society, persuaded by corporate advertising and politicians alike, has come increasingly to empty the domain of public morality of traditional imperatives of loyalty and obligation, and has come to see social life only in terms of the self-interest of the isolated individual. And now the end of the era of cheap resources is putting tremendous strain on the American system of government-guided capitalism by throttling the engine of economic growth.

The crisis of legitimacy or, as it is sometimes called, the crisis of authority is straining to their limits the cultural and intellectual resources of the liberal tradition.[6] The questioning of the basic assumptions of liberal society is of necessity a piecemeal process. Our ways of thought, like our day-to-day lives, have been formed through an historical experience of which liberalism is a major part. Yet, the sense of malaise is pervasive and the search for an understanding of our problems is opening up questions about the whole liberal conception of life. Such fundamental questioning of the premises of philosophic liberalism is necessary to gain an understanding of our possibilities as a people.

If our crisis is as severe as much current social analysis suggests, then a renewed sense of public commitment cannot be generated by a return to the earlier policy of economic growth or by appeals to self-interest alone. The larger problems dogging government require a confrontation with the hard questions of moral and political experience: what changes will have to take place in the

5. See Alexis de Tocqueville, *Democracy in America*, translated by George Lawrence (Garden City, New York: Doubleday, 1969), pp. 534, 540.

6. From the Left, the issue has been explored trenchantly by Jürgen Habermas, *Legitimation Crisis* (Boston: Beacon Press, 1975). Sociologist Robert Nisbet has addressed a similar problem from a neo-conservative perspective in *The Twilight of Authority* (New York: Basic Books, 1975).

United States if there is to develop a consensus about the general welfare that will arouse citizen initiative? Over the long run, the only alternative to a public process of struggling with these difficulties is an imposed social discipline. Social changes are inevitable.

Several contemporary social analysts are particularly helpful in grasping the dimensions of our contemporary situation. Fred Hirsch was until his death in 1979 an eminent British economist of world stature. Daniel Bell is a major American social theorist whose career has involved him for many years in trying to gain an overview of the changes our society is undergoing. Robert Heilbroner is also an American and an economist of extraordinary historical and theoretical breadth. All three thinkers have been deeply engaged in studying the workings of liberal society. They have likewise given prolonged reflection to liberal theories of government and culture, and yet display no unanimity in ideology or political stance. Thus it is particularly noteworthy that they all portray the liberal world as coming unstuck as the workings of its basic institutions generate effects destructive of the natural and social environment they depend upon for their survival. The whole liberal construction of an analytic science, an individualistic motivation, and an instrumental, utilitarian politics, which had seemed a complete and objectively secured—almost self-evident—view of human affairs, is now at sea.

It is as though a long-familiar background were suddenly being removed, a background so familiar it had become largely invisible, yet one which, it can now be seen, had been indispensable if the clearly etched foreground was to maintain its shape. The foreground is the world of liberal thought and practice, so long the focus of public discussion and interest. The rediscovered background is a dimension of moral and social life that liberalism has ignored or denied, yet one that is crucial if the values of liberal morality, particularly liberty and equal justice for all, are to be maintained and extended. Hirsch, Bell, and Heilbroner reveal in persuasive ways that the world of liberal individualism has depended for its viability upon moral and social relations of a quite different texture. The paradoxical effect of the growth of liberal capitalist society has been to undermine those social relations which have historically restrained and modified self-interested competition. Discussion of these relationships against this wider background will provide a perspective on the efforts of contempo-

rary liberal thinkers to address the problems of political legitimacy and social cohesion. Since the difficulties these liberal theorists encounter are bound up with the suppressed social and moral
background, a critical examination of their work will provide a
basis for attempting to recover a public philosophy more adequate
than liberalism, a civic philosophy that has been with us all along,
though it has often been eclipsed. Articulation of a renewed civic
philosophy is vital if the American promises of liberty and genuine
equality are to be extended—as they must be if the nation is to
survive as a free society. It is now time that civic philosophy again
find its voice.

:: II

Liberal philosophers and political economists since Thomas
Hobbes have been suspicious of claims to define the public good
and, like the American Federalists, have sought ways to deflect
these concerns into mechanisms that could reliably maintain social
peace while generating prosperity. This was to be done by harnessing private, calculative interests.

Fred Hirsch, though an eminent economist, has dramatically
departed from that tradition by construing the past two centuries
of Western economic development as an historically bounded
"transitional case" of social development. The defining feature of
this case has been its great concentration on and reliance upon the
exchange system of the market as a mechanism for social coordination. Liberal economics has in turn provided the conventional
rationale for this form of organization. But rather than the time-
less laws of growth that economists have sought to reveal, Hirsch's
analysis turns up self-generating constraints in successful market
societies. This is a result that sharply questions the adequacy of
the categories of liberal understanding for grasping the dimensions of our present problems.

The fundamental pattern Hirsch sketches is a shift from a relatively long phase of what might be termed market success to a new
situation of growing market failure. Market success can be understood as a situation in which there is a relatively high degree of
allocative efficiency. Such allocative efficiency refers to a relative
equilibrium of supply and demand among producers and consumers and a state of dynamic growth as well, since an efficient

market motivates productive activity and stimulates decisions to acquire skills and capital assets.

The history of the liberal market economies in the United States and Britain over the past two centuries shows a remarkable overall rate of market success, despite severe setbacks. This has been particularly true of the period between the end of World War II and the early 1970s. Yet, despite the immense increase in absolute productivity, the market system has also been characterized of late by rapid inflation and structural rigidities and imperfections. These have resulted in a slowing of growth and a waste of resources. Hirsch points out that these new kinds of problems have not proven susceptible to improvements through application of the fiscal controls developed since the 1930s, and the failure of these proven remedies must be explained. The basic reasons, Hirsch argues, must lie in aspects of the market system that have been previously overlooked. In fact, the categories of economic analysis may themselves conceal certain key aspects of our economic systems that the appearance of market failure has begun to reveal.[7]

Hirsch notes that, given the long period of successful economic growth, most economists begin their analysis with several core assumptions: that the valuations of individual consumers provide the stimulus for economic activity in a market economy, that production is shaped by the signals transmitted through the market, and, ultimately, that individual satisfaction is realized through prudent exercise of self-interest. The market, then, is seen as a successful institution in modern society and individualistic economic behavior as a successful principle of social organization. Hirsch comments, as have many others, that the novelty of the liberal capitalist order was that socially beneficial results flowed from harnessing the desire for maximizing personal advantage. As he puts it, "Good has been done by stealth."[8]

7. Fred Hirsch, *Social Limits to Growth* (Cambridge, Massachusetts: Harvard University Press, 1976), pp. 15-16. On this point Hirsch's work can be compared with other notable attempts to situate the categories of economic analysis in historical perspective. See especially Louis Dumont, *From Mandeville to Marx: The Genesis and Triumph of Economic Ideology* (Chicago: University of Chicago Press, 1977), and Albert Hirschman, *The Passions and the Interests: Political Arguments for Capitalism before Its Triumph* (Princeton, New Jersey: Princeton University Press, 1976).

8. Hirsch, *Social Limits*, p. 11. Compare Karl Polanyi, "The Economy as Instituted Process," in Karl Polanyi, Conrad M. Arensberg, and Harry W. Pearson, eds., *Trade and Market in the Early Empires* (Glencoe, Ill.: Free Press, 1957), pp. 243-69.

The ideal model of a competitive economy conceives of each producer and consumer making choices independently of the consequences their choices have for other participants in the market. In this ideal model, market prices will automatically work to distribute goods with maximum efficiency if each producer aims to maximize his own profits and each consumer seeks the fulfillment of his own preferences. In practice, the system does not function perfectly; instead, side effects of self-interested behavior do impinge on market efficiency and provide the rationale for government intervention. Hirsch's work emphasizes the increasing importance of these side effects or externalities on the nature and quality of individual consumption. To describe the interdependence entailed by mass consumption in a modern society, Hirsch develops his notion of social scarcity. By this he means that the supply of valued things is restricted not only by the physical limits of land, labor, materials, and technology, as depicted by neoclassical economics, but also by the social context within which they are used. Put another way, like the natural environment, the social environment imposes social limits to growth. Unlike natural environmental limits, though, some decisive social limits are generated by the market process itself.

Social scarcity becomes more understandable through Hirsch's distinction between material and positional goods. Material goods are the wide range of goods and services amenable to increased output through improvements in productivity without deterioration in quality. The material economy, defined in these terms, is the central focus of modern economics. Positional goods refer to the range of goods, services, occupations, and other social relationships that are either scarce in an absolute or socially imposed sense or are subject to crowding through extensive use. The allocation of positional goods is amenable to traditional supply-and-demand analysis but has rich sociological implications. The relationship between education and employment is a good example. Work in industrial society is hierarchically organized, so preferred jobs can be identified—i.e., those jobs that provide high degrees of income, amenities, and prestige. Preferred jobs are positional goods, valuable because their supply is limited; they are desirable relative to the bulk of employment opportunities. As incomes rise, effective demand for such jobs increases until it exceeds the available supply.[9]

9. Hirsch, *Social Limits*, pp. 41-51.

Hirsch's analysis emphasizes the lack of symmetry between individual action and the aggregate effect of many individuals' actions in a modern economy. A presumed symmetry between individual and aggregate effects is the core of the theory of economic liberalism, for while individuals can in some cases succeed in attaining desired positional goods, it is obvious that not all can. As the intensity of demand rises, the price of positional goods is driven up. This produces inflationary results, as more resources are diverted to the pursuit of positional goods with no corresponding increase in their supply. Or, if the supply is increased, as with automobiles or legal degrees, there is a negative effect on the quality of the environment that sustains the individual's pursuit. Thus, all cannot do what one can.

As these hidden costs of growth become widely recognized throughout the population, they affect conceptions of the opportunities for enhanced personal welfare, alter long-standing motivational patterns, and create new social cleavages. The self-regulating "invisible hand" does not, due to an internal logic of the market, allow all or most to advance their standing in the race for positional goods. Contrary to the expectations generated by economic-growth policy, there can be no general benefits or real growth in the positional area. Like Zeno's race between Achilles and the tortoise, this is a world of apparent but not real motion. Yet, as general material affluence has risen, it is precisely relative advance that has taken center stage in the public mind, and there is a growing recognition that new patterns of social stratification are emerging in modern societies. That is, even in periods of tremendous material affluence there remain unbridgeable gulfs between those with coveted positional goods, such as professional or managerial status, and those without them, who go on lacking them despite rising real income.

But if the pursuit of self-interest in the market cannot produce relative advance, let alone relative equality, in the social realm, nonetheless political and social egalitarianism is a dominant aspect of liberal society. As movement in the positional race has come to seem increasingly unattainable through individual market behavior, we have witnessed an intensification of efforts by collectivities—e.g., labor unions, professional associations, ethnic and racial groups—to advance or maintain their status in the positional race by political means. However, to have recourse to the state to deal with stratificational or distributional conflicts is to abandon the cornerstone of Western post-war social policy, that is, the dream of growth for all with minimum redistribution.[10] The new political efforts strike at the heart of the liberal justification for both market and government and challenge the ability of liberal policy or orthodox theory to assimilate such demands. Thus, political institutions that have based their legitimacy on their ability to "deliver the goods," to improve individual well-being through rising productivity and income, find themselves overloaded with demands they cannot meet and cannot restrain. Positional goods cannot be expanded indefinitely, nor do they trickle down to the poor.

These unexpected results strike at the heart of so-called libertarian defenses of the market as well. Frederick von Hayek, whose economic theory has influenced, among others, philosopher Robert Nozick, argues that economic progress is the result of an "echelon effect," a form of the trickle-down theory.[11] In Hayek's theory, inequality is actually the indispensable basis for the betterment of all in society. If Hirsch is correct, this could hold only for the "transitional case."

The meaning of Hirsch's analysis for politics and political theory is as striking as it is clear. The dominant formulations of liberal political theory, linked to the development of "interest-group" politics in the United States, have severed the connection between self-interest and general welfare. The notion of collective benefit has been simply presumed, when it has been referred to at all. The twentieth-century welfare state is expected to take care of issues of justice while relying on the "me-too" motivation of self-interest. This is consistent with modern liberalism's notion that politics is an extension of the pursuit of private interests through political bargaining. Like the ideal type of the market, the political "arena" is assumed to be perfectly self-correcting. As in the market, so in the polity: free pursuit of self-interest, now on the part of groups such as trade unions, corporations, ethnic organizations, even government bureaucracies, is trusted to produce benefits for all through economic growth.[12] Hirsch comes close here to opening the question about the positional, that is, culturally de-

10. Ibid., pp. 155-58.
11. Frederick A. Hayek, *The Constitution of Liberty* (Chicago: University of Chicago Press, 1960), pp. 42-43.
12. A representative argument is put forward by Robert A. Dahl, *Pluralist Democracy in the United States* (Chicago: Rand McNally, 1967).

fined, meaning of income in general. In fact, all goods are in an essential dimension positional and are never simply natural or material. An adequate income is in practice only definable as whatever combination of economic resources an individual or family needs in order to participate with dignity in the life of the community.[13] Seen this way, economic issues are always cultural and moral matters whose tacit premise is the good of a full sharing of social life, and Hirsch's paradox of affluence, while more acute than in the past, is no longer unique to contemporary capitalism.

But the liberal assumptions, if they were ever convincing, are simply no longer tenable. Continuation of a marketing society and a bargaining polity requires some mutual restraint on the part of the participants, even from the point of view of self-interest. But if self-interest really is the natural, inevitable, and decisive political principle, it finally remains in the interests of each group for *others* to show restraint and then for that group to reap the benefits. What is missing in the purely individualistic theory of liberalism is a convincing conception of justice and common values on the basis of which such an agreement might be reached.

The issues raised by Hirsch's critique of liberal economics and the growing recognition of the limitations of interest-group theory are therefore particularly interesting when set in a wider historical perspective. Hirsch's argument is reminiscent of the important critical challenge to utilitarianism and classical liberalism raised by Emile Durkheim in his critique of the work of Herbert Spencer.[14]

For Herbert Spencer, the structure of industrial society was based on economic exchange, on private contracts sanctioned by a laissez-faire state. Durkheim attempted to undermine this liberal view because, for him, a profit-oriented market economy that imposes limitless, maximizing activity upon its members is anomic and pathological. Contractual relations based on motives of self-interest are not a sufficient organizing device for society; they cannot produce sufficient solidarity to maintain social order. Durkheim's comments on this point are quite suggestive:

13. See the work of sociologist Lee Rainwater on the role of moral and cultural considerations in efforts to set quantitative measures for poverty and adequacy of income, especially *What Money Buys: Inequality and the Meanings of Income* (New York: Basic Books, 1974).

14. See Emile Durkheim, *The Division of Labor in Society* (New York: The Free Press/Macmillan, 1965), chs. 3 and 4.

If interest relates men, it is never more than some few moments. It can create only an external link between them . . . where interest is the only ruling force each individual finds himself in a state of war with every other . . . nothing is less constant than interest . . . it can only give rise to transient relations and passing associations.[15]

Thus, for Durkheim, social solidarity can never result from the free interplay of market forces; contractual exchange produces, at best, very transient harmony of interest. Social bonds based on the calculation of self-interest are too ephemeral to maintain a social order. Instead, solidarity requires a shared moral code, a framework of institutionalized norms establishing and sanctioning the conditions of reciprocity in personal affairs.

Because of these views Durkheim also argued that the liberal market was a transitional case. Specifically, he tried to show that utilitarianism and so classical liberal philosophy were symbolic representations of an extreme and aberrant form of individualism. In his view, utilitarianism was "contradicted by everything which history and comparative ethnography teach us about the moral life of humanity."[16] When society exists in a normal state, interaction occurs within a framework of institutionalized norms and values that are objective inasmuch as individual personalities reflect this *conscience collective*. Durkheim analyzed extreme departures from this state as pathological forms of social organization. In a normal state of society, institutions combine recognition of normative constraints with an internalized sense of personal commitment.[17]

In many ways, Hirsch's understanding of society is Durkheimian. Hirsch's historical analysis confirms and extends Durkheim's critique of the contract by demonstrating how the widening sphere of individualistic market behavior erodes the market's hidden infrastructure of traditional moral codes. Also like Durkheim, Hirsch shows how even the most enlightened intervention, e.g., Keynesian policy, cannot restore economic stability by appealing to self-interest alone.

15. Durkheim, *Division of Labor*, pp. 203-4.
16. Quoted in Dominick La Capra, *Emile Durkheim: Sociologist and Philosopher* (Ithaca, New York: Cornell University Press, 1972), p. 225.
17. For interpretations of this point see La Capra, *Durkheim*, and Robert N. Bellah's Introduction to *Emile Durkheim on Morality and Society* (Chicago: University of Chicago Press, 1973).

Hirsch treats this set of issues particularly well through his analysis of the problems of restraint and of the way in which the distributional compulsion of modern society raises the question of the legitimacy of the market. He notes that the social prerequisites of the market have been given much more attention by sociologists than by economists. In redressing this lack of economic analysis he employs his implicitly Durkheimian perspective effectively by discussing the various social controls that have conditioned, limited, and made possible the market as a sphere of modern society. In his view, such controls have performed three key functions. One was to soften the burden of market forces. Traditional norms of charity and aid have functioned as informal controls acting as a "distributional corrective." The second was the role of state action in providing necessary amelioration from outside the market system. The third was the normative behavior needed to allow the market process itself to operate; these range from norms of honesty and justice to acceptance of the legitimacy of the contract.[18]

As traditional moral codes are eroded restraints are weakened, making the economy less manageable and increasing the difficulty of achieving collective goals. The key sociological implication of Hirsch's analysis in this regard is that liberal capitalism was capable of harnessing the motive of self-interest without politically explosive conflicts.

The crisis of affluence has exposed the historically limited nature of the individualist assumption, common since Bernard Mandeville's *Fable of the Bees*, that private vice is public virtue in economics. Hirsch points to the fatal blind-spot of the liberal-utilitarian tradition in his analysis of the problem of externalities. The reason that individual self-interest taken in the aggregate cannot succeed as it can in the individual case is because no society, not even a capitalist one, is actually an aggregate of social atoms. Economic calculation and pursuit stand revealed as embedded in a social and cultural matrix not reducible to a sum of individual desires. The paradox of growth is ultimately the working-out in practice of the paradox of liberal public philosophy.

18. Hirsch, *Social Limits*, pp. 120-21.

:: III

In the end, Hirsch's analysis of the entropic tendencies of the capitalist market system presents a dismal prognosis for the moral cohesion of liberal society if those trends go unopposed. Under conditions of slower market expansion, the welfare state will be called upon to implement public planning of the economy which both reflects and creates an order of distributive justice. However, the usual utilitarian criterion of "delivering the goods," which has guided American policy over the past quarter-century, provides no basis for working out a conception of the general welfare that could support the political changes a policy of explicit distributive justice would require. Moreover, the internal contradictions of competition for positional goods, as well as the natural and international constraints of material scarcity, are long-term trends, indigenous to the modern world-market system, and they appear likely to continue.

There is ever more intense conflict among various classes and groups that has to be played out as a struggle over government economic policy, and there is the impending threat of political stalemate or anarchy as these groups must struggle harder to win gains through the government. Private economic frustration tends all the while to undercut citizens' willingness to support government, either by taxes or by voting. Thus at the time that a public reconsideration of the moral context of economic life becomes essential, the ability of American leaders to mobilize general support is very weak. Private expectations are being frustrated, but the habits of liberal capitalism and the forms of liberal political discourse undercut the kind of public understanding and reorganization that could better the situation: a cruel irony indeed.

Daniel Bell sees the problem Hirsch raises so forcefully, and by probing its fundamental dimensions he reveals more starkly the deep roots of the crisis in liberal culture. Bell presents contemporary American society as riven by a set of internal contradictions, and his sociological insight is that capitalist economic institutions, organized around competitive self-interest, are in danger of undercutting the motivations that sustain them. The reason for this is that motivation is maintained by shared practices and meanings which are embedded in forms of mutual solidarity. Acquisitive economic behavior erodes this background of trust by making reciprocal cooperation risky and, often, imprudent. Traditional societies for this reason saw acquisitive behavior as dangerous to the bonds of trust, respect, and sharing upon which social life depends. The peculiarly honorific status of acquisitiveness in the moral order of liberal capitalism has been based on an assumption that egoistic competition could be fostered and extended to many areas of social life without harm being done to the larger non-competitive context of solidarity. Liberal political theory since Hobbes has built upon the same curious assumption.

At a deeper level, liberal economics and political theory are based upon an instrumental conception of human action. Since Thomas Hobbes and John Locke, the liberal thinker has typically seen man as by nature a tool-using individual, as *homo faber*. It is characteristic of *homo faber* that anything has value—the term itself derives from liberal economics[19]—only inasmuch as it serves a purpose given by the individual's needs and wants. Goodness or value is thus subjective in origin, meaning that it is a quality that the active individual subject confers upon those objects and processes which fulfill his wants. Ends or purposes are, for the liberal thinker, subjective. They are also utilitarian, in that the criterion of value is always the relative adequacy or usefulness of a particular tool as a means of furthering individual wants. In Locke's view, for example, social and governmental institutions are merely nonmaterial tools which arise spontaneously or are constructed consciously as means to fulfill the needs of the individual: hence Locke's insistence that secure possession of the fruits of one's labor, which he termed the liberty to enjoy property, is natural to humankind and more fundamental than social ties as such. Both property and society receive their value with reference to the needs and purposes of the individual.

The kind of modern social theory whose perspective Bell accepts has developed in part as a reaction against the narrowness of this liberal instrumentalism. To the nineteenth-century students of society Karl Marx, Emile Durkheim, and Max Weber, the insufficiency of the liberal theory was patent; moreover, the corrosive effect of utilitarian capitalism on social and moral life was cause

19. See Raymond Williams's study of the rise of the instrumental-utilitarian conception of society in the nineteenth century and various intellectual responses to it, *Culture and Society: 1780-1950* (New York: Columbia University Press, 1958).

for genuine alarm.[20] That tradition of thought, despite its considerable internal variations, concurs in the idea that human beings are intrinsically social, meaning that language, consciousness, and personal identity all develop within, and only within, a context of interaction. A social context, moreover, is always and necessarily a moral order. Social practices and institutions embody relationships among persons that direct and orient the persons involved to act and feel in certain ways. Being a certain kind of individual is bound up with responding to others in accord with these practices. Thus personal identity is internally connected to shared gestures, activities, customary forms; to be human is to be at once a participant in social life and in a moral order. Institutions, then, are not mere tools external to the individual, which he can use or not use at will. His very will has been shaped by the customs he, often unconsciously, shares; this is no less true when the individual dissents from the common practices. It then follows that values inhere in forms of social life and that these in fact orient individual instrumental acts by explaining and giving them their significance. Modern individualism as a moral ideal is itself a collective achievement.

Instrumentalism, with its corollary, the subjective and finally arbitrary nature of value, is the deepest motif in liberal thinking. The most troublesome philosophical problem for liberal thought, accordingly, is to explain the interrelationship between instrumental and intrinsic values. For the liberal thinker, all value derives from utility, and *rational* means efficiently instrumental. Social and cultural values are only rational in this view when they efficiently achieve their utilitarian end, that of providing individual satisfaction. Thus a rational society would eschew custom and sentimental bonds and aim to be as explicitly contractual in its operations as possible. Again the market springs to mind as ideal type. Thus, to be consistent, liberal thinkers must try to explain those institutional values, and expressive acts like ritual and taboo which do not seem directly useful for survival, as fulfilling some

20. See Anthony Giddens, *Capitalism and Modern Social Theory: An Analysis of the Writings of Marx, Durkheim and Max Weber* (London: Cambridge University Press, 1971); and also C. B. MacPherson's analysis of Hobbes's and Locke's anthropology and social theory from a similar perspective, *The Political Theory of Possessive Individualism: Hobbes to Locke* (New York: Oxford University Press, 1964).

indirect instrumental purpose. So the "real" meaning of religion, art, manners, family customs turns out to be an attempt at control, a means to survival and to the satisfaction of needs.[21] The problem with this mode of thinking is that sooner or later the question of logical regress must be faced: "If *this* is a means to *that*, what is that for?" and so on. Following the logic of the liberal position strictly, there can be only one answer at the end of the process, and it is the same one that was there in the beginning: the value, the purpose of all social and cultural artifacts is the survival of the individual (or, in some versions, the group or species). But beyond this there is no rational probing. Hence, while more "primitive" societies tried to answer the question of orientation with myth, religion, and poetry, the liberal counsels us to be more mature and face the limits of instrumental reasoning by looking to our tackle as best we may. In the end, the notion of an intrinsic or self-justifying good is from the instrumental standpoint a literal *non sequitur.*

As Bell sees it, the dilemma of liberal capitalist society is that the dominance of instrumental, economic thinking in day-to-day life has produced a society of ever more effective techniques which are less and less closely related to any common goal. The only intrinsic value of an instrumental or functional organization like the market and the business corporation is efficiency. But that is simply another way of saying that the institution aims only to augment its own power. Capitalist society tends to create an ethos, as Bell calls it, of growth and expansion both on the level of economic institutions and in the realm of personal motivations. As a social theorist, Bell does not accept the notion that all values are utlimately instrumental or that a humanly worthwhile society can be organized around purely utilitarian goals; hence he sees the economic realm as needing subordination to what he calls the political realm. There debates about the social goals that ought to govern and orient the instrumental realm of the economy can be publicly carried out. He describes his position as that of a "social-ist in economics," because it subordinates instrumental processes and private aggrandizement to collective goals.[22]

21. The "economic explanation of history" is an extension of this utilitarian logic of liberal theory. It continues to be quite popular, as in the current vogue of sociobiology.

22. Daniel Bell, "Foreword: 1978," in *The Cultural Contradictions of Capitalism* (New York: Basic Books, 1978), pp. xi ff.

Where, then, do these collective values come from? The obvious answer, the polity, is deceptive. Bell tells us that he is a "liberal in politics," meaning that public debate and decision-making about the goals for economic and social life should be decided on the basis of equality among participants in the debate. Liberal government, for Bell, is a very different realm from capitalist economy, which generates inequalities of wealth. But why should the polity give citizens equal treatment under the law? Here Bell sees the tremendous limitation of liberal political theory, though his response to that limitation is not finally successful as a movement beyond it. The limitation is that liberalism's instrumental notion of reason gives no basis for the moral ideal of treating citizens with equal dignity. This sort of equality is not to be justified on grounds that it is most efficient for everyone in the long run, though that argument has been made. Liberal thinkers have usually turned instead to a conception of natural right, as did Locke and Kant. Ironically, the one kind of equality given by nature according to strictly utilitarian theory, equality in need and ignorance about moral absolutes, will not suffice to establish equality in political rights.

To uphold the liberal value of equality of rights and obligation, Bell is forced to look to a third realm of modern society. He calls this the cultural realm, within which reside those intrinsic values that enable us to distinguish the noble from the base, the human from the inhuman. In matters of culture he declares himself a "conservative," by which he means that he respects tradition and "the principle of authority" in matters of art and education and in matters of value itself.[23] In treating the realm of culture as analytically distinct, Bell reveals a fundamental "contradiction" in American society. His analysis is a consistent working-out of the conflicts between an instrumental society that "economizes" more and more of social life, thereby changing cultural values in the direction of hedonistic individualism, and those cultural values which tradition and authority, especially religious authority, teach are essential to any life that can be called human. These are values such as honesty, adherence to principle, neighborliness, concern for the common welfare. This conflict between hedonistic instrumentalism and traditional authority is being enacted in political

23. Bell, *Cultural Contradictions*, p. xv.

struggles, which Bell sees as a menace to the survival of liberal values in politics. Ultimately, however, Bell's conservatism does not escape the logic of liberal instrumentalism, which inexorably grinds down the forms of intrinsic value into means for self-aggrandizement.

Bell sketches a sociological history of the dynamics of Western societies, which suffer from a host of problems he enthusiastically catalogues: inflation, unemployment, racial discrimination. The central problem, however, is the loss of meaning and the weakening of belief in the legitimacy of coordinating institutions, especially the polity. This problem is fundamental and distinctive because it is not amenable to a technical or instrumentally managed solution.

> I write not of the events of the decade but of the deeper cultural crises which beset bourgeois societies and which . . . devitalize a country, confuse the motivations of individuals, instill a sense of *carpe diem*, and undercut its civic will. The problems are less those of the adequacy of institutions than of the kinds of meanings that sustain a society.[24]

Bell explicitly turns to Emile Durkheim, as Hirsch did implicitly, as a useful starting point for comprehending the cultural problems of society. He notes that, for Durkheim, religion is essentially the consciousness of society, and meaning arises from the cleavage between the realm of the sacred and that of the profane. Durkheim's reference to the eclipse of religion in modern society does not mean declining church membership but, instead, the dissolution of shared sentiments and affective ties. "The primordial elements that provide men with common identifications and affective reciprocity . . . have become attenuated and people have lost the capacity to maintain sustained relations."[25] This weakening of shared moral norms and symbolic understandings produces, through a process somewhat similar to the one described by Hirsch, intractable economic and political problems. For Bell, affluence leads to the replacement of a sense of calling and self-discipline by hedonism, in the form of an endless search for novelty and variety in consumption. Motivation toward virtuous character in the religious sense is displaced toward consumption, status display, and higher standards of living. The unforeseen result is that as growth

24. Ibid., p. 28.   25. Ibid., p. 155.

comes to be attacked as the cause of pollution, crowding, and decline in the quality of life, liberal theory is increasingly left without the cultural resources to counter narrow self-interest. As Bell puts it, "Without a commitment to economic growth what is the *raison d'être* of capitalism?"[26]

The traditional culture and the economy become ever more disjointed; yet, government is called upon to intervene in the regulation of the market, establishing a normative economic policy. This process has finally made direction of the economy by the federal government indispensable. Since the 1950s the state has also underwritten and stimulated many advances in science and technology and, since the 1960s, has added a growing commitment to normative social policy, e.g., civil rights, housing, and income supports.

Through the long period of post-war growth, the culture of liberalism has spread to the newly affluent a belief in the legitimacy and efficacy of advancing individual self-interest. Yet, the complex, interdependent nature of contemporary society requires fairly high degrees of agreement to achieve collective goals. The need for consensual agreement is particularly evident in the area of distributive justice. Here Bell sees political institutions as unable to manage societal problems because they cannot stem the tide of escalating demands on public resources. These demands are fueled by the hedonistic and acquisitive strains of the culture, which are themselves the result of increased affluence, the "economizing" of day-to-day life. The liberal polity lacks a viable tradition or ideology to mobilize public commitment and support for goals other than private acquisition. Here is the dilemma of capitalism. The culture crisis is thus manifested in the loss of what Bell calls *civitas*, the "spontaneous willingness to obey the law, to respect the rights of others, to forgo the temptations of private enrichment at the expense of the public weal."[27] For this loss Bell has no real replacement to offer, although his notion of the "public household" leaves open the possibility of a notion of politics different from the liberal one.

But this leads us to the problem of Bell's cultural "conservatism." He has chosen the term well. Modern conservatism arose as a political ideology at the end of the eighteenth century, with Ed-

26. Ibid., p. 80.   27. Ibid., p. 245.

mund Burke's work as a direct counterattack to the liberalism of
the French Revolution. Burke argued that the political excesses of
the Revolution stemmed from the revolutionaries' unfounded confidence in reason as a guide to politics.[28] By reason Burke meant just
what the Enlightenment liberals meant: analytical, instrumental
thinking. Burke anticipated Bell's argument about capitalism's
cultural contradictions in all its basic points. Against the whole-
sale "rationalization" of society on the basis of utility, Burke elo-
quently defended the unplanned accretions of social bonds, ties to
the soil, custom, and a tradition-hallowed hierarchy of value. The
"irrational" outgrowths of human history provided the web (one
of Bell's favorite terms) of significance that sheltered individuals,
nourished them, and gave them direction. Destroy them, and mankind is lost; nothing remains but the nihilism of the stark utilitarian desert. The Revolution had revealed how fragile these webs
were. Good statesmen must now consciously seek to preserve. They
cannot call into being by will those vital webs of meaning; those
can only arise without conscious intent.

Like Burke, Bell sees that modern liberalism requires a counterbalance of values that are not utilitarian in nature. But like
Burke, he is finally reduced to assertion and an appeal to religious transcendence to defend these counter-values. The reason for
this less than satisfactory position is that in the deepest sense Bell,
like Burke, accepts the liberal conception of human nature that
grows out of the idea of instrumental reason. According to that
conception, the realm of culture can only be the result of an evolutionary process which is finally instrumental in nature. The conservative thinker can point out the entropic effects of instrumentalism in historical action, but he is powerless to oppose it because
he, too, accepts the notion that social life is at bottom a kind of
instrument, a means to survival.

The dominance of the liberal ethos has been so great, particularly in the post-war era, that it has controlled the options for
viewing social life. Conservatism is the reactive mirror of liberal
instrumental individualism. For individual aggrandizement and
the calculation of utility it would substitute the solidarity of the
group and the hallowed ways of custom—above all, of authority.
But why are these things good, indeed, better than the liberal

28. See Edmund Burke, *Reflections on the Revolution in France* (Garden City,
New York: Doubleday, 1961), and also Williams, *Culture and Society.*

goods? Only because we need them to survive. There is no intrinsic good in any of these things, nor are there reasonable ways to
discuss or—crucially—to reinterpret tradition. To be able to talk
about these things would require a conception of value, society,
person, and, finally, reason that is larger than the liberal one. The
cultural contradictions of capitalism have created a great desire to
find such an alternative, but the route toward it must lie through a
critique of the reigning assumptions.

Bell sees with dismay that the tendency toward self-disintegra-
tion in affluent American society is generated by the successful
operation of its primary coordinating institution, the state-regu-
lated market. He portrays the dangerous consequences of the race
for acquisition when for the first time in history it becomes truly
generalized among all classes. The spread of relative affluence
after World War II did not alter the relative distribution of wealth;
that has in fact become more tightly concentrated than before.
Rather, dramatically increased productivity brought suburban living, automobiles, higher education, and various other positional
goods within the reach of many more Americans than ever before,
at the same time that the competition for these things heated up.
The erosion of traditional constraints in favor of hedonistic self-
interest among both the owners of wealth and the working class
thus represents not a contradiction but a working-out of liberal
capitalist culture, freer than in the past from the older social and
moral orders within which it rested. The contradiction, as Bell
presents it, is between the institutional tendencies of capitalist
society and the cultural values that could prevent its most destructive effects and upon which its own viability as a social system
therefore depends. The survival of liberalism itself as a moral and
political philosophy of individual dignity is thus threatened first
and foremost by the "economizing," utilitarian way of thinking,
which is concomitant with the liberal ideal of individual freedom.
Liberalism is caught in a contradiction, indeed: hence Bell's search
for moral authority and his otherwise strange assertion that the
defense of liberal politics has turned him to cultural conservatism.

Robert Heilbroner does not consider himself or his work conservative. He does not see social and economic egalitarian tendencies as inherent threats to political democracy. He approaches the
problems of contemporary liberal society from a long involvement
in economy theory and history marked by a strong element of

Marxist analysis. Thus it is especially noteworthy that his concerns of the past decade have brought him to a conception of the present crisis of what he calls "business civilization" that is similar to Hirsch's and Bell's. Heilbroner's chief interest is the profound change in popular conceptions of what individuals may rightfully expect from society and each other which has resulted from the huge growth in productivity the capitalist economies experienced after World War II.

Heilbroner calls the post-war conditions "social affluence" and sees their cultural impact as the generation of a new concern with relative position in the social order. There is widespread expectation of upward class mobility that is at odds with the escalator kind of development aimed at by government growth policy. Affluence has created, for half the population at least, greater demands for mobility, income, and economic stability. To the extent that these demands and expectations have actually been met, growth has also lessened the sense of economic insecurity among jobholders generally. This has weakened the sense of deference and willingness to restrain demands among both blue- and white-collar workers and so has set off inflationary pressures through competition for positional goods, while weakening the older group ties and deference that had restrained competition.[29] The pie has grown a lot, but the ranks of the aggressively hungry have grown even faster.

The increased expectations, inflated by government growth policy and relative stabilization of market cycles, have thrown into doubt the old verities linking hard work and success. The new concern for advancement, Heilbroner notes, poses severe problems for the market economy because it undermines individuals' motivations to seek enrichment by responding to shifts in supply and demand which do not always fulfill hopes for upward mobility. Yet, the new expectations are still clearly economic and individualistic in character. Social affluence has simply refocused the desires of individuals and groups for competitive success in a more political direction, pressing for government intervention to redress inequalities and advance the relative position of interest groups. This is the drive for greater equalization that so alarms the so-

29. Robert Heilbroner, *Business Civilization in Decline* (New York: W. W Norton, 1976), pp. 51ff.

called neo-Conservatives. It threatens the "career open to talent" beloved of the early liberals, where *talent* is defined by what the competitive market will bear. Ironically, this tendency to demand more from government action is the indirect result of the success of the very competitive values philosophic liberals like Bell and the neo-Conservatives promote.

Heilbroner points out that economic growth has brought an increased mobility, a desire and a competitive pressure to "rise" whenever possible, which has weakened the support individuals once received from family, neighborhood, and church. The mobile and relatively affluent now must obtain these supports by contracting for them in the market—consider the tremendous rise in middle-class expenditures for psychotherapy—or by pressuring the government for services. Much of the current dissatisfaction with government costs stem from a widespread belief of middle-income taxpayers that they do not get their money's worth, having "contracted" with government for services in exchange for taxes, not for a redistribution of wealth from the more to the less affluent. So the contemporary attacks on redistributive programs such as welfare should not be misconstrued as a blanket attack on government intervention or, better, "participation" in the private economy. They represent, as J.K. Galbraith has dubbed it, a revolt of the relatively rich against the poor, prompted by the slowing of economic growth.[30] Behind these movements lies a set of attitudes and cultural assumptions corresponding to the liberal premise that self-interest is the fundamental and legitimate social motivation— only now, thanks to social affluence, this is being acted out with less and less interference from traditional notions of deference or group solidarity.

The root of the problem, Heilbroner argues, lies in the modern overemphasis upon the economic machinery of capitalism and its attendant value system of individual utilitarianism. The primacy that both philosophic liberalism and Marxism have placed on an instrumental view of society has led to a self-fulfilling prophecy: assuming that need-satisfaction powers a politics of interests, modern societies have overemphasized the capacity of market and technical organization to shape successfully the temper of social life. In

---

30. See John Kenneth Galbraith, "Oil: A Solution," *New York Review of Books* XXVI, 14 (27 September 1979): 3-6.

fact, says Heilbroner, the adaptive capacities of capitalist societies in the face of recurrent cycles of economic boom and bust have come not so much from their economic "base" as from their political and cultural "superstructure." Historical change depends as much upon new political responses as upon material constraints, such as the ecological ones, which will shape all future development. Political movements are themselves aspects of deeper changes in cultural meanings, including more or less conscious development of new images of the good person, the good society, and the integrated life.[31] Consequently, the crisis facing American society is cultural as well as a problem of economic and social structure, and the utilitarian version of liberalism, which is so much a part of the world of social affluence, is the center of the problem.

Now, the effects of long downturns in economic growth on a society such as ours are not likely to be benign and the sort of struggles over distribution Heilbroner sees as arising will pit groups against one another in an extremely unequal battle. The less advantaged and less powerful are clearly likely to lose. The immediate problem, then, is how to manage politically a civilization like that of the United States, heavily dedicated to the accumulation of wealth when the limits and, indeed, internal contradictions of that goal are becoming apparent. The problem on the international level is, if anything, even more acute and more dangerous.[32] But if government has to be the agency of social management, presiding uneasily over a market dominated by vast corporate empires, and the earlier successes of economic growth have undercut the traditional moral bonds the state must draw upon for its own justification, what are we to do?

Heilbroner argues that a future of relative scarcity makes basing self-worth upon economic achievement socially disastrous. Without significant cultural changes away from the primacy of individual accumulation and the utilitarian mode of thinking that accompanies it, there is no way to avoid tightly controlled despotism simply as a mechanism for social survival. More consistently than Daniel Bell, Heilbroner perceives that the root of the destructive potential of individual self-interest is the liberal conception of

31. Heilbroner, *Business Civilization*, pp. 44-49.
32. Heilbroner has described a chilling scenario of the unequal international struggle between haves and have-nots in his *Reflections on the Human Prospect* (New York: Norton, 1974).

human nature itself. Repelled by liberal capitalism's exaltation of the acquisitive individual, Heilbroner has also been increasingly critical of the similar Marxist tendency to see human beings as exclusively creatures of need and interest and thus subject to nearly infinite change depending on socioeconomic conditions.[33] This puts him in a difficult position.

The essence of the structural crisis American society confronts in the new age of resource scarcity and international competition is a reorientation of its industrial system, prodigal in its use of energy, away from unlimited expansion in the pursuit of profit toward an unwonted thrift and egalitarian organization of its resources. Heilbroner is loyal to the traditional program of the Left in its concern with an egalitarian social and political order, but he argues that the new era will make simple redistribution a far less satisfactory solution than it once appeared. The whole premise of our industrial civilization built upon technology has been that human fulfillment is a struggle for material ends, for a world of physical abundance. The Enlightenment vision of progress is summed up by the instrumental and utilitarian notion of value at the heart of liberalism, a notion Marxism collectivized but also adopted.

Heilbroner understands clearly that it is this conception of history and progress which is in crisis. As long as a future of abundance seemed possible, then a politics of individual or class interest also appeared reasonable, postponing the question of mutual accommodation and justice till after reaching abundance in the liberal vision or until the revolution liberated the forces of technology, as Marxists saw it. But if the achievement of an egalitarian society waits upon technological abundance, then the entire vision of a liberated society is a chimera. For what Heilbroner sees as inevitable everywhere in the "post-modern" world is more social discipline. The only alternative to despotic, unequal management of scarcity is collectively self-chosen frugality, and that is the possibility which the spread of the culture of affluence has badly undermined.[34]

33. Heilbroner, "Reflections on the Future of Socialism," in *Between Capitalism and Socialism: Essays in Political Economics* (New York: Random House, 1970), esp. pp. 102-14.

34. Heilbroner discusses this issue at length in *Reflections on the Human Prospect*.

The gloom of Heilbroner's conclusion about the future of industrial society both liberal and socialist leads him, like Bell, to search for another way to guide social and private life, one not founded on the instrumental and utilitarian idea of progress. Also like Bell, Heilbroner evokes a vision of a post-industrial society in which "tradition and ritual" are to provide guidance and solace for life, now no longer organized around the struggle for material goals or individual achievement but ordered by communally and traditionally ordained patterns of living.[35] What is happening here? Heilbroner has accurately located the fallacy in the utilitarian vision of progress. If moral ties are instrumental for the satisfaction of individual needs, and a fraternal, just society is contingent upon fulfillment of these needs, then the collapse of the technological crusade against scarcity means giving up the dream of Jerusalem the Golden in the form of the abundant liberated society. But what are the alternatives? Heilbroner seems to emphasize one: reversion to some form of organic society in which scarcity can be endured, though not necessarily equitably, because its members are held in check by deference to tradition-sanctioned patterns of distribution. Edmund Burke has appeared a second time.

Yet, is this post-industrial customary society even a possible vision? Other thinkers, explicitly fearful of the rise of government tyranny though more sanguine about effects of the market system, have begun proposing a revitalization of "intermediate institutions" between the individual and the centralized state such as family, neighborhood, and church. Drawing inspiration from Alexis de Tocqueville, Peter Berger and Robert Nisbet have proposed that government intervene less in local affairs so as to allow these traditional structures breathing space. There is much merit to this argument, which would balance the individual and the centralized state through a vigorous local life. However, a simple appeal to intermediate structures is not in itself enough, precisely because of the culturally enervating effects of social affluence. These authors do not advocate changing the economic structure; yet, the effect of the modern corporate economy has been to create competitive pressures that have weakened networks of reciprocity and self-help. This effect in turn has often forced individuals to rely more and more on commercial services and governmental

35. Heilbroner, *Business Civilization*, p. 98.

bureaucracies to take care of social needs. Recent literature on the changing relationship of families to "expert services" documents this trend.[36]

The consequence is that households become more dependent on market and governmental powers while less tightly associated with others. The sheer difference in scale often precludes whatever kinds of community do flourish from competing with corporate giants and the state, a trend C. Wright Mills, writing in the 1950s, called the emergence of "mass society."[37] Given the strongly private cast to thought about goals and values in growth-oriented American society, Heilbroner's pessimism seems to undercut possibilities for change in the direction of renewed local community unless the policy of the national government were itself to be oriented toward fostering it.

Thus, the real conclusion is this. Without significant cultural changes away from the primacy of individual accumulation and the utilitarian mode of thinking that accompanies it, there is no way to avoid tightly controlled despotism simply as a mechanism for social survival. But where to look for such changes? For Heilbroner, utilitarian liberalism cannot help; it is a large part of the problem. The other models he sees are not directly applicable. They have been provided by one of modern Western civilization's most remarkable enterprises, anthropological research. Heilbroner urges us to learn, or relearn, from so-called primitive peoples to order society through tradition and religious authority.[38] How this is to occur Heilbroner does not tell us. So his analysis, too, points toward a picture of civilizational entropy, another gloomy coda to the West's faith in progress.

:: IV

Hirsch, Bell, and Heilbroner make out a strong case that liberal capitalist affluence finds itself entangled, indeed, nearly immobi-

36. In this connection see Kenneth Keniston, *All Our Children: The American Family under Siege* (New York: Harcourt, Brace, Jovanovich, 1977), and Christopher Lasch, *Haven in a Heartless World: The Family Besieged* (New York: Basic Books, 1977).

37. See C. Wright Mills, "The Mass Society," in *The Power Elite* (New York: Oxford University Press, 1956).

38. Heilbroner, *Business Civilization*, p. 98.

lized, by its own contradictions. These theorists of the social contradictions of affluence emphasize that economic and social analysis is always embedded in an historical and cultural perspective, and this understanding has enabled them to reveal the transitory nature of the social and cultural conditions that allowed liberal capitalism to flourish. We can then also see that the theoretical categories of liberal social philosophy—the self-interested, acquisitive individual, the self-regulating market, the instrumental conception of social relationship, the notion that politics is bargaining among interests—are themselves historically situated. They are not universal truths; they appear as self-evident only to people at home in a certain kind of society. But then we must realize that the categories of social analysis depend upon the interpretive context of the theorists who use them.

For both Heilbroner and Bell, older liberal assumptions about human nature and society have lost their status as obvious truths. They see that the economic view of human life is too narrow either to explain or, in the long run, sustain itself. Both thinkers, along with Hirsch, argue that the liberal fascination with the economic, instrumental conception of life has done much to undo the subtler bonds of shared understanding within which individuals always stand before they operate as self-interested agents. They see that utilitarian individualism is practically dependent upon a nonutilitarian context of meaning and moral orientation.

However, none of these theorists really goes beyond a liberal understanding. They view those practical contexts of meaning as mysterious webs of support descending from earlier days, which, once dissolved by utilitarian actions, fade into cultural decomposition—that is to say, that the evaluative aspects of social life cannot themselves be grasped in the terms of liberal means-end rationality. And there is profound insight in this. But to treat communal meanings as simply accidental, nonrational precipitates of experience, as the modern conservative tradition largely does, is to stop short of a genuinely radical critique of liberalism. Implicitly, the conservative thinker accepts the liberal definitions of intelligence and value as bound to means-ends efficiency. Consequently, Hirsch, Bell, and Heilbroner see communal ideals as having little vitality in the present, as a sort of nonrenewable cultural capital: hence the extreme pessimism of their conclusions.

Yet, at the same time, particularly with Heilbroner, there are moments that suggest an active alternative to resignation.

If there is a thread of meaning that prevents pessimism about the possibilities of liberal society from becoming acquiescent despair, it is the realization that grasping the problems of the liberal conception of society already implies another understanding. Discourse about community and justice still has relevance in American society, if only because the efforts of the dominant public philosophy to do without it have led to the theoretical and practical contradictions of social affluence. It does not require social scientific investigation to realize that persons question the conditions of their lives, expecting and often giving justifications in terms of values to which they are committed. Justification, on this common-sense level, implies that in practice people trust that some accounting can be given of why a certain form of life is right and good. Behind this assumption lie basic common understandings about the conditions of existence, frequently religious in nature, to which people refer in making or refusing claims to justification.

In times of great cultural change such as the American present, such questioning and justification become more frequent and widespread. They also become essential for individuals and communities in order to find their bearings in a situation of cultural turbulence. The discussion and tumult do not take place in a value-neutral situation of pure logical argument, which is sometimes upheld as the proper plane for reaching truth, but neither is this everyday process of justification a mere epiphenomenon, a simple reflex of economic interests or other structural forces in the society. If modern social theory has taught us anything, it is the barrenness of either a pure "idealism" or "materialism" in which human action is reduced to ideas or to material forces.

In fact, the language people use to understand their situation and take a stance toward it is itself an important part of their world. Persons are moral agents in that they can question themselves and their situations and take responsibility for the stances they adopt. They are not simply counters in a systemic map, moved from without. Indeed, language is a living matrix as well as a medium.

Since the rise of the positivistic ideal of social science in the last century, it has remained an article of methodological faith that social activity may be analyzed objectively both "without" as institutional patterns and "within" as meaningful action. But, according to positivist dogma, one cannot rationally pursue the question of the truth or validity of the life-forms analyzed. Max Weber accepted this limitation as the necessary boundary of scientific social inquiry. The necessity for going beyond this positivistic conception of social science to a view that can encompass the issues of values and morals is a latent conclusion of the critique of social affluence. The central importance of cultural, especially moral, conceptions in maintaining a social life is obscured by the usual liberal language of formal legitimacy. The very premise of the concept of legitimacy is the descriptive-evaluative dichotomy of modern positivistic social science. For comparative and taxonomic purposes, Weber's idea is an important summarizing one, but it obscures the fact that has proved so decisive for understanding our contemporary situation. It fails to recognize that social functioning, let alone meaningful life, is not a ratio between a spectrum of possible "value choices," on the one hand, and institutional "goal attainment," on the other. Rather, the cohesion of a society, the authority of a polity are concretely, subtly woven by the kinds of moral meaning within which its members live.[39]

Civic spirit in America has been weakened by the effects of social affluence, and this has been exacerbated in that growth itself has been very inequitably shared. Yet, criticism of these conditions and the ability to pose questions about the equity and worth of contemporary social life are themselves hopeful; they mean that all is not lost. Some measure of moral solidarity continues to resist the erosion process, an implicit civic sense of justice and equity continues to rouse dissatisfaction for many with the idea of a purely self-regarding life. The analyses of Hirsch, Bell, and Heilbroner ride on the practical condition that there is a sharing of ideals with which the theoretical description resonates and which it articulates, even though the usual conceptions of mainstream social science obscure this vital practical dimension.[40]

39. Liberalism's instrumental notion of politics as technique, along with its blindness to the foundation of political power in social power, makes the idea of legitimacy a very vexed one in contemporary America. See John Schaar's illuminating piece, "Legitimacy in the Modern State," in *Power and Community: Dissenting Essays in Political Science* (New York: Vintage Books, 1970).

40. Richard J. Bernstein has provided an acute characterization of contemporary

If American society is to weather the remainder of the present century, those shared meanings and ideals must be rearticulated and reassessed. This is the most compelling project for both moral-political philosophy and the human sciences. The reconstitution of a genuine national political society requires widespread parti-cipation in working out a more explicit moral understanding of citizenship and the dignity of human rights that is embodied in the life of the citizen. Revival of these themes of politics—in its classical sense—in terms redolent with the republican tradition of the American past is essential to the task of reforging a language of political discourse that can articulate the meaning in contem-porary conditions of the ideals of justice, dignity, and the common good.

---

mainstream social science and its problems in *The Restructuring of Social and Political Theory* (New York: Harcourt, Brace, Jovanovich, 1976), esp. pp. 1-54.

TWO

Meeting the Crisis:
The Resources of Philosophic Liberalism

:: I

One consequence of the fragmentation of the contemporary intellectual milieu is that an intelligent assessment of any issue bearing on public life requires crossing the boundaries of a variety of academic disciplines. The concerns central to a public philosophy are pursued, often by mutually conflicting methods and in several different technical languages, in the fields of sociology, economics, history, law, and psychology, as well as philosophy and political science. Yet, as Chapter One tried to show, a kind of coherence has emerged, at least about the chief difficulties confronting democratic societies. The loss of public confidence in heretofore dominant political and economic institutions, as in the cultural and intellectual traditions which have sustained them, has been widely noted and analyzed. This so-called crisis of legitimacy has touched off not only efforts at understanding but, perhaps more important, projects that aim to revitalize and reinterpret those widely held creeds which, though now tattered, have for a considerable time formed and animated public culture.

In American society during this century, philosophic liberalism has provided the chief intellectual matrix for both public discussion and more specialized intellectual discussions of political and economic matters. If there is a crisis in public culture at present, it is not surprising that many Americans, including intellectuals, have looked to the inherited teachings of liberal individualism to provide philosophic direction. Whatever the presumed hold of

European, especially socialist, ideas upon American academic thinkers, the waning of the attitudes of the 1960s has clearly brought into prominence a pronounced enthusiasm for philosophic individualism and the political theory of the social contract. Indeed, the issue historically is whether the matrix of philosophic liberalism can provide American society with an understanding of itself that will be capable of advancing democratic self-government in the difficult conditions of the present.

However, there are good reasons to doubt the capacity of liberalism to continue to provide a public philosophy adequate to a self-governing society. The next two chapters attempt to provide these reasons through an examination of the works of several important contemporary exponents of the liberal tradition in moral and political philosophy and psychology. At the outset of this endeavor it is valuable to focus on the relationship between the present problem of public life and the historically formed characteristics of philosophic liberalism in order to develop a conceptual and historical context within which to examine the claims of contemporary liberal thinkers.

The widely discussed crisis of legitimacy analyzed in the preceding chapter is deeply troubling because it concerns the cohesion of modern industrial democracies such as the United States. The problem is that the citizens of these societies appear to be losing the kind of fundamental agreement or acquiescence in public norms and values which has formerly sustained a measure of social solidarity as well as having moderated and checked self-interest. The interpretation being presented by many social theorists today differs in important ways from the older analyses according to which alienation from politics and social norms was the result of poverty and of the failure of the market economy to meet social needs. It is not that poverty amid affluence no longer exists or that it fails to generate alienation but, rather, that there is a *new* alienation growing even among the comparatively well-off, that is, among just those groups for whom market capitalism appears to have been a success.[1]

According to the usual analysis of alienation caused by poverty,

---

1. In general outline the analyses of Fred Hirsch, Daniel Bell, and Robert Heilbroner (discussed in Chapter One) are paralleled by that of the German social theorist, Jürgen Habermas, in *Legitimation Crisis* (Boston: Beacon Press, 1975).

the failure of the market economy to provide jobs and a socially adequate income erodes, among those suffering such effects, acceptance of the moral validity of the liberal capitalist norms of work and reward according to economic competition. By contrast, the new alienation does more than weaken general acceptance of the competitive work ethic as a fundamental moral order.[2] It also represents an apparent collapse of belief in the importance of certain institutional procedures claiming to provide justice, and creates cynicism about the equity of social arrangements in general. Moral confusion about public life then intensifies the appeal of self-interested individualism as a practical ethic among both political leaders and persons at large. The dynamic of the problem points toward a weakening, even a dissolution, of social bonds— in the extreme vision, a reenactment of the philosophical state of nature. Thus the problem presents itself, at once on a practical and a theoretical plane, as how to reinvigorate the social and moral bonds of American society, as how, in effect, to renegotiate the social contract.

Given this situation, the near-desperation of the proponents of philosophic liberalism is understandable. Liberalism as a tradition of thought is ill-equipped to provide guidance in an undertaking that is aimed at nothing less than revitalizing—and recasting—the moral basis of social life. The chief strength of liberal thinking—and its great appeal to entrepreneurs, practical politicians, and architects of national policy—has been its denial of the need for any substantive agreements about the ends of coordinating social institutions such as law, government, or economic enterprises. Instead, liberalism has preached the virtues of purely formal, procedural norms to regulate public conduct. Liberal thought has thus denied that public institutions should or can express in their organization or function a consensus about the kinds of goals they aim to foster, beyond a generalized freedom to pursue private ends.

Seen in broad perspective, liberalism represents a decisive break

2. See Herbert G. Gutman, *Work, Culture and Society in Industrializing America* (New York: Knopf, 1976); also Daniel T. Rogers, *The Work Ethic in Industrial America: 1850-1920* (Chicago: University of Chicago Press, 1978). The term *decline of the work ethic* is obviously vague and clichéd, and it can be misleading. It would be a step toward clarifying this issue to view it in historical perspective.

with the long tradition of civic republican thought, which argued that a self-governing society requires a shared general understanding that there is a scale of substantive ends and values upon which the vitality of social practice depends. In the civic republican view, the aim of public, especially governmental, institutions was precisely to express this general understanding of the ends of social life and to cultivate the kinds of practices that nurture both those ends and the character of the citizens. Liberalism has traditionally relegated these concerns to the private sphere. Given the experiences of early liberals with the Old Regime or, indeed, the example of modern totalitarian regimes, this attitude is comprehensible. However, in practice no political philosophy can ignore the moral and social bases of public life, and liberalism was able to be silent about them so long only because other, nongovernmental institutions provided a secure context within which the limited liberal version of procedural consensus could operate. This symbiosis between the liberal public institutions of government and market economy on the one hand and substantively committed forms of life, particularly family, religious and local community, on the other was noted by as early a social analyst as Alexis de Tocqueville. The distinguishing aspect of the contemporary crisis of legitimacy in liberal societies, as even liberal social analysts point out, is precisely the breakdown of that symbiosis, a situation which has, over time, come to alter substantially the practical moral and social meaning of liberal institutions and culture.

In sum, without the stabilizing effects of vital community and religious forms of life, the market-centered culture of competitive success has generated a situation in which the traditional liberal values of individual security and general welfare are undermined by the workings of "liberal" institutions. In this climate, technocratic and authoritarian remedies for increased atomization are readily propounded and, when they are couched in benign rhetoric, may find a hearing. The problem is exacerbated by the dominance of liberal culture in most public discourse, so that the central symbols of philosophic liberalism—individualism, the purely instrumental nature of institutions and social relationships, the primacy of analytical, scientific thinking, the alleged naturalness of a competitive, acquisitive stance toward life—all remain widely accepted as the only possible terms of public discourse. But these notions at best can provide only a highly problematical account of social and moral life. Moreover, they tacitly rely upon a social understanding of human life bound up with substantive commitments.

:: II

The concepts of philosophic liberalism were forged in polemic, as weapons for emancipating European social life from what early liberals regarded as the destructive and inequitable dominance of special privilege and monopoly in the regimes of early modern Europe. Liberal thought has never wholly lost this emancipatory edge, and from the seventeenth century to the present the defense of freedom for the individual has been its major theme. The Old Regime in Europe tied political, ecclesiastical, social, and economic institutions together, justifying privilege by appeals to tradition. Thus emancipatory liberalism easily associated escape from injustice with freedom conceived as an end in itself. Since traditional religious authority generally supported the feared and hated state, liberalism exalted independent reason, especially in the new scientific form, and sought a fresh basis for politics in the claim that individuals were endowed with rights in isolation from any associations except those that they deliberately formed for their own ends.

In order to escape the ties of tradition as well as to establish civil peace on a secure basis, intellectuals of the seventeenth and eighteenth centuries who created liberal discourse, preeminently Thomas Hobbes and John Locke, revolutionized thinking about moral and political life. Their new individualism gave primacy to man's relation to external, nonhuman nature rather than to human social bonds. This extraordinarily bold break with tradition had vast ramifications. The later liberal moral theory and the liberal theory of human nature emphasized that the rights and the psychological composition of human beings derive from this primary relation between the individual and nature. This is the image of *homo faber*, of the human being fulfilling his desires through work on the world. Relations with his kind come second, are logically derivative from and practically ancillary to this primary image of the individual working on nature. From this first postulate comes the liberal emphasis upon freedom understood as security of possession. This security becomes possible, in the absence of interhuman ties, only on the basis of control of material conditions: hence the strong tendency of individualist doctrines (and societies) to exalt both economic possession and technical dominance over nature.[3]

The second dominant feature of liberal thinking is its instrumental view of social relationships. This follows from the first premise, as does the utilitarian conception of value, which is the third aspect. As the basis of human life is seen to be the relation of the individual with nature, work comes to be humanity's defining characteristic. Relations among persons, including the biologically necessary one of reproduction of the species, are then seen as means for reproducing and enhancing the primary function. Relationships and institutions are then simply instruments and tools of another type, serving the same end of enhancing the individual's security and control over the world. As will be noted presently, this notion creates problems for liberal moral theory, which is rooted in the postulate of the natural rights of individuals.

The utilitarian standard of value complements the individualist picture of human nature. According to the liberal view, man is propelled to work upon nature for the purpose of fulfilling desires that are innate and private in origin and satisfaction, first of which is the desire to survive. Fulfillment of these desires or passions is the great human imperative, fundamentally directing all other aspects of human life. Desires are seen as drives seeking satisfaction, and they are believed to be infinite. This, too, is consistent with the individualist premise, since the overriding need to secure survival presses the individual toward a strategy of controlling not only immediate conditions but the conditions upon which immediate survival depends, and so on without limit.[4] Conditions are valued insofar as they enhance individual welfare; thus value is an aspect of the logic of control aiming to secure that welfare. In

3. See Louis Dumont's discussion of this conceptual revolution in his *From Mandeville to Marx: The Genesis and Triumph of Economic Ideology* (Chicago: University of Chicago Press, 1977). This notion of man as controller of nature for his own purposes stands beneath and gives coherence to the other aspects of liberal individualism, especially the emphasis upon freedom of possession: see C.B. MacPherson, *The Political Theory of Possessive Individualism: Hobbes to Locke* (New York: Oxford University Press, 1964).

4. Thomas Hobbes is explicit and graphic on this point: see *Leviathan*, edited by Michaelf Oakeshot (New York: Crowell-Collier, 1963), ch. 11 (pp. 63-64), ch. 13.

the absence of confidence in ties based upon mutual trust, concern with security sets in motion a logic of control that defines *the good* exclusively in strategic terms.

Fourth, liberalism has conceived of reason as a tool, an important instrument at the disposal of the passion-driven individual that he may use to extend his control over circumstances and thus increase his security and satisfaction. The early liberals took as their model the natural science of the seventeenth century, which utilized a new analytic and mathematical form of thinking. Seeing science able to achieve a dramatic control over nature by means of a studied application of the new kind of reasoning, they hoped to develop a comparably effective application of scientific techniques to human society. They thereby began a project which has continued through the Enlightenment to the utilitarian political economists of the nineteenth century to those contemporary social scientists who still see themselves as at last rendering human investigation "scientific." Almost simultaneously that philosophic departure began a parallel line of moral and political theory which has attempted to reconcile the premises of liberal social philosophy with its assertion of natural rights.

Moreover, there has been a close affinity between the individualistic, utilitarian aspects of liberal theory and commerce, between liberal politics and political economy. If by definition human desires are infinte, the only long-term ways to minimize conflict among self-interested, striving social atoms are either authoritarian control or a means of ensuring that there will be a growing quantity of satisfactions. The tremendous appeal of commercial capitalism to the liberal theorists of the eighteenth century from Mandeville and Montesquieu to Adam Smith was the hope that *le doux commerce* would provide continually expanding elbow room to lessen social conflict and make possible mutual adjustment without sacrifice of freedom on anyone's part. It is fair to say, viewing the matter this way, that the eighteenth-century liberals did not see vicious competition as a likely consequence of organizing society around the market system but as a general betterment and calming of social turbulence. Montesquieu, Hume, and Adam Smith all hoped the new age would be a cosmopolitan one, escaping the harsh and bitter antagonisms that had been the odious underside of traditional loyalties and ties.

Indeed, the fundamental utilitarian assumption about what is good and what confers authority commits a liberal society to a program of economic expansion. And since desires are understood as private both in origin and in satisfaction, with self-interest as the "natural" motivating force in mankind, the goal of life becomes acquisition of things or experiences that fulfill those desires. Both modern liberalism and its great opponent and critic, Marxism, derive much of their appeal from their common promise to provide happiness by fulfilling those desires. Rival social systems can thus be understood as competing to bury their opponents in a cornucopia of satisfaction. At its worst, this aspect of utilitarian liberalism fosters the potlatch atmosphere of conspicuous consumption and *ressentiment* that seems an inherent part of the capitalist ambiance. Yet, the inherent egotism of the utilitarian principle has also proven an immensely powerful solvent of the bonds of traditional authority and parochial loyalties. As Marx saw clearly, once one defines life's goal as the satisfaction of passion and desire, the old taboos, the sacred aura surrounding tradition-hallowed ties and relationships, rapidly lose their power to enthrall. Judging worth by its consequences for one's own well-being has proven the most subversive philosophy ever devised.

In this way the utilitarian assumption is the counterpart in the realm of ideas to the capitalist market considered as an institution. Indeed, the "emancipation" of market motives and behavior from traditional social restraints would have been impossible without the ideological solvent of utilitarian moral attitudes. It was part of that long revolution which has changed forever a world of custom-hallowed relationships in which men and women lived and saw themselves as groups that reflected a cosmic order of things. The outcome has been the creation, often with great violence, of the brave new world of contractual society whose chief metaphor for itself is "the system," a fabricated set of linkages among individuals pursuing their own, largely economic, interests. The process has been both cheered and regretted, with liberals defining themselves as the "progressive" chorus, the advocates of rationality and modernity.

The great transformation of society set in motion in early modern Europe has been at once effect and cause of the triumph of liberalism, and no single factor has been more important to that process than the establishment of science as the ideal of reason. Indeed, since the seventeenth century the canons for political understanding have been those of an explanatory science. Hobbes referred to the proper procedures of science, including what were then called the moral sciences, as "resolutions," reduction of everyday experiences to analytic elements, or "simples," which were presumed to be subject to rigorous logical definition and quantitative measure.

The new method, for British empiricists and continental Cartesians alike, was resolutely, self-consciously analytical. Truth lay in the "simples" to which complex wholes were to be reduced. The self-consciousness of the experiencing or cogitating individual was the Archimedean point to which thinkers looked to secure their claims. The new mathematics provided a metaphor (actually a new logic) by which this atomistic conception of the world could be convincingly articulated. The reduction of the *zoon politikon* and *animal rationale* of classical and medieval thinking to the passion-driven individual was bolstered by Hobbes's assertion that truth meant the display of logical relations among atomic parts. The "new science of politics," like the new science of nature, derived its initial plausibility from the supposition that a discourse describing human activity as mechanical relations among elements forming a logical system would display the nature of man not as an ideal but as it really is, for the new ideal of knowledge was the ability to describe successfully the observable appearances of events in the language of "simples" and to display their mathematical-logical coherence. These mathematical-logical relations became the "forces" of seventeenth-century physics. Knowledge, then, was knowing things as facts. The vehicle of knowledge was scientific theory.

Hobbes was well aware that this new method represented a massive reorientation of what had been known as the moral sciences. Indeed, the intensity of his polemics against Aristotle suggests how necessary he thought it to battle the classical, teleological conception of knowledge. Yet, so effective were Hobbes and the great intellectual revolutionaries of that "century of genius" that the definition and ideal of knowledge in the human sciences today remain largely that of reducing social and political events to the outcome of conflicts among social forces and individual drives. It is important to try to neutralize some of the mesmerizing effects of this all-too-familiar groove of thought, not only to see what was lost to the human sciences but to realize why so much intellectual labor in our own century has been devoted to articulating an alternative.

Knowledge in human affairs has been an ambiguous term since the Greeks. In its Hobbesian sense, knowledge is about objects. To *know* means to account for activity by means of reductive explanation. There have been a plethora of variants on this scheme, of which behaviorism is perhaps a nearly ideal type. But there is an opposed understanding of knowledge which runs deeper in common sense than the logical-reductive one and was, until the Hobbesian epistemological revolution, an important philosophical ideal. This notion stresses the understanding of the meaning an act has in its context both for the actor and for the perceiver. Understood in this way, knowledge is an aspect of a relationship between the knower and the known. Knowledge in the moral sciences before Hobbes was always a knowing *with* the other, understanding the other in a dramatic context. Since Hobbes, knowledge has come to be respectable only when the other could be exhaustively talked *about*. Not that insight disappeared—it simply ceased to be called knowledge in any respectable sense.

Hobbes's project was, then, nothing less than a conceptual revolution. He came to redefine the meaning of knowledge and of both theory and practice. Although it was his intent to deny the ethical and persuasive dimension of the human sciences by casting them as dispassionate investigations of the supposed machinery of society and politics, Hobbes was in fact a moral thinker of the first order. The new meanings knowledge and theory acquired in the seventeenth century powerfully show, when compared to the language of traditional political philosophy that Hobbes was opposing, the moral and persuasive dimension of the human sciences, even when this dimension is consciously denied.

In Hobbes's polemic against Aristotle's science of final causation, more was at stake than the meaning of theory. There was a displacement of one conception of life by another, a cultural revolution of vast dimensions. Classical philosophy had distinguished a variety of modes of knowledge corresponding to the subject matters under investigation, and Aristotle's terms *theoria, praxis,* and *techne* distinguished among three different ideals of knowing. *Techne* refers to the kind of knowledge associated with a craft, in which the producer is in complete charge of his material and forms it in accord with a preconceived plan. By contrast, knowledge of human action, *praxis*, requires a kind of participation and involvement Aristotle called *phronesis* or prudence.[5] Unlike production or *techne*, practical activity and practical knowing were understood as skills that cannot be set aside at will. That is, one does not, indeed, cannot "rest" from applying one's sensitivities about how to live. They have become essential parts of one's personality, so that a person is who he or she is only through exhibiting a kind of practical understanding and skill. Practical knowledge forms the personality of its practitioner and so is inseparable from his identity. Aristotle concluded from this that the possibility of coming to understand a form of cultural life requires competence in moving within that life. Practical involvement is the precondition for reflective clarification, which in turn plays its role in deepening the person's comprehension of how to live his life. Human affairs require practical experience to be understood; purely formal, mathematical knowledge is impossible here. Furthermore, knowledge of political affairs is only possible for the virtuous person, the one who has already in practice learned to revere the intrinsic values of the life of the citizen, and that in itself requires a measure of self-mastery.[6] Thus practical knowledge is always engaged in a kind of circle in which progress means not escaping one's initial understanding but, rather, deepening and expanding it.[7]

Theoria, the third of Aristotle's basic types of knowledge, is neither a productive nor a practical understanding; it issues neither in product nor in action but in a kind of transformation of understanding through which the knower comes to participate in the nature of the known and so to transcend a purely egocentric point of view.[8] There was thus a decisive practical, existential aspect to

5. Aristotle summarizes the various modes of knowing, especially in terms of their value in inquiry in human affairs, in his *Nicomachean Ethics* bk. VI.

6. See Aristotle, *Nicomachean Ethics* bk. I, ch. 3.

7. Hans-Georg Gadamer has provided a rich interpretation of Aristotle's notion of prudential understanding by relating it to the conception of the "hermeneutical circle." See Hans-Georg Gadamer, *Truth and Method*, edited by Garrett Bardau and John Cummings (New York: Seabury Press, 1975), esp. Part Three. See also Martin Heidegger, *Being and Time*, translated by J. Maquaric and E. Robinson (New York: Harper and Row, 1962).

8. Hans Jonas has developed the contrast between the ancient idea of theory as a participation in the world that transforms the knower from an egocentric to a common social, then, finally cosmic point of view, and its very different modern counterpart. Jonas argues that the implicit aim of the modern theory is to control

theoretical knowledge as the Greeks conceived it, but that aspect disappeared in the seventeenth-century scientific understanding of theory, which continues today as the ruling interpretation in much of philosophy and the human sciences. In the classical conception, theoretical knowing was grasping the *telos* or immanent end of natural processes, a kind of knowing that is available, Plato insisted, only to participants in a dialogical process of inquiry in which both cognitive and existential understandings are at stake and subject to transformation.[9] To know something was to be affected by it, to share its form or *eidos*. This form was not conceived simply as an underlying simple or logical structure but as a motivating purpose which can be grasped only by adopting a new standpoint of understanding—literally, to stand in a new way toward the situation. To know in this way is thus a kind of passion; one undergoes a change. To know truly, to be wise, is a transformation of one's basic loyalties, described by the classical philosophers as an identification with the immanent end of the cosmos: hence the inescapable persuasive, rhetorical dimension of classical reason.

Plato's *Phaedrus* is a *locus classicus* for this topic. The dialogue seems to argue that if knowledge is always transformative experience, then it can only be communicated by shared practice of that experience; the unenlightened must, as Plato puts it, first have trust (*pistis*) before he can have knowledge (*episteme*). The classical thinkers saw that the means of persuasion and communication are internally connected to and decisive for self-transformation. Speech about human affairs, in the Platonic understanding, is always an evocation of a problematic situation in which our response plays a crucial co-defining role, though it is a response to an encompassing involvement rather than an act of manipulative will. Even Aristotle's apophantic or revealing speech presupposes

---

the world for the knower's advantage—the reverse of the classical notion. Theory then becomes a branch of technique. See Hans Jonas, "The Practical Uses of Theory," in his *The Phenomenon of Life: Essays toward a Philosophical Biology* (New York: Harper and Row, 1966).

9. In his discussion of the epistemological presuppositions of ancient as opposed to Hobbesian political science, John W. Danford has brought Wittgenstein's philosophy of language to bear: see John W. Danford, *Wittgenstein and Political Philosophy: A Reexamination of the Foundations of Social Science* (Chicago: University of Chicago Press, 1978), esp. ch. 7.

that background of existential participation which moderns find
hard to see in nature but do find in the human creation of art.[10]
Alfred North Whitehead summed up the point when he noted that
the Greek view of nature was inherently dramatic.[11]

But if the classical conception of philosophical knowledge was
thus laden with moral and, in particular, political meaning, it
gave rise to continual and ferocious debate about the relation of
everyday life in the *polis* to these philosophic claims to depth of
understanding. The philosophic questioning of common sense
posited a powerful tension between the immanent authority of
custom and the claims of reflective insight. It carried potentially
subversive political implications. The theme of the philosopher
and the city created a continuing tension in European history that
was magnified by the Christian assertion of nonpolitical sources
of authority. By Hobbes's century, religious claims to transcendent truth connected to secular power had disrupted European life
with bloody religious wars and even, in Hobbes's England, done
the unthinkable: beheaded a reigning monarch and replaced him
with a Commonwealth.[12]

Against this background Hobbes's system of reductive empiricism, with its assault on classical philosophy and its total redefi-
nition of political thought, reveals itself as anything but an isolated theoretical revolution. Hobbes's political theory is not a
thorough-going empiricism; the ethical, rhetorical, transformative dimensions of theory are not forgotten.[13] Hobbes's "logic machine" is a rhetorical invention by which the dangerous and disruptive opinions of men can be toned down and rechanneled along
predictable and manageable paths, like the forces of the new
physics.[14] But first men had to be persuaded that there can be no

10. See Eric Voegelin, "Reason: The Classic Experience," in *Anamnesis*, translated by Gerhart Niemeyer (Notre Dame, Indiana: University of Notre Dame Press.
1978).

11. Alfred North Whitehead, *Science and the Modern World* (New York: Macmillan, 1927), p. 7; cf. R. G. Collingwood, *The Idea of Nature* (New York: Oxford
University Press, 1957).

12. The shock value of the execution of Charles I, which should not be under-
emphasized, has been described by Michael Walzer in his *Regicide and Revolution:
Speeches Made at the Trial of Louis XVI* (Cambridge, England: Cambridge University Press, 1974).

13. See Leo Strauss, *The Political Philosophy of Hobbes, Its Basis and Genesis*
(Chicago: University of Chicago Press, 1952), esp. ch. 1.

14. The phrase "logic machine" is Norman Jacobson's. See his *Thomas Hobbes*

merit in philosophers' and saints' claims of understanding a lofty *telos* for mankind. The possibilities of moral knowledge had to be deflated before the fevered patient could be manageably reoriented. Hobbes noted:

For it is evident to the meanest capacity, that men's actions are derived from the opinions they have of good or evil, which from those actions redound unto themselves; and consequently, that men once possessed of an opinion that their obedience to the sovereign power will be more hurtful to them than their disobedience, will disobey the laws, and thereby overthrow the commonwealth and introduce confusion and civil war; for the avoiding whereof all civil government was ordained.[15]

This law of nature, finally, is not a law actually governing human existence before the men, in whom it lies as a disposition toward peace, have followed its precept. . . . Only when they have covenanted to submit to a common sovereign, has the law of nature actually become the law of a society in historical existence.[16]

So the whole apparatus of the "logic machine," the reduction of striving for virtue to the "simples" of fear and defense, is employed for a purpose. This anti-teleology created, was designed to create, a profound change in political teleology.

A close reading of Hobbes shows that the alliance between liberal political philosophy and reductive empiricism was not simply fortuitous. The liberal concern with what, from classical and Christian standpoints, were the lower parts of human nature was justified epistemologically by the reductive empiricism of the new political science. The scientific conception that theoretical knowledge confers, in Bacon's phrase, power to improve the bodily happiness of mankind further persuaded morally concerned thinkers to apply analytical knowledge to regulating human activity in order to secure public order. The early modern liberals—Hobbes, Locke, Bacon, Montesquieu, and Adam Smith—saw and presented the new mechanical metaphor of social life as cause for optimism for the future, and their new moral psychology complemented their politics both as a theoretical structure and as a rhetorical construction.

---

as Creator (New York: Educational Learning Press, 1971), and also his *Pride and Solace: The Functions and Limits of Political Theory* (Berkeley: University of California Press, 1978).

15. Hobbes, *Leviathan*, p. 355.   16. Ibid., p. 94.

But the development, indeed, the triumph of individualism and utilitarianism has generated moral ambiguity and contradiction within liberal culture. The analytical character of this modern rationality, once enacted as a moral style, has achieved much for which the early modern proponents of the new science of man only wished. Freed from traditional social forms and prohibitions, Western men have advanced the control of nature, the division of labor in society, and the production of wealth. It is now clear that this project required the reduction of unique qualitative claims of value and authority to the common coin of quantitative measures. That process of analytic reduction, of working over qualitative contents, went on in virtually every area of social life, generating the new conceptions and professional spheres of science, economics, politics, and law. Throughout, the advocates of liberal modernity aimed at the ideal of a mutual adjustment of interests, of making the system work. The reality, however, has proven more complex than the liberal vision.

It was essential to the emancipatory strategy of liberal thinking that cultural meaning be analytically separated from power and instrumentality and, likewise, that the individual be conceived of as outside social bonds. Anthropological individualism was designed to serve as a buttress for moral individualism in the form of the doctrine of equality of natural rights. In opposition to classical philosophy, which had argued that equality was a goal and outcome of civic culture, liberalism declared the moral equality of individuals to be an intrinsic aspect of their personhood, having no determinate relation to social life.

There is a difficulty here. Are rights to be derived from human nature as revealed by analytical reasoning? The fundamental assumptions of the liberal theory of human nature made that project impossible. To justify postulating the moral dignity of persons within the liberal framework, one cannot appeal directly to the nature of human psychology as understood by the new reductive view of man. Rather, liberal moral thinkers sought to develop a new approach to ethics based, like the early modern epistemology of Descartes and the rationalists, upon the characteristics of moral conscience and the formal structure of moral reasoning itself.

There is thus a crucial ambiguity in the way equality has developed in liberal commercial societies, and this ambiguity began to create uneasiness for liberal thinkers very early on. On the conceptual level, the difficulty liberalism finds in surmounting these ambiguities provides strong evidence of its inadequacies as a political vision for our time. To order social life toward a dynamic equilibrium of mutual adjustment of private satisfactions, the seventeenth-century founders of the new politics sought a common scale by which to measure moral goods and render them subject to an impartial procedure of calculation. Thus to process traditional understandings, the "superstitions" and "taboos" of the old moralities with their religious and cosmic interpretations required a general leveling of qualitative differences and authoritative claims. Those goods that could not be so measured became frills of no consequence for the rational calculation of political and individual utility. In passing, we should note that from its beginning the modern view of man showed clear affinities with the demands of centralized administration as well as those of commercial life. Hobbes advocated efficient royal administration; Montesquieu saw bureaucracy and mercantile life proceeding hand-in-hand, as did Bentham. Aspects of Fabian socialism continued to link calculative reason and central administration.

The leveling of qualitative differences for calculative convenience produced as a practical as well as theoretical consequence the doctrine of the equality of desires—desires, not moral claims, since what else could the ideals of conduct and customary behavior of nobles or peasant families now appear to be, once played on the dissecting table of the new science of society? Individual pleasure and preference became the standard of value. The new calculative politics, supported by analytical science, in fact proceeded with complete certainty that the utilitarian logic of consequences provided the one universal criterion of goodness. The qualitative claims of the old morality were of course untranslatable into this kind of consequentialistic language and thus were judged, ipso facto, rationally indefensible. Those qualitative claims denied the equal validity of subjective desires. More, they generally claimed that some ideals and practices constituted unavoidable duties and obligations which bound individuals because of the intrinsic righteousness of the ideals, regardless of subjective desire or wish.

This was the problem of moral as opposed to political order in Hobbes that Locke endeavored to address by invoking a noncalculative natural law, an idea he took over from earlier Christian philosophy. Without a principled commitment to treating others as due the same consideration as himself, what is there to prevent the enlightened utilitarian from judging social practices and moral codes, including those that prohibit certain acts against persons, as dispensable instruments in the pursuit of his interests? And if we substitute the business corporation or the state for this interested individual, the gravity of the problem clearly grows.

The question for liberalism, then, is whether it can provide a rational justification for a principled commitment to moral restraint or the education of self-interest. Once one accepts the basic anthropological assumptions bound up in the program of progress through liberation, this becomes a formidable question. The unfettered pursuit of desires, the increase of technical control over nature and society can as logically give rise to competitive struggle as to benign calculation of mutual adjustment; indeed, struggle appears to have proven the empirically more common result. We live in Hobbes's world at least as much as in Locke's.

:: III

In its origins, as in its later recasting as a struggle to appropriate surplus, the liberal view of human development has seen history as liberation of desire and of technologies for the satisfaction of desire. The nub of the theory is the ideal of instrumental control, of power whose orienting locus is the individual. Yet, the individual is ultimately conceived of as the creature of its passions. Freedom's development is thus stalked by an all-consuming power, its own monstrous shadow. Conceptually, this is the consequence of trivializing cultural meaning by subordinating it to the status of a mere accompaniment to the instrumental process. In the liberal conceptual machinery designed around individual or social utility, human dignity finds no basis of support. Natural right becomes an assertion which must scramble elsewhere to find a reasoned basis.

To counter the reductive logic of its empirical claims about human nature and to provide at least a rudimentary social vision without challenging the logic of the basic scheme, liberalism has sought in moral philosophy a basis for natural right and social obligation. This is particularly true of much contemporary liberal moral theory, which wants to use the idea of rights as a corrective to the utilitarian logic of modern public policy and economics.

The difficulty is that a right is an aspect of the relationships human beings have with one another, while the postulate of individualism commits philosophic liberals to the notion that relationships are essentially means to instrumental, utilitarian goals. The relational aspect of the notion of rights is the basis for the entailment a right implies. For example, a negative right, traditionally a chief concern of liberalism, is a claim not to be the recipient of certain kinds of acts. Such a right obligates all others to refrain from making the bearer of that right the recipient of such acts. The same is true, conversely, for positive rights, which entitle an individual to goods or opportunities. Obligations and rights are reciprocally related because they are aspects of social relationships.

Liberalism's reduction of relationships to the model of pure instrumentality represents an extreme narrowing of conceptual focus, setting a fundamental problem for liberal moral thinking. Since its model of rational action, like its notion of human psychology, is instrumental and individualistic, the "rational" human actor becomes the egoist. How, then, can one construct reasons that can compel a rational thinker to accept a doctrine of natural rights, with its concomitant obligations? Historically and conceptually, liberal philosophy has produced two sets of answers.

The first has been the style of ethical thinking known as utilitarianism, which begins from the premise that moral values derive exclusively from the consequences of action, so that the basic structure of all moral reasoning is finally reducible to a choice of actions on the basis of their consequences. The standard by which consequences are evaluated is individual judgment of pleasure and pain, taken either singly or in the aggregate.[17]

While utilitarian thinking is thus based upon the familiar premises of liberal psychology, the second tradition of liberal moral psychology is more complex and ambiguous in its relationship to that theory of human nature. This second style takes its direction

17. The classic and most developed philosophical statement of the doctrine is John Stuart Mill's *Utilitarianism* (Indianapolis: Bobbs-Merrill, 1957). For an account of the development of the utilitarian current in liberal thought, see Elie Halévy, *The Growth of Philosophical Radicalism* (London: Faber and Faber, 1952). The conceptual structure and problems of the utilitarian notion of action are explored by Talcott Parsons, *The Structure of Social Action* (New York: Free Press, 1949), esp. vol. I, pp. 93ff.

from the idea of the social contract. The social-contract theorists—
Hobbes, Locke, Rousseau, and Kant—sought in various ways to
modify the instrumental and utilitarian tendencies inherent in
liberal anthropology by postulating a second kind of moral reasoning which could justify social obligations within a theoretical
framework of individualism. The contractarians hoped thereby to
civilize the libidinous freedom of the emancipated man of liberal
imagining without attacking his autonomy of will. The leading
contemporary American defenders of liberal moral philosophy
(whose work occupies the next several chapters), have returned to
contractarian teachings as the basis for their defense of rights and
obligations.[18] However, because it never wholly abandons the individualistic premises of liberal anthropology, the contractarian-
tradition understanding of what is required for genuine public
philosophy, like that of the utilitarian tradition, remains inade-
quate. This can be seen by examining each approach in turn.

For utilitarian liberals, the aim of public policy is much the
same as the good of an individual: to maximize the net balance of
satisfactions. From the viewpoint of contemporary contractarians,
the chief failing of utilitarian reasoning is that when considered as
a social ethic it is indifferent to the distribution of satisfactions or
pains among individuals. It is a doctrine of the aggregate and so
subordinates the claims of individual rights and liberties to their
utility for producing, in the aggregate and over time, an optimal
distribution of satisfactions.[19] Indeed, this aggregative conception
of the collective good follows directly from liberal psychology, as
all goods are such only as they produce or are in themselves desirable consequences for individuals.

Strictly speaking, utilitarian thought lacks a notion of social
order beyond the instrumental bonds of contracting to enhance
the sum of individual satisfactions. Practical reasoning, for utilitarians, thus finds its ideal case in instrumental action, which
receives moral justification from its success or failure in achieving
a desired satisfaction or in serving as a means to such satisfaction.

18. For example, see John Rawls's appeal to the contract doctrine in his influential *A Theory of Justice* (Cambridge, Massachusetts: Harvard University Press,
1971), pp. 11-22, and his critique of utilitarian doctrines, pp. 22-33, 158ff.

19. See David Lyons, *The Forms and Limits of Utilitarianism* (New York:
Oxford University Press, 1965), and Henry Sidgwick, *The Methods of Ethics* (London, 1907).

However, moral reasoning as such has since classical philosophy been concerned with what ought to be enjoined upon men, and a necessary part of any morality has been the criterion that general maxims be consistent in their application to all similar cases. Thus even for utilitarians a mere counsel to act so as to maximize one's pleasure is not yet morality. But moral maxims such as "thou shalt not steal" gain their legitimacy only because they are judged actually to improve the likelihood of satisfaction in the aggregate.[20]

Utilitarians such as J. S. Mill have been sensitive to the potential of this sort of consequential reasoning to break down into simple self-interest. This occurs in situations in which following a general moral maxim works against one's immediate desires. Therefore, utilitarians have argued that the principle of consequential reasoning commits us to consider the overall benefits to be gained from adherence to moral maxims even when they contravene self-interest in a particular situation. Maxims are to be selected according to the relative desirability of the consequences of their application compared to the aggregate effects of following alternative courses of action. "Rule utilitarians" like Mill argue that the goal of secure satisfaction commits a rational calculator of self-interest to a "supreme principle" or morality, that of consistently following tested substantive maxims.[21]

Thus rule utilitarians claim that all have an interest in respecting rights and obligations because such adherence to principle has the consequence of increasing the sum of satisfactions obtainable, thereby rendering individual pursuit of satisfaction more predictable and stable. But this reasoning holds only if individual desires are compatible in the aggregate. What if experience suggests that attention to certain claims to rights and obligation does not further the maximization of aggregate satisfactions, or what if desires turn out to be so conflicting that generally satisfactory rules for regulating their pursuit cannot be agreed upon? These are not merely hypothetical questions. They reveal that consequentialist thinking becomes a possible structure of moral thinking only under certain fairly specific circumstances in which individual desires

20. See W. K. Frankena, *Ethics* (Englewood Cliffs, New Jersey: Prentice-Hall, 1963), and D. P. Gauthier, *Practical Reasoning* (Oxford: Clarendon Press, 1963).
21. Mill, *Utilitarianism*, ch. 5.

can be mutually compatible, at least over the long run. In other words, rule utilitarianism presupposes a certain type of social environment, together with corresponding types of character and cultural understandings. The harmonious operation of its self-regarding logic tacitly depends upon a certain social and moral ecology.

A moral ecology is a social world in which psychological motivation is formed through a pattern of relationships interpreted and sustained by shared understandings. In this way motives and acts are oriented to social interactions, which are partly constituted by mutually shared symbols. However, by reducing human motivation to the expression of organic drives, liberal psychology lost sight of this social reference of desire. By similarly reducing the complexity of socially structured and symbolically mediated action to instrumental utility, liberal thinking isolated the individual actor from his context, which was then denied any necessary part in an understanding of the actor's motivation or thinking. Finally, liberal moral thinking has attempted a herculean labor by accepting these rather impoverished premises and then seeking to link the self-interested individual to a life of moral relationship by principles of reasoning which must also be divorced from substantive context.

Compared to utilitarian ethics, contractarian liberalism gains greater conceptual power by providing a skeleton of social relationship from which one can attempt to flesh out a full social and moral ecology by tracing the lineaments of suppressed but implied social contexts. This will enable us to recover the "ground" of the Gestalt whose "figure" is partially described by theorists of the social contract. This reconstruction is an essential step in a critique of liberalism that can point us toward a viable understanding of public philosophy.

American liberal culture depends heavily upon the social-contract doctrines of both Locke and Hobbes, whose understandings of the contractarian idea are not entirely compatible.[22] This is

22. The Lockean elements of American constitutionalism have been continuously emphasized and eulogized: see Louis Hartz, *The Liberal Tradition in America: An Interpretation of American Political Thought since the Revolution* (New York: Harcourt, Brace, 1955). The Hobbesian cast of the system has been less celebrated, but see James Coleman, *Exploring the Foundations: The Hobbesian Origins of American Constitutional Thought* (Toronto: University of Toronto Press, 1977).

because they derive their respective assumptions about human psychology from different moral ecologies. The differences become instructive when seen in this way. Hobbes conceived the state of nature as dangerous and unstable, a futile struggle for dominance among mutually threatened egoists. The decisive move from that state, which is exemplified by warfare among nations, to the security of the social contract, enforced by the strong arm of the Sovereign, was propelled by fear of the violence of that natural condition.[23] However, Hobbes's hypothetical contractors, to the degree that they accept the contract through reason, are persuaded by a logic different from the kind implied in Hobbes's description of the state of nature. They must somehow come to appreciate that mutual recognition of rights and the corresponding trust that the other will meet his obligations make for a more secure life than does each individual's pursuit of control over all the conditions affecting his life. They must in effect be persuaded to act as though they trusted one another.

However, on Hobbes's psychological premises it is difficult to see how such a switch in perspectives can be made permanent. The social ecology of the state of nature is such as to generate continual anxiety and mutual hostility. "Natural" men are unable to assure their own survival. This is because the natural state lacks rules. Men have no status, no meaningful relationship. They confront one another in desperate competition. Self-interested pursuit of individual welfare appears to these men as a "logical" response to this situation; yet, when viewed from the perspective of the system of relations as a whole, it is evident that no individual can effectively secure his control over the conditions of his satisfactions in any stable, long-term way. Hobbes introduces the contract to resolve this problem by providing the rules that can ensure individual survival, but the Leviathan does not alter the psychological nature of the contractors.

Within Hobbes's social contract, individuals are still motivated by fear, only now it is fear of the Sovereign. Thus the new stability is highly precarious. Its maintenance depends on a policing power that prevents egotistical actings-out of the sort characteristic of the state of nature from recurring or, more crucially, from paying off. If "crime" were to pay on a sufficient scale, if the Sovereign were

23. See Hobbes, *Leviathan*, ch. 12, esp. pp. 63-64.

ineffective, the social contract would dissolve, and the state would sink back into anarchic struggle. The superior wisdom of the contract becomes dependent on a social ecology in the absence of which reasoning and action revert to radical egoism.[24] The difficulty is that Hobbes's conception provides little hope that the requisite social ecology can be maintained. Hobbes is forced to this dismal conclusion because his reductionistic psychology conceives of human desires as untouched by social experience. Action is always instrumental for Hobbes, and because it is, Leviathan must be a police state without a convincing answer as to *quis custodet custodes*.

Locke's revisionism did not challenge this core of the Hobbesian theory. Instead, Locke substituted a different reading of the nature of the fundamental desires characteristic of natural man. Locke's social contract was predicated on the potential combatibility among individual desires for security and satisfaction.[25] In essence it was this far more attractive teaching which gave liberalism the optimistic tone of a message of political betterment and provided the root idea that was amplified through Adam Smith's concept of the natural complementarity of the division of labor.[26]

Locke's contractors have a greater likelihood of developing a viable civil society because their condition by nature better disposes them in that way than does Hobbes's state of nature. By postulating a natural compatibility between desires and a capacity for adherence to divinely given moral law, Locke in effect begins his theory with individuals who, though egoists, share a measure of mutual recognition and obligation. Locke's state of nature already has rules; it is already a culturally ordered world. The contractors share a moral ecology that disposes them to understand the superior rationality of restraint and obligation without which their security and satisfactions—in Locke's language, freedom and rights—could not be ensured.

The difficulty in Locke's theory is the problem of accounting for the existence of this kind of moral insight and social interac-

24. Ibid., ch. 13.
25. An admittedly general summary of Locke's argument in *Two Treatises of Government*, edited by Peter Laslett (second edition, London: Cambridge University Press, 1967), 2:376ff.
26. See Albert Hirschman, *The Passions and the Interests: Political Arguments for Capitalism before Its Triumph* (Princeton, New Jersey: Princeton University Press, 1976).

tion among creatures who are described as essentially isolated and private in their motivations and identities.[27] Locke presents a bifocal picture of human beings. They are naturally self-interested and desirous of private satisfactions. Their practical reasoning is thus of the same instrumental kind as that of Hobbes's men and is likewise aimed at controlling the conditions of satisfaction. These are characteristics of the social ecology found in Hobbes's state of nature. On the other hand, Locke's state of nature has a more secure structure because it is culturally shaped: the individuals associate within practical patterns that stabilize their identities and satisfactions by incorporating them within a system of mutual recognition of worth. The state of nature thus appears to be a moral community. On the other hand, the desires and reasoning of Lockean men are driven by amoral wants of a private and strategic type. To such beings, appeals of a moral sort—such as an appeal to support the social contract—would be entirely unavailing. The doctrine of compatibility of desires explains how egoists could come to shed the antagonism of Hobbes's war of all against all and arrive at a state of mutual disinterest, but it cannot compel the egoist to enter and continue in the moral community without external constraint, which Locke eschewed.

Indeed, it was not Locke but Rousseau who described these two psychologies as opposing images of human nature. One was the isolated, instrumental individual, while Rousseau recognized the other as the classical character of the citizen. By reconstructing the social and cultural contexts for the contract doctrines of Hobbes and Locke, Rousseau demonstrated the incompatibility between the premise of liberal individualism with its attendant psychology and the moral bonds required by the interdependency of social life.[28] So long as the individualistic psychology of desire remains in place, Locke's formulation of the contract will tend to collapse

27. A strong contemporary effort to present Locke as having proposed a good answer to this difficulty is that of John Dunn, *The Political Thought of John Locke* (London: Cambridge University Press, 1969). However, Dunn admits that the relation between moral conscience and desire is an unresolved issue in Locke (p. 1).

28. See Judith N. Shklar, *Men and Citizens: A Study of Rousseau's Social Theory* (London: Cambridge University Press, 1969). For the importance of Rousseau's contributions to the development of Kantian liberalism and its criticism by Hegel, see George Armstrong Kelly, *Idealism, Politics and History: Sources of Hegelian Thought* (London: Cambridge University Press, 1969), pp. 75-180.

back into Hobbes's, which, as we have seen, provides no real basis for social life. The problem Rousseau posed has remained decisive for contractarian thinking and, indeed, for the liberal tradition as a whole.

Rousseau revealed the abstractness of earlier contractarian thinking by arguing that the transition from the pre-social state of nature to civil society demanded a thoroughgoing change in the psychology of the contractors. His answer to the question as to how society is possible, the idea of the general will, reestablished a conceptual link between moral reasoning and the pattern of social relationships, the link the earlier liberals had severed. The general will explained what conditions would have to prevail in order for the social contract to be achieved and remain viable. Those conditions of possibility amounted to a mutually regarding moral ecology in which individual desire could be formed and stabilized through reference to an authoritative pattern of social identities. There the "objectivity" of classical ethics, the point of view that sees the common good of the community of individuals related through cultural forms, becomes as "natural" a standpoint for thought and motive as the utilitarian perspective seems "natural" to the Hobbesian man. The moral point of view thus appears as an essential aspect of human life as social existence.

Seen in this way, Rousseau's critique and reconstruction of the contract doctrine meant that the transition from utilitarian self-interested reasoning to moral understanding was one with the development of character within the social life of a moral community. However, this aspect of Rousseau's thought ran contrary to the dominant thrust of liberal culture. By reviving the importance of social life and virtue in ways that recalled classical republicanism, Rousseau's thought also emphasized the interdependency of human life and with it the issue of the authoritativeness of practices and moral insights. But that raised the specter of a traditional social order still very much alive in the eighteenth century.

Rousseau wrote within a context shaped by the emancipatory program of Enlightenment liberalism, which was an integral part of the great social transformation then in progress in Western societies.[29] That process sundered countless historical and custo-

29. See Karl Polanyi, *The Great Transformation* (New York: Holt, Rinehart and Winston, 1944).

mary connections in European culture, though it seemed to liberal thinkers to provide new opportunities for individual self-determination and, later, for the self-determination of classes and religious and national groups. There was truth behind their optimism; yet, there were also the painful disruptions occasioned by the swift ending of the old order, the whirlwind described by Marx a century later, in which "all fixed, fast-frozen relations, with their train of ancient and venerable prejudices and opinions, are swept away; all new-formed ones become antiquated before they can ossify. All that is solid melts into air, all that is holy is profaned, and man is at last compelled to face with sober senses his real relations of life and his relations with his kind."[30] Still, like a good Enlightenment liberal, the Marx of the *Communist Manifesto* celebrated the solvent effects of the new world order, based upon capitalist relations of exchange, as the necessary condition for a cosmopolitan civilization based at last upon recognition of man's "real relations of life and with his kind." In that setting it is hardly surprising that Rousseau shared with liberals several key premises, in particular a distrust of traditional institutions and social groupings. Indeed, Rousseau accepted the convention of the atomized state of nature (which reflected in ideal form the tendencies of capitalist social transformations) as the way to pose the question of how collective life is possible.

The wills of the contractors are conceived as free not only of the determinism of desires and natural causes but of the socially formed motivations of traditional society as well. The leap to the general will does create a new context of social relations, including a moral ecology, that is not merely a summing of individual desires or a common denominator among individual wills. But the moral ecology of the general will remains abstract in that the common project which gives the general life its authority has no substantive content, and this is consistent with Rousseau's conception of will as abstracted from any historical context.

Much in Rousseau's work indicates his sensitivity to the importance of the concrete, contextual aspects of social life. In the *Social Contract* he turns to the idea of a "civil religion" as a way to instill motivational content in the wills of his citizens, and Rousseau certainly knew that republics like his native Geneva depended

---

30. Karl Marx and Frederick Engels, *Communist Manifesto*, in *Selected Works* (New York: International Publishers, 1968), p. 38.

upon the nurturing of a strong moral ecology.[31] These aspects of his thought suggest that the viability of the contract depends on a notion of a general good and a conception of the intrinsic values of collective life that is able to provide the conditions necessary for creation of a general will. Without such a substantive content, Rousseau's general will tends to fall back into the atomistic moral psychology of Locke, which, in the absence of a substantive moral ecology, creates conditions of conflict requiring a Hobbesian order for their solution.

Several of Rousseau's intellectual heirs, most notably Hegel and Tocqueville, have been acutely sensitive to this problem of the abstractness of the general will.[32] Tocqueville regarded the viability of American republicanism as a function of the ability of local communities and associations, together with religious morality, to provide substantive loyalties sufficient to sustain the social contract. In Tocqueville's view, the American republic was able partially to solve the contractarian problem through the historical good fortune of having inherited a social and moral ecology that could anchor and counterbalance the anomic tendencies of utilitarian capitalism. But this American "solution" was largely a tacit—indeed, an accidental—one, due to the social and cultural circumstances attending the founding and early years of the United States, particularly its convenantal religious orientation and long habits of republican self-rule. It was not a "liberal" solution in the philosophic sense.

:: IV

The main line of contractarian thought after Rousseau, the Enlightenment thinking which influenced American republicans as well as European theorists of liberalism, continued to ignore or

31. See Jean-Jacques Rousseau, *The Social Contract*, translated by G. D. H. Cole (New York: Dutton, 1950); *Politics and the Arts: Letter to M. D'Alembert on the Theatre* (New York: Free Press, 1960). In a study explicitly informed by Rousseau, Benjamin Barber has presented an analysis of the interrelationship between Swiss republican institutions and the maintenance of specific forms of social and cultural life. See his *Death of Communal Liberty: The History of Freedom in a Swiss Mountain Canton* (Princeton, New Jersey: Princeton University Press, 1974).

32. For example, see Charles Taylor's recent presentation of Hegel's philosophy as both an acceptance of Rousseau and an attempt to anchor the will in a new conception of nature: *Hegel* (London: Cambridge University Press, 1975).

to downplay the dependence of the contract upon the practical context of a moral ecology. In part this was a direct if ultimately ironic consequence of liberalism's emancipatory strategy. As the institutions of the old order in Europe tottered, were discredited and, occasionally, were eclipsed, older notions of authority were challenged in the name of a new principle. This was the idea of self-determination, which the eighteenth century termed *autonomy*. The novelty lay less in the term than in the new context of discourse within which it functioned. The individual appeared starkly in early modern Europe, the one moral entity surviving amid the decomposition of traditional structures and the erection of the new impersonal machinery of economic order. The new market relationships of contract and exchange were one part of the picture. The on-going conflict between centralizing royal power and other social groupings was another. The genius of liberalism was to provide an account of all this in which it became possible for thinking persons to locate themselves as morally significant participants, able even to challenge sovereignties old and new.

However, the climate of expanding state sovereignty, capitalist social relations, and the powerful new scientific ethos posed formidable intellectual difficulties. The dead hand of traditional bonds could be effectively removed from the individual by dividing social life into a public sphere of formal, contractual relationships regulated by statute and a discontinuous private realm, largely hidden from public view in both theory and practice. There the economic individual was also husband, son, father, Christian, Jew, or free-thinker, living within often highly traditional contexts of social mores. The new political theories concerned themselves largely with sovereignty, contract law, and public order. When the mores were discussed, it was usually in a context framed by the liberties of individuals, usually male householders, as defined in contractual terms.

The notion of autonomy also provided a way out of the physical determinism that appeared to be the upshot of the new science of nature. That new science had seemed to Hobbes and many of his followers to demolish the older conceptions that had rooted morality and institutions within a meaningful natural order. This conceptual change emancipated instrumental thinking from any specific set of given ends, but it also made human action into the causally determined effect of physical forces, since both the desires of the individual and the interests of society must similarly be effects of these deeper causes. But if one could show that there was a class of human actions that followed not from the push of desire but from an aspect of the individual independent of natural determinism, then the moral dignity of the individual might be rescued in a way that was free of the fixed ends of the old order of nature. Autonomy would provide both the basis for emancipation from traditional bonds and the moral basis for the new order of contract.

Indeed, the most cogent and elaborate defense of the liberal view of society as contract, that given by Kant, took the autonomy of the will as its focus and ground. Emancipation as Enlightenment thinkers generally understood it was premised upon freeing the individual from paternalism and the coercive power of custom and tradition. In opposition to the authority of tradition, which had been the customary guide for action, Kant set a conception of reason as a procedure for making judgments so compelling that they could be employed from any individual's point of view and yet be agreed to by all. The model for Kant's notion of rationality was, of course, the procedures of the natural sciences, particularly physics. As Kant saw it, the great success of physics lay in its use of canons of reasoning that emphasized consistency in applying principles to cases as well as coherence among the principles themselves. For Kant, these qualities defined the meaning of rationality and set the standards to which all thinking should aspire. Kant's genius was to employ this insight in an effort to make ethics a thoroughly rational enterprise and so to provide a firm basis for the theory of social contract.[33]

Kant aimed to provide a rational account of the freedom of the will which would give autonomy the same self-evidence that the principles of Newton's physics and Euclid's geometry enjoyed during the Enlightenment. By so doing he would provide a logically consistent defense of individual moral dignity while also obligating all to respect the dignity of each. Kant thought that he could secure this moral framework against the corrosiveness of skepticism and practical utilitarianism, which had destroyed the tradi-

33. Stephen Toulmin has characterized Kant's project as making ethics a "quasi-discipline," "grounded" by the internal coherence and consistency of its principles: see his *Human Understanding* (Princeton, New Jersey: Princeton University Press, 1972), esp. pp. 406-11.

tional framework of natural law. His notion of morality as systematic and universal procedures of judgment tied the autonomy of the self to its obligations by making rational judgment the essential character of the will. Rousseau's emphasis upon the will was developed by Kant to mean that individual autonomy is tied to a kind of thinking that derives its validity not from any particular desires, interests, or commitments but from the sheer internal necessities of reason itself.

Thus Kant provided the contractarian tradition with both a new moral basis and, he thought, a definitive control upon the disruptive, amoral tendencies of instrumental, utilitarian thinking. To do this he invented a new and subsequently very influential notion of practical reason. For Kant, all reasoning was a matter of forming judgments, an analogy to the logical operation of subsuming particulars under universal principles. The novelty of his philosophy was to try to ground or secure these judgments not by appeal to the nature of things but by reconstructing the frameworks of rational consistency within which the various types of judgment were made. The frameworks themselves, of which the "pure" or theoretical reason underlying mathematical and scientific thinking was the paradigm, were justified by their conceptual necessity, their inescapability as the logical contexts within which alone the ordering of judgments could be intelligible.

Practical reasoning was for Kant a framework distinct from theoretical reason because it was concerned with acting, that is, with the will in Rousseau's sense. But for Kant it resembled theoretical reason in that it too was a matter of judgment or, to be precise, a matter of decisions about particular cases dictated by general principles. Moral philosophy became ethical theory, reconstruction of the logical framework necessary to support ethical principles. The context was assumed to be characterized by its own kind of logical universality and inescapability. Thus practical reasoning in the Kantian tradition became "deontological," a method of making consistent decisions through application of general principles to particular cases. Ethics became established as a peculiar realm in which the will is free, yet obligated. This provided a new contractarian reply to self-interested egoism.

Kantian ethics invoked against simple self-interest or egotism the criterion of logical, systematic coherence. The argument runs that to be rational means to submit claims about truth or goodness

to an impartial forum in which even-handed procedures of judgment can be brought to bear. Clearly, mere self-interested calculation does not do this when it looks to the simple fulfillment of its
desires as the universal overriding principle. Then, says the Kantian, there is something defective, something incomplete about the
egoist's claim to be rational. The pull of desires and inclinations
distorts the operation of a fully rational reflection, and so rationality must be grounded in some faculty other than desire and
inclination. It must be grounded in the will.

But what conditions must prevail for such truly rational thinking to take place? First of all, the moral thinker must be able to
submit his interests to a forum of impartial reason. And an attempt to "give reasons" to justify a moral judgment already implies such a forum. If he does, then he is by nature not only a
calculating egoist but also a rational being. Since rationality by
Kant's definition considers universal principles, the moral thinker
as a rational being must judge according to these universal standards. However, since rationality, again by definition, is common
to all rational beings per se, our thinker is forced to conclude that,
to be reasonable, a rational decision for himself would have to be
the right decision for any rational being in such circumstances. He
cannot think morally without making decisions he would wish
any rational being to make. Finally, then, he is brought to accept
his essential equality with all other rational persons before the
moral law, since the duty imposed by his own rational nature is to
treat himself with no less, but also no more, concern and respect
than he treats others.

Kant's defense of an ethic of obligation tries to outflank and
encompass utilitarian reasoning. Obligation is grounded in the
demands of reason that we treat ourselves and others in the same
way. Equality is a corollary of the dignity and respect owed to
human beings as other autonomous beings who are, according to
Kant, ends in themselves; it does not rest on an empirical judgment of equality of needs and interests. Kant's conception of moral
freedom understands freedom and rationality to coincide because
to be free really means to be uncontrolled by self-interested motivation. Thus the utilitarian is not free, because he is not completely reasonable, and he is not completely reasonable because he
does not employ entirely universal moral judgments.

Kantian teaching continued the Christian conception of the

moral life as a struggle on the part of a "higher" nature to bring the lower under its control,[34] and Kant's "good will" as the agreement of the individual person, as rational being, with the harmonious system of universal principles contained an echo of classical moral philosophy.[35] But the deontological ethics did not challenge the utilitarian premises of liberal moral psychology. The theory of obligation attempted to tame the most savage effects of self-interest by interpreting the principle of utility as an incomplete part of a higher rationality. It did this by postulating a kind of second tier of selfhood, a free, rational self irreducible to the desire-controlled personality of liberal psychology. This free core of the self could be known only through our experience of action and moral decision and not by means of behavioral observation. It was the mysterious center of the person, the will, the noumenal self, and it was the basis of the claim to moral dignity for all persons.

For Kant, the argument against pure utility held plausibility because he had already conceived rationality to be a single, universal system of intrinsically compelling principles. Those principles he saw as compelling in that peculiar rationalistic sense of the phrase "self-evident": that is, so coherent that they could be denied without self-contradiction. That, in fact, was the intent of the Categorical Imperative. It claimed that a rational person must accord equal respect to all other rational persons as agents of their own actions if he is intelligibly to claim such dignity for himself.

However, the Kantian formulation left the core of the utilitarian conception intact, a fact with tremendous implications for the future of contractarian liberalism. The ethics of obligation limited the moral validity of calculative egotism by imposing its second tier of rationality, but it also accepted the utilitarian conception of action as a calculus of consequences whose notion of good is the subjectively pleasant and useful. Thus there could literally be no *reasonable* disagreement over taste or preferences, that is, about mores. Ethics ceased to speak about the good in the classical sense

34. Kant defined moral virtue as an imperative of reason, "the command, namely to bring all powers and inclinations under his control—hence the command of self-mastery": Immanuel Kant, *The Doctrine of Virtue*, translated by M. J. Gregor (New York, 1964), p. 70.

35. Kant, *Fundamental Principles of the Metaphysics of Morals*, translated by T. Abbott (Indianapolis: Bobbs-Merrill, 1949), p. 11.

and became a matter of the *right*, according to which moral reasoning is conceived as imposing a framework upon desires but has nothing to say about the quality of those desires except as they are judged and controlled by the operation of its general principles.[36]

In political philosophy, Kant the theorist of moral obligation in a strange way still follows Hobbes's utilitarian psychology. Public order is for Kant the sole legitimate goal of politics, and law and the state are essentially coercive, appealing only to fear and greed to produce conduct supportive of morality. Since moral acts by definition issue from an unbiased "good will," they serve as measures of political right and wrong. But politics is seen as a system for regulating behavior which cannot itself be moral, though, at its best, politics may parallel the moral order.[37]

By disjoining in principle the realm of nature and history from the regulative sphere of free moral reason, Kant sought a defense against both instrumental reduction of moral bonds and the demonic claims of religio-political absolutism. However, he thereby also canonized the Hobbesian view of the political realm as the arena in which struggles of self-interested passion play themselves out. Nature and history are now so shorn of intrinsic value that the relationship of the "private" individual to the "public" world is instrumental and purely self-interested. Political morality at most imposes limits on this jungle, and the social contract is invoked here as a moral ideal to guide policy in fostering social peace.

Kant's achievement was to provide the frame for subsequent understanding of the nature of moral reasoning and the grounds of political obligation. Yet, as the basis for a public philosophy Kant's contractarianism is indeed thin. The best-developed effort from within philosophic liberalism to provide a consistent under-

36. The long-standing hegemony of this way of thinking over moral philosophy, which is related to the dominance of instrumental calculation as a model for the psychologies of action, has been challenged in recent Anglo-American philosophy of action as well as in Continental phenomenology. For examples see the essays by Bernard Williams, "Person, Character and Morality," and Charles Taylor, "The Self in Question," in Amelie Rorty, ed., *The Identities of Persons* (Berkeley: University of California Press, 1976). See also Stuart Hampshire, "Morality and Pessimism," in his *Public and Private Morality* (Cambridge, England: Cambridge University Press, 1978), pp. 1-22.

37. Kant's clearest discussion of these relationships between morality and politics may perhaps be found in his essay "Eternal Peace," in Carl J. Friedrich, ed., *The Philosophy of Kant* (New York: Modern Library, 1949), pp. 434ff.

standing of human life that affirms the value of moral conduct and the authority of public institutions, it stands together with the utilitarian philosophy of J. S. Mill as a principal resource of liberal public discourse. But the decisive issue for American culture is whether or not the resources of liberal individualism permit development of a new and authoritative public vision. It is a challenge of moral imagination.

THREE

Context and Reason:
Recent Developments in Liberal
Political Philosophy

:: I

A public philosophy is a process of discerning and articulating the common project of a society and those things which make that project deserving of loyalty and commitment. There can thus be no public philosophy in general but only specific, historically conditioned public philosophies tied to the experience, contingencies, and moral vision of the societies which produce them and whose lives they in turn form. A public philosophy is an expression and vehicle of practical reason in its classical sense, embodied in the life of a people and bound up with that people's reflection upon itself and its project. To define a public philosophy is thus itself an historically situated act, an always arguable effort to understand and shape a shared enterprise.

There is no purely neutral position from which to assess the spirit of any people or historical undertaking, much less one's own, and disputes over how to define moral and political topics are themselves always moral and political conflicts. Moreover, moral and political assessments cannot be defended without at the same time defending the understandings of the matters from which the assessments spring. Not the least valuable part of the civic republican heritage is its continuation of the kind of practical reason that makes these insights intelligible.

On the other hand, philosophic liberalism has from its beginnings been committed to a mode of discourse and a notion of rationality thoroughly at odds with these interpretive principles. Liberalism has understood rationality as a property of certain systems of concepts and the rules governing them. Rationality has been defined independently of the activities of human beings, particularly as those activities were tinged by change and history. Liberal ethics and political theory have consequently sought grounding in canons of rationality and objectivity independent of all historical and cultural traditions. And yet liberal thought, as it has entered into and formed Western societies, has ineluctably itself become a specific tradition, but one whose understanding of itself has prevented recognition of its situation.

However, as liberalism and its economic and governmental forms have shaped habits of thought and action in America, the present disarray of those institutions is in part the consequence and expression of the inherent dynamics of liberal society. To resolve these difficulties will require reorientation of significant aspects of our life as a people, and this demands that we devise better ways to understand the relationships between American institutions and the habits of everyday life. Since any way of understanding is shaped by the investigator's moral and political vision and commitments, this effort is at bottom a critical self-reflection.

We can begin this investigation by considering that while liberal categories have for a long time dominated American self-reflection and powerfully formed our political vision, other important influences have also been at work. Although civic republicanism explicitly understood has not been a continuous tradition in the American mainstream, serious social and political reflection has never wholly lost the crucial insight that institutions, practical understandings, and self-awareness are always interrelated. Since the Enlightenment, Western political and social thought has struggled with two conflicting visions of the kind of society that ought to replace the old regime. In reality, this has been a struggle over the meaning of emancipation. The liberal alternative has projected instrumental organization and formal contract as its ideal of social life. That tendency has been opposed by a succession of thinkers and movements promoting the ideal of a self-governing community. Typically, while the former position has emphasized relations of command and the proper structuring of institutions as the keys to human betterment, the counter-liberal tradition has

insisted that institutions and authority must be seen as aspects of a
more inclusive social life lived meaningfully for ends beyond
power and the satisfaction of private desire.[1]

As the culture of liberalism falters, articulation of new public
philosophy can proceed by reweaving the strands of the civic republican tradition. These have begun to make an appearance even
in the works of liberal thinkers. Perhaps it is only because the
dynamics of the contemporary world seem to have outstripped the
capacity of liberal culture to account for them convincingly that a
radically different sort of understanding can be heard in the mainstream of discourse; however, this in itself is a hopeful beginning
for untangling the contradictions to which the liberal project of
emancipation has led.

There is little question that moral dignity is a concern deeply
embedded in the American political tradition from the opening
sentences of the republic's founding Declaration onward. However, it is also true that while equal dignity for all has generally
been given at least formal assent in American life, the practical
implications of this commitment for the structure and conduct of
government, law, economic, and social life continue to be disputed.
Moral dignity is at the root of concerns with justice and the equal
application of the law, and in America early proponents of liberal
thought joined traditional republicans in rallying to the defense
of the rights of citizens against tyranny. In that way emancipation
has been a constitutive aim of the American republic, though it
can be understood as citizenship in a sense that is wider than the
liberal conception. To assert the dignity of persons is to claim that
the kinds of social relationships that recognize this dignity in
practice have thereby a special value. In some measure most Americans readily recognize the presence or absence of the kind of relationship that provides for mutual respect in everyday life. And the
sense of outrage elicited by cruelty, humiliations, violence, and

1. This characterization is a paraphrase of Sheldon Wolin's argument in *Politics
and Vision* (Boston: Little, Brown, 1960). New light on the archaeology of this
opposition between an institutional and a cultural focus has been provided by
Quentin Skinner in *The Foundations of Western Political Thought* (2 vols., Cambridge, England: Cambridge University Press, 1979): see esp. vol. I, pp. 59-60. John
Dunn has given a sharp if pessimistic assessment of forms of contemporary political
understanding and their prognoses: see his *Western Political Theory in the Face of
the Future* (London: Cambridge University Press, 1979).

theft testifies to the presence of this understanding. This moral sentiment contrasts sharply with the popular liberal notion that politics, and social life more generally, is an impersonal arena for the pursuit of self-interest.

However, as early as the beginning of the nineteenth century, Alexis de Tocqueville noted the peculiarly American tendency to explain virtually all actions, especially those in public life, as the result of self-interest. Americans talked that way even when there was a clear discrepancy between the language of interest and practical situations in which citizens frequently acted with care for the welfare of others, even to the detriment of their own particular interest. The disposition to treat others with dignity and respect is not simply a result of intelligent self-interest; rather, as Tocqueville acutely noted, respect for others is rooted in a deeper sense of mutuality and an habitual readiness to acknowledge worth in the other's point of view.[2] These qualities describe a sense of life that grows out of the reciprocity of a community of active solidarity in which mutual respect is an expression of trust and part of a sense of self-worth. Yet, curiously, this practical moral sense has until recently been little considered by the formulators of liberal culture.

It is both a peculiarity and a defining characteristic of philosophic liberalism that it understands human action as essentially and unavoidably self-interested. Because liberalism postulates the individual self as morally and logically prior to relations with others, the desires and values of the individual are held to arise without intrinsic relation to those of other selves, so that social relationships are always and only a means to individual gratification. This pattern of thought was originally designed to free the individual from the oppressive bonds of hoary tyrannies and privilege, and these liberal assumptions reflect rather accurately the practical assumptions an individual needed to take part in a market economy. Thus it is not surprising that in American culture, by the early nineteenth century already deeply involved with market economic life, individuals came to describe even their relationships outside the market in the economic language of liberal thought. That has remained a continuing feature of American life, though it has become increasingly problematical.

---

2. Alexis de Tocqueville, *Democracy in America*, translated by George Lawrence (Garden City, New York: Doubleday Anchor, 1979), vol. II, ch. 8.

This tendency of liberal thinking, with its affinity for economic categories, poses a major difficulty for contractarian liberals who wish to construct a discourse about the dignity of persons as the moral foundation of the republic. Robert Nozick and John Rawls, while representing divergent positions in the contemporary debate on political matters, share the liberal conception of politics and morality, and their common idiom of expression, analytic philosophy, also shares many of the conceptual roots of philosophic liberalism.[3] Their work, representative of that context, is revealing and suggestive about the current state of articulate liberal culture.

For liberal thinkers political philosophy is always a derivation from and application of moral philosophy. Within the liberal tradition, it was Kant who made the most ambitious and complex effort to develop a compelling argument that could secure morality by a kind of practical reasoning which was not reducible to self-regarding effort. Nozick and Rawls are both, to varying degrees, influenced by the Kantian project, though neither accepts it whole-heartedly. Kant recognized that the analytical and instrumental modes of thought upon which earlier liberals had relied reduced human beings to objects for manipulation and provided no ground for a defense against tyranny and the subjection of one self-interested competitor to another. His solution was to postulate that the moral law to which Locke had appealed was founded on a certain intuition about human conscience: that all persons are to be treated as one should treat oneself. That meant treating every person with equal dignity.

For Kant, the morally right was the rational, that is, it was the application of universal principles to conduct. If men were to act in accord with moral duty, they would escape enslavement to their naturally determined drives, especially the tyrannical drive of self-interest. They would at the same time find themselves in harmony with one another, since their principles of operation would be universal and in that sense objective. Ethics in a Kantian spirit erects a second level of reasoning on which is grounded a very different understanding of human nature from the one postulated by liberalism's empirical moral psychology. Moral law is rational

3. See Robert Nozick, *Anarchy, State and Utopia* (New York: Basic Books, 1974), and John Rawls, *A Theory of Justice* (Cambridge, Massachusetts: Harvard University Press, 1971).

command derived from universal principles that check and restrain the operations of the phenomenal self. In a strict sense, politics, the state, and the law can only open the possibility for morality, though moral thinking is essential for directing the correct engineering of political machinery.

Since the liberal view so separates morality as rational will from empirical desires, morality tends to become identified with moral reasoning, even with moral theory in the sense of speculative general considerations. Morality is thereby rendered highly abstract and connected to the realm of practical desire largely as an opponent, lawgiver, and restrainer. These tendencies, which are typical of contractarian ethics, disclose a mistrust of the moral meanings embodied in tradition and contingent, historical experience.

On the one hand, liberal thought conceives of important features of social life as describable in the mechanistic, reductive language of strategic action. All else is either defined as the enemy of rationality—e.g., custom, tradition, and, above all, authority— or as somehow tolerable if atavistic—e.g., kinship and unaccountable individual preference. Morality, on the other hand, searches in the realm of general principles to define what duty requires and what are the limits to permissible self-interest, so that it becomes a matter of applying principles and rules to situations. The older classical and Christian tradition of morality as character formation concerned with virtue is ruled out *a priori*, since it depends on forming desires and dispositions to accord with moral sense, which cannot be done on the grounds of liberal theory.

Government, law, and, ideally, the mechanisms of the market are practical means for keeping conflicts among striving individuals within the confines of moral law. Political theories, such as those of Nozick and Rawls, that are based upon this kind of moral philosophy are efforts to articulate how the moral duty to respect persons ought to temper the pursuit of individual advantage through the mechanism of social control. While they do in fact consciously aim to persuade, these theories are formed by the canons of liberal rationality, especially as these operate in American university departments of philosophy still dominated by Anglo-American analytic philosophy continuing the tradition of liberal analytic reason.

Philosophy is conceived in these circles as a professional activity, on the model of the scientific societies. Thus, like science, philosophy is understood to have a delimited sphere of competence in a specific subject matter, approached by means of a peculiar research methodology. Since its inception early in the century in Britain and Europe, whence it spread to America just prior to World War II, analytic philosophy has drawn much of its inspiration from the practices of the scientific professions, or at least from philosophers' idealized conceptions of those professions. The founder of analytic moral philosophy, G. E. Moore, titled his work *Principia Ethica*, harkening back to Newton's great *opus*. Moore in effect elucidated a "research strategy" together with canons of judgment about what would count as success in moral inquiry.

Analysis is an apt term for the general features of this kind of philosophy. Since Kant, *analysis* has meant the effort to comprehend experience as a set of rule-governed relationships among elements. These elements are in turn conceived to be primitive or irreducibly basic constituents of the experience being described. Early analytic philosophy attempted to "reconstruct" the knowledge of the empirical sciences, aiming at an ever more coherent and unified set of accounts of experience. The ideal of logicality propounded by Rudolph Carnap and the Vienna Circle summed up a conception of the role of philosophy as logical criticism and reconstruction of science, an effort to produce a coherent unification of knowledge. While the notion of an ideal unified science has largely been abandoned by philosophers, the assumption that greater logical precision and coherence among our basic ideas take us closer to truth remains a central tenet of this tradition. Thus, moral philosophy is also seen as progressing by means of criticism and reconstruction of systems of moral concepts.

This ideal of reductive logical analysis lends legitimacy to the notion that moral philosophy is summed up in the task of discovering, through the analysis of moral rules, both primitive elements and governing principles that must apply to any rational moral system, *rational* here meaning "logically coherent." The search for such a "deep structure" of moral systems is taken as a purely formal inquiry not based upon any substantive commitment as to the value of the ends of action.

An important corollary to this ideal of moral philosophy is the atemporal character of the universal principles refined by analysis. By this reasoning, moral theory as a branch of analytic moral philosophy need make no reference to the past tradition of moral

philosophy, except for examples of one or another set of principles. This view takes for granted that one can develop sufficient
clarity about the premises of any moral tradition to reduce its
substance to a system of statements proceeding more or less logically from certain starting points. Moral systems, including the
philosopher's own, are thus conceived of as detachable, without
significant loss, from the historical and cultural contexts in which
they appear. All this has been described clearly by John Rawls.[4] As
contemporary thinkers, however, Nozick and Rawls are more sensitive to the importance of history and social experience in human
life than were the classic liberal thinkers. This is partly due to
the influence on Anglo-American philosophers of Wittgenstein's
ordinary-language philosophy. By acknowledging the importance
of the intrinsically social and historical dimensions of human
experience, they introduce new tensions into the analytic tradition.

:: II

Liberalism has associated human freedom and happiness with
a society and way of life in which rationality and institutions
consciously constructed according to its principles would replace
custom and tradition as the shapers of moral discourse and political action. At the center of that faith has stood the notion that
reason could be defined by certain formal properties, most notably
consistency and coherence, which elevated rationality into a circle
of discourse that transcended all particular, historically formed
patterns of understanding. It was generally believed that reason,
exemplified in science, would provide the Archimedean point from
which to reorder human affairs in its image. The search for the

4. See John Rawls's presentation of this point in his "The Independence of
Moral Theory," *Proceedings of the North American Philosophical Association*
(Presidential Address, 1974), 48 (November 1975): 5-22. The historical and social location of modern philosophy is attracting more attention within and
without the discipline: see Albert M. Levi, *Philosophy as Social Expression* (Chicago: University of Chicago Press, 1976), and Bruce Kuklick, *The Rise of American
Philosophy: Cambridge, Massachusetts, 1860-1930* (New Haven, Connecticut: Yale
University Press, 1977). Both these studies single out the narrowing of the range of
philosophy into a professional specialty and its almost complete identification
with academic institutions as the dominant trend. Since the death of John Dewey
shortly after World War II, no professional American philosopher has played a
major role in American cultural and political life outside specialized circles.

foundations of ethics in formulations of pure reason was then the necessary step toward a true political and social science.

In this perspective the liberal moral and political philosophers' new sensitivity to historical and cultural context is noteworthy. It may suggest a new uncertainty about the background assumptions that have long guided liberal philosophy.[5] But can insights into the historically and socially rooted nature of moral understanding be coherently integrated within the liberal framework without bursting it? The previous history of such efforts by thinkers such as Hegel, Tocqueville, and, in the United States, John Dewey suggests a negative answer.

Contemporary liberal thinking faces a peculiar dilemma. Earlier challenges to liberal orthodoxy were not dismissed or ignored because their arguments could be decisively crushed, since that is not possible in a disagreement upon the question of what constitutes rationality.[6] Rather, the cultural hegemony of liberalism could continue, particularly in the United States, because the dominant institutional complex of modern society which incarnated liberal modes of thought and action appeared internally coherent and fundamentally sound, despite such bad moments as depression and war.

Today, however, questioning of those institutional forms has become widespread and even America seems to have lost its innocence. As the dysfunctions of market behavior, the instrumental orientation of the state, and the dangers of scientific technology coupled to those processes reach public consciousness, the situation of liberal culture is changing. As the guardian of established power and an institutional structure it has celebrated as the embodiment of reason, liberalism has lost its emancipatory and prophetic stance. The traditional liberal notion of reason has come to be seen as a dogma that may inhibit and distort understanding. Liberal culture has become conservative in a practical sense.

The difficulty in liberal moral philosophy concerns nothing less than its core conception of rationality. Should that concep-

5. Rawls and Nozick are not alone in reflecting this new interest; for example, see the recent essays by William Frankena collected as *Perspectives on Morality: Essays by William K. Frankena*, edited by Kenneth E. Goodpaster (Notre Dame, Indiana: University of Notre Dame Press, 1976).

6. For discussion and development of these issues by a variety of thinkers, see Brian Wilson, ed., *Rationality* (New York: Harper and Row, 1970).

tion prove no longer convincing, the structure of liberal ethical and political thought will certainly lose the cogency it has long enjoyed. In such circumstances the maintenance and continuation of the emancipatory aims of liberal democracy will have to be carried on by other, though no less democratic, forms of discourse and political life.

We can take Robert Nozick's recent work as a case in point. In *Anarchy, State and Utopia* Nozick tries to provide a strong argument, in the style of analytic philosophy, for the kind of peculiarly American conservatism currently associated with libertarian politics. In marshaling his argument Nozick makes three crucial assumptions, all recognizable as classic liberalism. The first is that at least for the concerns of political philosophy, desires are individual in nature and social relations are instrumental, the idea of which is therefore exchange. His second assumption is that rights—which he calls entitlements—as well as duties attach to individuals alone. No moral claims upon individuals can be made by collectivities present, past or future, except by the individual's consent.[7] Nozick's third and most crucial assumption is the moral worth and autonomy of individuals, in a Lockean interpretation that emphasizes free choice and consent.

While the conventions of analytic philosophy demand an ahistorical approach to moral and political issues, Nozick's work resonates with a Lockean interpretation of the spirit of the American republic. He considers equality of respect as tied to the capacity for autonomous will and choice, and from these he attempts to derive moral norms that set limits to individual acquisitiveness; Nozick's moral theory thus attempts to restate a Lockean notion of the social contract.[8] In this effort his work has the virtue of logical consistency.

Nozick tells us, however, that he is at pains to persuade his readers that his theory is not merely logically consistent but gives moral credibility to his social vision. He advances a conception of human life that carries considerable rhetorical power, calling to mind the image of Robinson Crusoe. His ideal individualism evokes self-sufficiency, a sense of exploration, and a freedom from constraining obligation. Since liberty is understood as security, as in Locke, and coercion is the great evil, there can be only one legiti-

7. Nozick, *Anarchy*, pp. 32-33, 167.   8. Ibid., pp. 74-80.

mate cause for coercion, and hence for the state: the restraint of unjust coercion. Nozick's theory emphasizes this point by making nonviolation of others' rights an absolute constraint on the kinds of liberty one may exercise:

> In contrast to incorporating rights into the end state to be achieved (i.e., Justice), one might place them as side constraints upon the actions to be done: don't violate constraints. The rights of others determine the constraints on your actions.... Political philosophy is concerned only with certain ways that persons may not use others: primarily physically aggressing against them.[9]

Thus, justice is served if each individual pursues his own affairs without violating the basic side constraints on action. All persons are equal in regard to rights in this sense, though not necessarily equal in the kinds or amount of satisfaction they may achieve.

It is crucial for Nozick's defense of laissez-faire to retain the Lockean notion that individuals are autonomous in such a way that they can be obligated only by their consent. Morally justified state action is to be confined to enforcing certain rules of market procedure. This is Nozick's image of the "night-watchman state." Justice as entitlement finally means simply that there are natural constraints on the ways in which one may acquire and transfer holdings. Should these constraints be violated, the state may legitimately employ coercive means to rectify the violation so that transactions can again proceed freely. This theory is familiar: it is a form of the Invisible Hand.

In theory, the mechanism of exchange can balance conflicting desires with utility so that there is no need for economic, particularly distributive, justice and so no justification for redistribution of income or wealth to achieve a just society. F. A. Hayek extended this position by arguing, as Nozick summarizes:

> Since in a capitalist society people often transfer holdings to others in accordance with how much they perceive these others benefitting them, the fabric constituted by the individual transactions and transfers is largely reasonable and intelligible.... The system of entitlement is defensible when constituted by the individual aims of individual transactions. No overreaching aim is needed, no distributional pattern is required.[10]

If properly regulated by a strict observance of "side constraints," the Invisible Hand provides a way of organizing social life which

---

9. Ibid., pp. 29, 32.   10. Ibid., p. 159.

is just, that is, which respects the rights of individuals. Thus Nozick calls upon Americans to return to Lockean fundamentals with a view innocent of large-scale enterprise, financial concentrations, or the national security state. From this basis Nozick claims that his theory shows the way to a just society through rectification of past injustices, even should this require a more than minimal state. After rectifying property claims—an aspect he leaves very vague—we are told that the market and the watchman state could then run smoothly, leaving us to form intentional communities of our choosing.[11]

But throughout Nozick's discussion of the individual and the state, the relation of the individual to what he calls "society" in the above quotation is never an object of systematic reflection. At times he, like other libertarian thinkers such as Hayek, appears to think of all social relations as reducible to some form of exchange relationship, entered into for wholly utilitarian reasons.[12] However, when Nozick turns to discuss the basis for side constraints, he can no longer avoid the issue of the social dimension of moral psychology. He points to an account of human activity according to which the ability to form a "life with meaning," rather than exchange, is the fundamental fact about human beings that entitles us to equal dignity.

How are we to understand that capacity and how does it affect Nozick's moral theory? Are the two really compatible? He rather abruptly breaks off his "conjectures" to return to his Invisible Hand derivation of a justified protector state, and he gives no further basis for Locke's natural right. "The completely accurate statement of the moral background, including the precise statement of the moral theory and its underlying basis, would require a full-scale presentation and is a task for another time. (A lifetime?)"[13] Through the brilliant flashes of argument on the surface one senses a chasm. Despite his view of moral philosophy as argument, in the end Nozick presents a rhetorical appeal that his vision of a capitalist exchange network supporting a plurality of intentional communities is "not uninspiring." He simply abandons in midstream

11. Ibid., pp. 230-31.
12. Cf. F. A. Hayek, *The Constitution of Liberty* (Chicago: University of Chicago Press, 1960), esp. chs. 2 and 3.
13. Nozick, *Anarchy*, p. 9.

his efforts to explain the moral basis of Lockean rights from the root idea of "life with meaning."

Yet in its starkness Nozick's lack of a ground for equality of respect provides an important insight into the conceptual strains within contemporary liberal thought. Liberal premises have never actually sufficed to defend the values for which the liberal tradition has stood. Locke was able to argue that a bargaining society could preserve both social order and individual autonomy because he could assume among his readers a belief in a natural teleology of the individual toward God and in an ideal universal community. To bolster his arguments Locke was able to draw upon Christian and Stoic sources of the medieval notion of natural law that conceived of a moral order of social relationships. "Mankind are one Community," Locke wrote.

And were it not for the corruption and viciousness of degenerate Men, there would be no need . . . that Men should separate from this great and natural Community and combine into smaller and divided associations.[14]

This rhetoric cast the problem as a matter of developing social and political institutions that could bring human beings, corrupt, degenerate, and self-aggrandizing as they were, into harmony with the divinely established norm of justice. For Locke this meant showing that self-interest could be used to produce the functional equivalent of mutual concern. Practically, for all the early liberals it meant advocating a new social engineering to harness economic drives. By reckoning on the baser passions of men "as they really are," those thinkers hoped to provide a more secure social order which would also protect individuals from violence and oppression.

Nozick argues that the market and the minimal state are still our best and only morally consistent choices for realizing a just society. His rather elaborate apparatus is a design for a "functional equivalent" of distributive justice very much in the spirit of John Locke. In the view of classical political philosophy, distributive justice was a working out of the claims that individuals make on communal resources, and the basis for these claims was understood to be the citizen's participation and membership in the com-

14. John Locke, *Two Treatises of Government*, edited by Peter Laslett (second edition, London: Cambridge University Press, 1967), vol. II, p. 128.

munity.[15] By contrast, Locke located the basis of individual claims in the individual's labor, his working on the world, thus making property in the sense of power to dispose of the results of one's labor absolutely fundamental to human nature. The relational focus of classical and medieval natural law was displaced by the self-contained striving of the individual to manipulate the world for his security. This shift in perspective had vast implications. In particular, it narrowed the conception of those social relationships that could be relevant for moral and political considerations to that of a set of instrumental and strategic interactions among otherwise unconnected individuals.

These atomistic premises of liberal thinking have made it difficult to conceive in a positive way of social relationships that embody shared convictions as opposed to negotiated compromise or exchange: hence the deep liberal suspicion of authority, tradition, or nurturant relationships, even though these are all persistent aspects of the lives of social beings. Historically, the suspicion was often justified, but the limitation of viewpoint built into liberal understanding has made it extremely difficult to appreciate the historical and social nature of human life. This limitation has in turn sustained the simplistic dichotomies of reason and custom, autonomy and dependence, which reduce political life to a visioning of contracting individuals indifferent to each other, sharing nothing except a nervous regard for certain rules of procedure.

Nozick's return to free-market fundamentalism is plausible only if respect for the worth of individuals can be maintained in a social and cultural context of economic competition. Yet, Nozick's principal conception of morality considers such respect as a constraint on self-interested striving, implying an at least potentially antagonistic relationship between human decency and the practical psychology of everyday economic life. On the other hand, Nozick's rhetorical appeals to "consensual communities" and the human need for a meaningful life point in a different direction, toward social experience as capable of somehow reconciling both self-interested desire and human regard. However, were he to de-

15. See Aristotle, *Nicomachean Ethics* bk. V, chs. 2, 3, 6, 7; *Politics* bk. VII, chs. 1 and 2. William A. Galston has attempted to make a contemporary case for the Aristotelean view in his *Justice and the Human Good* (Chicago: University of Chicago Press, 1980).

velop that insight further, the antagonism that liberal ethics postulates as existing between the psychology of economic calculation and regard for rights would have to become problematical
and would thus make his assumptions jar with his concluding
vision. Thus, although Nozick is aware that morality has a social
reference, the horizon of his moral and political thinking is an
individualist anthropology. He does not trace the relations between
moral meanings and social practice beyond postulating that an
ideal balance would result from fair market competition.

Liberals have defined the social and cultural conditions sustaining moral dispositions as empirical matters outside the prov-
ince of moral reasoning as such. Nozick proceeds, aside from forays
into the basis for his side constraints, on the assumption that
normative ethical questions can be analyzed in isolation from
historically contingent social relationships. This dichotomy between the utilitarian moral psychology of liberalism and its ethic
of personal worth and autonomy is of a piece with the familiar
positivist conception of reason that sharply distinguishes "facts"
from "values." Liberal thinkers have traditionally feared that any
effort to situate moral insights within an understanding of social
life will necessarily subordinate the freedom and dignity of the
ethical individual to a social or historical determinism and so will
undermine the credibility of any moral stance. However, in practice that dichotomy has led to the dominance of purely utilitarian
conceptions of human action or, at best, to a tense compromise
between subjective moralism and a cynicism often masked as hard-
nosed realism. The history of liberal thought affords some heroic
examples—such as John Stuart Mill and Max Weber—of struggles
to live out this tension without collapsing its poles into one another (though these remain truly exceptional cases).[16]

On the other hand, significant modern thinkers dissatisfied with
the narrowness of the liberal account have worked to reestablish a
discourse that could link moral understanding to social and historical awareness. That project had its roots in the Scottish Enlightenment of the eighteenth century but received major impetus

16. For a brilliant presentation of this central problem of liberal politics, though
in a radically different context from the American, see Max Weber, "Science as a
Vocation" and "Politics as a Vocation," in Hans Gerth and C. Wright Mills, eds.,
From Max Weber (New York: Oxford University Press, 1946).

in the nineteenth from the many appropriations of Hegel. Besides Marxism, the "social liberalism" of T.H. Green and L.T. Hobhouse in England can be seen in this light,[17] as can John Dewey, whose work exercised a major influence on American philosophy during the first half of this century.

Dewey summarized the direction of this kind of liberal revisionism by arguing that

integration and cooperation between man's beliefs about the world in which he lives (Ises) and his beliefs about the values and purposes that should direct his conduct (Oughts) is the deepest problem of modern life. It is the problem of any philosophy that is not isolated from that life.[18]

The career of this revisionist social liberalism is instructive. Its central theme was the conception of the self as a moral entity that develops within relations structured by shared moral understandings. The revisionists denied the primacy that liberal thought since Hobbes had given to instrumental relations, on the grounds that instrumental action requires a context of meaningful non-instrumental interaction for its orientation. Instead of conventional liberal atomism, they argued for a holistic notion of social relations in which the individual is a moral being in reciprocal relations with others, so his motivations are necessarily tied to these relationships and the context within which they develop. Thus even competitive, self-interested behavior depends upon some prior context of cooperation, even if flawed or incoherent, for its development and maintenance. The revisionists attempted to recover a vision of social life as moral ecology.[19]

The insight that the moral self is a social reality formed in an historical community was not an original discovery of the social liberals or of Hegel but, rather, a recovery of a central tenet of classical political philosophy. Dewey in particular saw the implication of this insight for the whole edifice of liberal thought, especially its exclusive identification of reason with theoretical knowledge and analytic reduction. If the self is rooted in shared,

17. For example, see L.T. Hobhouse, *Liberalism* (New York: Oxford University Press, 1911); also T.H. Green, *Lectures on the Principles of Political Obligation* (London: Longmans, 1963).
18. John Dewey, *The Quest for Certainty: A Study of the Relation of Knowledge and Action* (New York: Putnam, 1960), p. 255.
19. The term *moral ecology* was discussed in Chapter Two.

active practices that form a whole not reducible to the sum of its analytic parts, then function and teleology return to serious discourse about human action. Thinking is always the thought of an interested, involved interpreter of action. And with that comes, of necessity, evaluation, practical commitment, and questioning as the fundamental, not derivative, features of reflection. Practical reason is thus rehabilitated in a sense closer to that of Aristotle than of Kant.[20] The upshot of Dewey's revision of liberal dogma was to make moral reflection a dimension of all inquiry about the world, since inquiry was conceived of as finally concerned with the question of the ends and worth of action.

In the long run the revisionist cause failed to reorient the fundamental categories of liberal thought, but the more socially oriented understanding has had the effect of influencing the contemporary context of discourse so that today even a Lockean or Kantian moral theory must somehow take into account the socially conceived moral psychology that the revisionists struggled to introduce into the mainstream of philosophical discourse. However, although contemporary thinkers may be compelled to accommodate the notion that values are essentially rooted in social life, liberals still assert that the justification of moral insight, if not its genealogy, requires holding fast to traditional liberal categories.

:: III

For John Rawls, too, moral philosophy aims to enunciate and justify substantively neutral procedures for choosing rightly among alternative courses of action or social policy. Rawls's *A Theory of Justice* has become an important reference point for contemporary moral philosophy.[21] In that work, Rawls tells us

20. However, Dewey is not wholly free of the utilitarian and anti-Aristotelean notion that the good is a matter of combining and balancing various valued projects: see John Dewey, "The Construction of Good," in *Quest for Certainty*, pp. 254-86. By contrast, an ethic of virtue is guided by a practical reasoning (*phronesis*, in Aristotle) formed through fidelity to certain understandings that define the self and shape the harmony of its projects: for example, see Charles Taylor, "The Self in Question," in Amelie Rorty, ed., *The Identities of Persons* (Berkeley: University of California Press, 1976), for a statement of that position in contemporary philosophical idiom.

21. For example, see the useful collection by Norman Daniels, ed., *Reading Rawls: Critical Studies of "A Theory of Justice"* (Cambridge, Massachusetts: Har-

that he is concerned to provide a "standard for the distributive aspects of society," which can apply whether the economic organization is capitalist or socialist.[22] Rawls's thesis is that democratic self-government is founded on an equality of respect and concern among the members of a society and that this moral insight has specific implications for how society should distribute entitlements and responsibilities among its members. His effort is to show that this insight is not an arbitrary assertion but instead is rationally convincing. To do this Rawls appeals to traditional motifs of liberal thought both in his notion of what counts as convincing argument in moral affairs and in the general strategy of his approach. However, Rawls acknowledges that his moral insight, or "intuition," is socially and historically situated, a position that clashes with his conceptual apparatus, in particular his notion of practical reasoning as formal and atemporal. There is thus a major conceptual tension between the substance and the form of Rawls's work.

A Theory of Justice is focused and guided by what Rawls calls a social vision which he tells us informs the whole, even though it is not part of the theory of justice properly speaking. This social vision explicates the intuition of justice Rawls sees as necessary to guide a democratic society. By contrast, *theory* proper means a consistent account of the intuition in accord with the ideal of logical coherence and completeness. Thus Rawls's theoretical account proceeds in typical liberal fashion, while the informing vision, itself historically contingent, conceives of human nature in an explicitly social and historical way.[23]

---

vard University Press, 1974), Brian Barry, *The Liberal Theory of Justice: A Critical Examination of the Principal Doctrines of Justice by John Rawls* (New York: Oxford University Press, 1973), and Robert Paul Wolff, *Understanding Rawls: A Reconstruction and Critique of "A Theory of Justice"* (Princeton, New Jersey: Princeton University Press, 1977).

22. Rawls, *Theory*, pp. 5-9.

23. Since liberal moral philosophers and social scientists have viewed the "real" nature of social life, or at least its historically progressive form (*pace* Marx), as utilitarian and guided by interests, they have generally discounted or given little attention to the continued vitality of nonutilitarian (and non-deontological) morality embodied in social movements upon other kinds of solidarity. However, historians such as E.P. Thompson and Lawrence Goodwyn have begun to broaden our comprehension of the moral basis of democratic movements. For a discussion see Harry C. Boyte, "Populism and the Left," *Democracy* (April 1981): 53-66.

To say that man is a historical being is to say that the realization of the powers of human individuals living at any one time takes the cooperation of many generations (or even societies) over a long period of time. It also implies that this cooperation is guided at any moment by an understanding of what has been done in the past as it is interpreted by social tradition.[24]

The point of Rawls's complex conceptual apparatus is to show that the historically specific political tradition of liberal democratic society is a morally valid one which can be justified by appeal to ahistorical and universal principles of moral right.

For Rawls a good society is a "well-ordered" one, by which he means a society whose basic institutions are both "designed to advance the good of its members" and regulated by principles of justice that are known and accepted by all members of the society. Furthermore, such a society will be stable and self-regulating because of this widely diffused sense of justice. This vision culminates in an ideal of society as a "social union," a society in which each individual can share common ends and activities that are valued for themselves.[25] The formal principles of justice that Rawls's theory sets out to justify are, he tells us, derived from this conception of social cooperation which makes possible a well-ordered, stable society facilitating "social union" among its members. Thus the social vision of the well-ordered society—Rawls's moral intuition spelled out—supplies the conditions of possibility for the intelligibility and conceptual necessity of his principles of justice.

The point of Rawls's rational reconstruction is to show that the moral intuition represented by these conditions of possibility is identical with those maxims of practical reasoning which express generalizations valid for all rational beings. That intuition is "fairness" and the maxims are the two "principles of justice." In *A Theory of Justice* Rawls never seems to question that establishing this point should mean starting with a model of "free and equal rational beings" capable of taking up a viewpoint "that everyone can adopt on an equal footing"[26] and then assuming that these beings are concerned to advance their own interests, mutually disinterested, and in agreement that "systems of value are not ranked in value."[27] That is, Rawls's reconstruction postulates a

24. Rawls, *Theory*, p. 525.   25. See ibid., pp. 453-62, 520-29.
26. Ibid., p. 513.   27. Ibid., pp. 17-19.

"rational choice" which in its pure form is individually self-interested and constrained by no commitments about various ends but only by the formal value of universalizing whatever choice is made; that is, the only commitment is that all like cases should be treated alike.

The well-ordered society is the historical project interpreted by social tradition to which Rawls refers above. It is recognizable as the vision of contractarian liberalism, heavily influenced by Kant. It presents a specific though abstract moral ecology, one in which identity is partially shaped by explicit principles of distribution governing various unspecified institutions. (There is no discussion of relations of production.) Indeed, Rawls's form of this social contract, the original position, is meant to demonstrate why all rational beings would choose this moral ecology, since it provides the only model of social cooperation that is truly consistent with the contractors' sense of (rational) morality; that is to say, it provides the conditions of possibility, the logical framework, within which truly generalizable maxims could be effective.

However, there reappears the old contractarian problem of how the contractors are to make the conceptual leap from the practical psychology of self-interest to the moral ecology of cooperation. Rawls's answer, "By their capacity for practical moral reasoning," begs the question as to whether this capacity is available to agents living outside the moral ecology of cooperation, with its presupposition of mutual concern and respect, and it commits him to reconstructing that moral sense from purely formal criteria. It is significant that he finally reintroduces substantive notions from the presumed moral ecology as a "thin theory" of the human good, that is, a theory of human ends, to make his reconstruction work.

In an early version of his theory (published in 1958), Rawls emphasized that moral understanding is, ultimately, practical disposition manifest in action rather than an inner or mental attitude. Referring to Ludwig Wittgenstein's conception of "language games"—in this case, moral language—Rawls wrote:

Acknowledging these duties in *some* degree, and so having the elements of morality, is not a matter of choice, or of intuiting moral qualities, or a matter of the expression of feelings and attitudes (the three interpretations between which philosophical opinion frequently oscillates). It is simply the recognition of one of the forms of conduct in which the recognition of others as persons is manifested.[28]

According to this view, morality is an understanding manifest in the practices of a form of life shared by a community.

On reflection, it is evident that this means that moral understanding moves in a kind of circle in which the practical consensus is guided by a tacit sense of importance that is presupposed even as it is brought to light through discourse. That consensus is ultimately not a system of beliefs, though it may be interpreted as such, but is, rather, embedded in ways of seeing and acting. The task of moral reflection is then inherently circular—though not viciously circular, since it aims at insight into this practical moral understanding. Moral reflection becomes in the first instance a task of interpretation.

However, to have continued to develop Wittgenstein's insight would have led Rawls from a liberal ethics of principles toward an ethics of virtue, which gives character a central place in moral understanding. For an ethics of virtue, character or the intentionality of the agent provides the connecting syntax through which the various acts and projects of the agent attain consistency. That consistency is rational in that it is describable through reference to intentional categories, such as the virtues of temperance or courage, that guide the agent's action and reflection.[29] However, this is a rationality which unfolds and can be displayed only by a narrative of an intentional project. This is of necessity a contingent process whose assessment depends in part upon the agent's own terms of reference, that is, upon the agent's most deeply held images of self. In a virtue ethics, the norms of practical rationality guiding the agent cannot be wholly reduced to maxims such as

28. Rawls, "Justice as Fairness," *American Philosophical Review* 67, 2 (April 1958): 164-94 (quotation on p. 182).

29. An important stream of thought in recent Anglo-American philosophy, called the "theory of action," has developed the insight that intentionality, or purposiveness and agency, is an inherent dimension of human language and practice that must figure in understanding human action: for examples see Stuart Hampshire, *Thought and Action* (New York: Viking, 1960); A.I. Melden, *Free Action* (New York: Humanities Press, 1964); Alisdair MacIntyre, *Against the Self-Image of the Age* (New York: Schocken, 1971); John Searle, *Speech Acts* (Cambridge, England: Cambridge University Press, 1970); and Charles Taylor, *The Explanation of Behavior* (New York: Humanities Press, 1964).

"Always do the brave (or just, or temperate) thing," since discrimination of the meaning of these injunctions depends not only upon the syntax of the maxim or the structure of the situation but, importantly, upon the disposition and understanding of the agent as well.[30]

Development of the skills of practical discrimination and action which make up the agent's character is most powerfully guided by symbols and paradigms of action and understanding rather than by rules of procedure or general principles. The proof of one's knowledge of the good, according to Aristotle, is the ability to discern the good person.[31] Continuity of discrimination through varying situations describes a tradition. A tradition of moral life is not, then, a continuity of decisions made according to the same principles so much as continuity in the kind of character and vision of life that define the actual projects of people over time. A living tradition is a continuing, often dramatic and conflictual, dialogue concerning those things which matter most deeply to its participants. A moral tradition of virtue is thus a continuity among varied forms of activity that is recognizable, at least to those participating in its practices, as valuable by reason of the sense of self and world that it sustains.[32]

30. The disposition of the agent is critical to prudence, or Aristotle's *phronesis*, in the virtue-ethic tradition, but disposition must not be understood as simple conditioned habit. It is, rather, a trained capacity to discriminate and comprehend situations with reference to dominant intentional commitments, the fundamental loyalties through which character is formed. See G.E.M. Anscombe, "Thought and Action in Aristotle," in Renford Bambrough, ed., *New Essays in Plato and Aristotle* (London: Routledge and Kegan Paul, 1965), pp. 151-52.

31. Aristotle, *Nicomachean Ethics* bk. I, ch. 7, 1097b.

32. Alisdair MacIntyre has called the core insight of the virtue-ethics tradition a "rule of practice." He distinguishes this notion, according to which the good of the practice is defined *internally* to the practice, from an "institutional rule." This is the idea of "constitutive rule," employed by John Austin and John Searle to describe social practices without attention to the defining value which the goods internal to the practices have for participants: cf. John Searle, "Ought/Is," in *Speech Acts*, pp. 277ff. As long as the intrinsic—because defining—nature of the goods internal to rules of practice is not seen, social practices appear as merely "institutional" practices whose authority, as in liberal theory, derives only from the (context-independent) individual's will. But this is to misunderstand the whole approach of classical virtue-ethics: see Alisdair MacIntyre, "Objectivity in Morality/ Objectivity in Science," in H. Tristram Engelhart and Daniel Callahan, eds., *Morals, Science and Sociality* (Hastings-on-Hudson: The Hastings Center, 1978), pp. 21-39; see also Allan Bloom, "Justice: John Rawls vs. the Tradition of Political Philosophy," *American Political Science Review* 69, 1 (June 1975): 648-62.

For the ethics of virtue and its allied tradition of practical reason, to imagine that one can transcend the horizon of one's own moral understanding immediately into a universal and "objective" context of rationality is a serious error. Such an effort narrows the understanding of human activity by viewing historical and social variation as so many alternative forms of life presumably available to a universal, contextless rational thinker. What disappears in such an account is that defining, authoritative role of the substantive paradigms of the good society, the good person, and good life practices. For those within the moral horizon, whose characters and vision of the world are shaped through fidelity to an understanding of virtue, the contingent and risky wagers about the good are in fact what makes life worthwhile.

Furthermore, the usual liberal appeal to purportedly universal standards of reason often beclouds and falsifies the thinker's understanding of himself by making invisible the dependence of his way of seeing upon its own authoritative tradition. This problem arises for John Rawls as he attempts to define moral rationality without reference to substantive goods. When he finds himself compelled to introduce into his theory a conception of substantive human ends he turns out to assume, not surprisingly, the usual liberal position that generic goods can be defined in abstraction from commitments to specific ends.

Rawls is working in the spirit of a Kantian deduction of the conditions of possibility, which reconstructs the context of intelligibility within which the general principles organizing moral experience are coherent and consistent. The reconstruction thus tries to show the conceptual necessity of holding those principles. Rawls's moral intuition, which he describes as "our settled conviction," is that justice means fair and equal treatment for all. Rational reconstruction then operates in a circle, beginning with an interpretation of historically contingent "settled convictions" about morality and asking under what conditions it would be consistent for all rational beings to hold these moral convictions. Specifically, Rawls asks under what hypothetical conditions it would be reasonable for human beings to choose to act according to principles of fairness, adjusting both conditions and principles of action as necessary until the conditions of choice logically entail the principles. If such a "cognitive equilibrium" is reached, Rawls

argues, we have grounds for asserting that our settled moral conviction is defensible as a universal moral imperative.[33]

Rawls proposes that commitment to the equality of persons
manifested as universal rules of procedure entails accepting two
general principles. The first principle states that each person is
entitled to an equal right to "the most extensive total system of
equal basic liberties compatible with a similar system of liberty for
all." This implies that, from a moral point of view, human beings
are to be respected as capable of choosing to act autonomously, in
the sense that individuals are able to determine their own goals
however they may reach that determination. The second principle
has two parts. Social and economic conditions are to be equal,
with inequalities tolerated only if they meet the conditions of
being: "(a) to the greatest benefit of the least advantaged...(b)
attached to offices and positions open to all under conditions of
fair equality of opportunity."[34] This is also known as the "difference principle." The two principles explicate a "general conception," as Rawls explains: "All social primary goods...are to be
distributed equally unless an unequal distribution of any or all of
these goods is to the advantage of the least favored."[35] It is an
egalitarian ideal organized so as to regulate the distribution of
social and economic goods among individuals.

Rawls constructs his own version of a social contract, seeking a
cognitive equilibrium between his principles of justice and hypothetical moral agents characterized by the ability to think consistently about the possible bases for social cooperation from an
"original position":

> The aim of the description of the original position is to put together in
> one conception the idea of fairness with the formal values expressed in the
> notion of a well-ordered society, and then to use this conception to help
> us select between alternative principles of justice.[36]

Rawls follows contractarian tradition by starting from the standpoint of hypothetical individuals "mutually disinterested" and
independent of any social and historical context. In the original
position, the self is a generic one that is a moral being precisely by

---

33. Rawls, *Theory*, pp. 20-21, 48-51; also Rawls, "Independence of Moral
Theory," p. 6.
34. Rawls, *Theory*, p. 302.
35. Ibid., p. 303.   36. Ibid., p. 549.

virtue of its rational powers, which enable it to rise above concerns particular to itself and to make decisions from a general point of view. However, among the traits Rawls's contractors are described as possessing are those which do not readily coincide with the conception of the moral self as transcending particular interests, for while the contractors are described as rational in being able to give reasons for their choices and possessing a moral sense of the kind just described, they are "concerned to further their own interests as well." In the original position, the contractors' characteristics are actually a reconstruction of the conditions necessary for rational moral choice. Thus, Rawls seems to say that rationality includes the intelligent pursuit of self-interest.

Indeed, Rawls does include, and give considerable importance to, the utilitarian notion of practical reasoning as intelligent pursuit of self-interest, though he argues against a purely utilitarian moral theory on the grounds that a teleological morality of purpose and consequences such as Jeremy Bentham's must always refer to subjective criteria of evaluation such as pleasure.[37] Rawls claims that only formal, universal procedures of moral choice that define the right, not the good, of actions can avoid this wholly subjectivistic standard; yet, it is the private, utilitarian conception of the self and action that necessitates the general and abstract notion of moral reasoning.

Thus the device of the original position seems to accept a private and utilitarian conception of value as in effect setting the problem that moral theory is developed to resolve. The contractors are composite, even contradictory, beings. They can be persuaded to equality of respect as explicated in the two principles of justice only by recognizing their rational and generic nature as manifested in universalizable moral thinking, which overrides all particular interests.[38] So Rawls has constructed another version of the state of nature that sets the problem of how to secure a stable basis for social cooperation. His solution to the problem of social order is for the contractors to agree to a well-ordered society organized according to his two principles. But does Rawls have a convincing solution to the old problem of how hypothetical contractors—or any human beings—can be brought to think and act in accord

37. Ibid., pp. 27-33.
38. Compare Immanuel Kant, *The Conflict of the Faculties*, in H. Reiss, ed., *Kant's Political Writings* (London: Cambridge University Press, 1970).

with moral rationality? One answer might be that generalizable moral reasoning is possible for any adult at any time, and that one need not appeal further. However, Rawls's awareness of historical and psychological development seems to have ruled out such an option. Another answer would be to propose that living in the practices and ideals of something like a well-ordered society inclines the contractors to make their choices rationally, and so ethically. But this contextual approach would tie moral understanding to a specific moral ecology and leave no ready basis from which Rawls could establish universal, context-free canons of ethical reasoning.

However, liberalism's individualistic and utilitarian vision of human nature has compelled contractarian thinkers to base their social contract upon a moral will that is discontinuous with the desiring nature of the human self. And in the end Rawls does not depart from this tradition. For contractarian liberals, morality limits how individuals and groups may rightly relate to others and defines the moral self in terms of obligations imposed through consistent application of general principles: hence contractarians have sought to base the moral sense in the rational faculty of individual consciousness and have tried to ground and guarantee it by the universality, completeness, and consistency with which moral principles are applied. By following this tradition Rawls hopes to gain a cognitive anchoring for his moral position, to secure rights and obligations in a world of instrumental relations; yet, Rawls's notion of moral theory inherently disjoins this discourse about principles of right from considerations of the relation of social practices to the formation of motives and conscience.

By defining morality as formal completeness and defending it in the same way, moral theory encourages us to forget that theorizing is in reality situated in contexts of moral understanding and practice. Admittedly, Rawls himself seems aware of this tendency of moral theory and has tried to offset it at least partially by stressing the historical and social dimensions of the moral vision that guides his theory. However, he seems at odds with himself, or, more precisely, as with other contractarians before him, his ends and means do not fit together coherently. His theory tries to reconstruct the moral ecology of the well-ordered society as the necessary context for instrumental action. It shows that only such a society can provide stable conditions under which the actions of individuals can achieve security, self-esteem, and fulfillment of private desires. Rawls then uses formal principles of reasoning derived from Kant to check the validity of the reconstruction against the norms of consistency and universality.

To produce the "fit" of cognitive equilibrium, Rawls tries to persuade "rational egoists" through the device of the original position. Rawls's starting point is thus the utilitarian logic of action characteristic of traditional liberal psychology. His quasi-Kantian argument aims to show that purely self-interested action is less consistent than morality and also is unable to provide an enduring basis for the primary goods human beings most want—above all, security and self-esteem. These goods can only be obtained in a social situation of mutual trust and commitment. Thus the argument for the superior rationality of the contract invokes a conception of human nature that depends on an implicit moral ecology. This is an historically specific understanding at odds with liberalism's psychology of self-interest. To make the original position viable, Rawls must postulate certain moral capacities for his hypothetical egoists, for example, the capacity for empathy and the capacity for moral imagination—the ability to conceive of the effects of generalizing principles and courses of action. Rawls considers this moral sense implicit even in self-interested human action. Thus rational reconstruction of the moral sense points beyond purely formal criteria of reasoning toward the question of what conditions must prevail in order for this moral sense to be realized.

While Rawls admits the historical specificity of his moral intuition and that it is rooted in the moral ecology described by his social vision, he remains committed to moral reasoning in its Kantian sense as a forum of universal, substantively neutral principles. Yet, his rational reconstruction of moral reasoning emphasizes its dependence on certain contexts and conditions, particularly the notion that human character is socially formed; hence his theory moves in the direction of reconstructing the logic of the development of this moral consciousness. But to remain consistent with the liberal tradition, the rational reconstruction of this developmental process would have to be possible without appealing to any postulate beyond the formal principles of right. It would have to proceed without dependence upon an ethic of character or commitments to any substantive ends of action. The credibility of this final step in rational reconstruction, as Part III of Rawls's *Theory of Justice* suggests, is tied to the social vision and the necessary conditions of its development and maintenance.[39] This cannot be divorced from the question of how human moral capacities actually develop. In the end, Rawls's theory is closely linked to the viability of liberal moral psychology and its conception of human action.

39. See Rawls, *Theory*, pp. 396ff.

FOUR

A Failure of Moral Imagination: Liberal Psychology and the Matrix of Care

:: I

The new concern of liberal moral philosophy with the role of social life, history, and tradition in the development of important liberal values does not in itself signal the breakdown of the liberal paradigm.[1] It is not a continuation of the revisionist social liberalism of John Dewey and associates. The usual liberal conventions concerning the nature of reasoning, society, and politics are still in place in the work of thinkers like Rawls whose aim is to justify the historically specific notions of liberal culture before the bar of a reason presumed to be universal and trans-historical. This justification takes the form of "rational reconstruction."

Rawls's theory attempts to provide such an account for the liberal notion of justice as reciprocity, yet his attempt differs importantly from Kant's classic reconstruction of duty. Rawls explicitly recognizes that he can only hope to provide reasoned arguments within a context of agreement about at least some features of human psychology and practices of discourse.[2] This means that

1. Sympathetic critics of Rawls have gone further, noting the apparent discrepancy between Rawls's notion that moral and reasoning capacities are rooted in cultural and social life and his reliance in his social contract (the original position) on the traditional liberal perspective of the self-interested individual. See Joyce Beck Hoy, "Three Conceptions of Autonomy in Rawls's Theory of Justice," *Philosophy and Social Criticism*, no. 1 (1979): 57-78.

2. See the discussion in Chapter Three, Part III. Contrasted with the claims of earlier liberals, Rawls's work implies the awareness voiced by William A. Galston in *Justice and the Human Good* (Chicago: University of Chicago Press, 1980): "Moral

moral theory must acknowledge its dependence upon an interpretation of moral intuitions and certain features of human action. Moral philosophy thus acquires an interpretive dimension.

The aim of rational reconstruction is to turn an interpretation into a formal explanation. It attempts to define the rules that govern the meaning of competence for some class of thoughts or actions. These rules would then explain why a given decision or action makes sense and so fits coherently into a given context of thought or activity. For example, modern linguistics has tried to reconstruct the rules of grammar and syntax in a way that would enable observers who understood those rules to judge the competence of speakers of a given language. Speakers of a language can and do make such judgments of competence, and the linguists' assumption is that what makes such discrimination possible is the existence of a logically coherent set of rules governing the use of language to which all speakers of the language tacitly subscribe. If the theory-informed judgments of the linguists match those of the native speakers, the reconstruction is judged to be correct. Rational reconstruction thus tries to make explicit and systematic the "conditions of possibility" of an ongoing community of practice.

Applying this method to moral theory means reconstructing the context of rules governing the moral practices of a community. The members of a moral community, like the members of a linguistic community, discriminate between competent and incompetent performances, valid and invalid moral intuitions. Rawls's reconstruction of the intuition that justice is fairness tries to show that one can construct a coherent context of general rules on the basis of which any rational thinker could explain the intuitive judgments of members of that moral community about which acts are morally competent or "just." But Rawls goes further than this. A rational thinker can be convinced of the genuine and universal validity of this moral intuition of fairness because it in fact is the one he would hypothetically choose for himself and for all. The moral is the universally rational. This is going a step beyond the usual limits of theoretical reconstruction. Rawls wants to show

---

philosophy is the sum of the destruction of immediate purposes and our enduring needs for grounds of action. It seeks to provide reflective grounds capable of withstanding skeptical corrosion" (p. 15).

the inescapability of his moral norms for all rational actors, regardless of community context.

But, as we have seen, Rawls's intuition contains the claim that rationality is importantly related to his conception of human nature, specifically, to its social character. While the theory of justice is established by formal criteria, the plausibility of the theory is strongly affected by the empirical question of whether his theory grasps the morally significant aspects of human action. Particularly important is the question of how the kind of rationality liberalism assumes to be characteristic of moral action is actually developed—specifically, whether development of a sense of the right is actually separable from a commitment to a sense of the good. Thus the contemporary enterprise of justifying the norms of liberal moral and political philosophy becomes once again importantly connected to moral psychology.

Separating the right from the good seems unproblematical to liberals in political practice as well as in moral philosophy, because their notion of theory, including rational reconstruction, assumes that moral intuitions and sentiments are logically describable as rules independent of discriminatory and interactive skills. Thus liberal thinkers believe that they can explain a moral sense independently of the substantive commitments that are an aspect of practical moral life and character. Rational reconstruction of a moral sense gains credibility if one can show empirically that the moral sense reconstructed in the theory is developed through a process of more inclusive and coherent reasoning that is independent of any specific substantive commitments about the ends of action. For this reason Rawls appeals to the cognitive psychology of Jean Piaget and, in particular, Lawrence Kohlberg.[3] Kohlberg's theory provides a kind of empirical test of whether the development of the sense of justice underlying the social contract is possible within the context of a theory of the self and reasoning compatible with liberal tradition.

For its claims to be convincing, liberalism needs an empirical moral psychology. Such a psychology would have to show that rational autonomy and justice, as the liberal tradition has understood these ideas, are intelligible and practically possible as the

3. See John Rawls, *A Theory of Justice* (Cambridge, Massachusetts: Harvard University Press, 1971), pp. 460-61.

outcome of patterns of social interaction and the development of reasoning. But the liberal moral ecology is founded on procedural, not substantive, public commitments. To show that it is viable, a theory must also demonstrate that the development process can be understood in a language which is itself free of references and commitments to substantive public commitment; otherwise, liberal moral commitments and the liberal image of society would appear less than self-sustaining, would appear to depend upon other more inclusive kinds of understanding.

The novelty of Kohlberg's work, on the other hand, is its claim that it incorporates Jean Piaget's cognitive-developmental psychology. Piaget's theory of a natural, invariant progression through stages of cognitive and moral development provides Kohlberg with the way to present a "non-indoctrinative" education that is not value-neutral. He can do this because Piaget's psychology put forward as science—a genetic structuralism—justifies a hierarchy of stages of reasoning and judgment as culturally universal. These mature stages of moral reasoning correspond to the moral philosophy of the social contract as developed by the contractarian philosophers, especially Kant.

Kohlberg classifies moral reasoning into a sequence of three *levels*, each of which consists of two *stages*. These move toward progressively more inclusive and differentiated principles of reasoning.

At Level One, moral value resides in external, quasi-physical happenings, in bad acts, or in quasi-physical needs, rather than in persons and standards. Stage One is characterized by the obedience and punishment orientation, egocentric deference to superior power or prestige, or a trouble-avoiding set, and by objective responsibility. Stage Two is characterized by the naively egoistic orientation. Right action is that which instrumentally satisfies the self's needs and, occasionally, the needs of others. There is awareness of relativism of value to each actor's needs and perspective, a naive egalitarianism and orientation to exchange and reciprocity.

At Level Two, moral value resides in performing good or right roles, in maintaining the conventional order and the expectancies of others. Stage Three is characterized by the good-boy orientation to approval and to pleasing and helping others, conformity to stereotypical images of majority or natural role behavior, and judgment by intentions. Stage Four is characterized by the authority and social-order maintaining orientation to "doing duty" and to showing respect for authority and maintaining the given social order for its own sake, and by regard for earned expectations of others.

At Level Three, moral value resides in conformity by the self to shared or shareable standards, rights, or duties. Stage Five is characterized by the contractual legalistic orientation, by recognition of an arbitrary element or starting point in rules or expectations for the sake of agreement. Duty is defined in terms of contract, general avoidance of violation of the will or rights of others, and majority will and welfare. Stage Six is characterized by the conscience or principle orientation, not only to actually ordained social rules but to principles of choice involving appeal to logical universality and consistency with orientation to conscience as a directing agent, and to mutual respect and trust.[4]

The theory presents us with an account of both the empirical development of moral thinking and a philosophical explication of the liberal conception of universal *a priori* moral principles as the logical, natural climax of cognitive maturation. Kohlberg's theory differs from the more conventional liberalism of Rawls in rejecting the individualistic, atomistic assumptions of traditional liberal moral psychology. For Kohlberg, moral meaning is derived not from solitary wills but from the ongoing fact of social participation. This is the influence of John Dewey's mode of thinking. Piaget's structural account of cognitive maturation shares the pragmatic insight that reasoning arises from participation in problematic situations and, ideally, progresses toward wider, more inclusive interactions between individual and environments. Yet, Piaget, unlike Dewey, sees these operations as ultimately reducible to describable transformations of a structure of elements whose intelligibility derives from a certain conception of language and logic which Piaget calls "structuralist."

As will become clearer as the discussion proceeds, the logical and epistemological commitments of Piaget's structuralism turn out to have close affinities to the liberal-Kantian metaphor of moral reasoning as legislating. The Deweyan, operational sources

4. See Lawrence Kohlberg, "Stage and Sequence: The Cognitive-Developmental Approach to Socialization," in David Goslin, ed., *Handbook of Socialization Theory and Research* (Chicago: Rand McNally, 1969), p. 376.

of Kohlberg's theory press in the opposite direction, toward a situational, prudential understanding of moral reasoning that includes an interpretive aspect in strong contrast to the Kantian or the structuralist paradigm. Tracing these conflicts within Kohlberg's theory will bring us again to the limits revealed when one asks about the adequacy of its understanding of moral reasoning and moral life.

In recent years Kohlberg has responded to criticism of his work, which has been ongoing since the 1950s. The fortunate side-effect has been more explicit discussion about the conceptual and philosophical issues raised by his theory. Kohlberg parallels the linkage in Piaget's work of epistemology with genetic developmental psychology to the relations Kohlberg thinks investigation of the epistemological status of moral ideas ought to have with investigations concerning the facts of moral development.[5]

Kohlberg emphasizes the connection of his conception of moral psychology with the main tradition of philosophical and political liberalism. Further, he distinguishes two schools within liberalism. One, the naturalistic or utilitarian school, is represented in the works of J. S. Mill, Sedgewick, Dewey, and Tufts. The other is represented in the works of Locke, Kant, and Rawls.[6] This distinction is important for an understanding of Kohlberg's work. It explains why the starting premises of his developmental theory are Deweyan but the philosophical justification for the ideal of justice as the end of moral development proceeds along the lines of Kant's deontological or duty-ethics.

The Deweyan basis of Kohlberg's work, to which Kohlberg himself often alludes, is easy to mark. Dewey's "progressive ideology," we are told, derives from a functional epistemology that equates knowledge neither with measurable "sense data," as in behaviorism, nor with "self-insight," as in existential or phenomenological epistemology. Knowledge is instead understood as "an equilibrated or resolved relationship between an inquiring human actor

5. Kohlberg, "From Is to Ought: How to Commit the Naturalist Fallacy and Get Away with It in the Study of Moral Development," in Theodore Mischel, ed., *Cognitive Development and Epistemology* (New York: Academic Press, 1971), pp. 154-55.

6. Lawrence Kohlberg and Rochelle Mayer, "Development as the Aim of Education," *Harvard Educational Review*, vol. 42, no. 4 (1972): 472-73.

and a problematic situation."[7] Behavior and internal states are thus integrated in a functional conception of mind in which competence is ideally measured on the basis of systematic and reproducible observations of performance coordinated with interpretations of that performance by the performer. This pragmatic conception of maturation as a process of "equilibrating" interactions is not a merely descriptive observation, however; it explicitly contains an evaluative claim that the correct direction of maturation is toward "ego-strength," understood as the ability to take up a position as a member of a community whose transactions are characterized by mutual respect.[8]

The moral ideal guiding Dewey's functional conception of development has shaped the categories of that theory. Dewey early postulated three stages of growth in ego-strength. In his scheme the expressive, subjective, or self-centered orientation of childhood was to be transformed by moral education into a second stage of morality understood as propriety. This in turn was incomplete until criticized and guided by an ethical understanding of a more universal and self-reflective scope.[9] Dewey's scheme was really an interpretation of human psychological maturation. Kohlberg rightly notes that this insight requires one to take empathy and identification of self with the other as the fundamental datum in psychological maturation. He writes: "Empathy does not have to be taught to the child or conditioned; it is a primary phenomenon. What development and socialization achieve is the organization of empathic phenomena into consistent sympathetic and moral concerns, not the creation of empathy as such."[10]

Kohlberg's well-known three stages of moral reasoning roughly parallel Dewey's scheme. Kohlberg's pre-conventional level is characterized by ego-centered, consequential reasoning, largely on the basis of reward and punishment. However, that stage is normally transcended into the level of conventional moral reasoning, characterized by loyalty and identification. For Kohlberg as for

7. Ibid., p. 460.

8. Kohlberg, "Moral Education in the Schools: A Developmental View," in Robert E. Grinder, ed., *Studies in Adolescence* (New York: Macmillan, 1969), pp. 237-41.

9. See John Dewey, "Outlines of a Theory of Ethics," in *Early Works: 1882-1898* (Carbondale: Southern Illinois University Press, 1972), vol. 3.

10. Kohlberg, "Stage and Sequence," p. 394.

Dewey, it is precisely the underlying primary phenomenon of empathy or role-taking that makes this transition possible, as long as the child's environment provides opportunities for identification. Kohlberg's culminating phase is, like Dewey's, a kind of generalized empathy or identification which enables the moral reasoner to transcend the limited and particular loyalties and proprieties of his particular context of transactions. Kohlberg's conception of personal maturation as a moral being is at the same time a normative ideal of adulthood, of what it means to be a moral self.

Again following Dewey, Kohlberg takes it as a premise that moral behavior is always more than conditioned response, that it has a cognitive aspect. This is because any transaction of organism with environment is already an "interpretation" or "definition" of the situation. By selecting some aspects of the environmental conditions as more important than others, as more deserving of attention and response, the organism is introducing teleological agency into the scene; hence affect is seen as an internal experience of a functional interaction that is interpreting the situation by discriminating certain conditions as means to a desired future outcome. For Kohlberg, "socially communicated symbolic definitions determine the actual felt attitudes and emotions experienced by the individual . . . the basic way in which affect is socialized is not so much by punishment and reward as it is by communication of definitions of situations which elicit socially appropriate affect."[11] Like Dewey, Kohlberg's normative understanding of psychic development links inner and outer life, affect and cognition, thought and performance; "values" become a real, even a controlling, element in basic experience.[12]

However, Kohlberg seems to have reservations about the philosophical adequacy of Dewey's naturalism, and also about the epistemological adequacy of Dewey's theory as scientific psychology. Kohlberg asserts that his own progressive ideology "rests on the value postulates of ethical liberalism" according to which "traditional standards and value-relativism" are rejected in favor of ethi-

11. Ibid., p. 393.
12. See John Dewey, *Experience and Nature* (New York: Open Court Publications, 1925), ch. 10; also "The Construction of Good," in *The Quest for Certainty: A Study of the Relation of Knowledge and Action* (New York: Putnam, 1960), pp. 254-86.

cal universals, principles "formulated and justified by the method of philosophy, not simply by the method of psychology."[13]

If we assume that the things we do are valuable because they fulfill our needs and desires, and prize this quality of usefulness above all others, it is clear that aside from fear, the only thing that can persuade us to a course of action will be hope of gain. On the other hand, suppose human beings to have dignity as ends in themselves, suppose that this dignity means, above all, being able to gather oneself together in pledging one's word, in making a free commitment of oneself, then acts are right or wrong depending on whether or not they conform to this essential dignity. Deontological ethics, which begins from the notion of unconditional moral duty, states this premise in the principle that only a course of action that can be generalized for all and that does not violate any person's fundamental dignity is truly right. Clearly, there is a great disparity between these two ways of understanding moral life. The utilitarian form of reasoning can be checked by a person who accepts the deontological morality of autonomy but, strictly speaking, this means switching the criterion of value at some point. Liberal philosophy has never succeeded in finding a smooth continuity between the two.

Kohlberg's theory of moral reasoning aims to resolve that troublesome incoherence without heating up latent conflicts over ultimate values. To do this, he must show that his theory of the growth of moral reasoning is truly universal, that it is true for all people everywhere, for Americans and Chinese, men and women. He must prove that he has discovered a genuine science of human development. If he can do these things, Kohlberg will have made a persuasive case for his theory as a coherent guide for our personal and our collective lives in these difficult times. He will have provided an incontrovertible principle of moral authority in a pattern of reasoning that inevitably leads us from the crude hedonism of utilitarian thinking to the dutiful civility of the deontological ethic.

The doctrine of cognitive stage theory presupposes that reasoning can be mapped out as a set of rules for organizing and relating contents or elements. These rules are actually statements of biologically adaptive patterns of behavior. For Kohlberg, adaptation

13. Kohlberg and Mayer, "Development," pp. 472-73.

is a process that aims at "conserving" the fundamental structures of an organism while its patterns of activity change in interaction with its environment. The famous six stages of the theory are examples of this adaptive process, "the transformations of simple early cognitive structures as these are applied to (or assimilate) the external world, and as they are accommodated to or restructured by the external world in the course of being applied to it."[14]

Kohlberg's original postulation of the pre-moral, the conventional, and the principled levels, each divided into a relatively less and a relatively more differentiated stage, came as a development of Jean Piaget's suggestion that there is a natural progression from moral reasoning based on fear and conformity to others' expectations toward an ethic of self-imposed principles. Following Piaget's work regarding levels of cognitive development, Kohlberg proposed the theory that the maturing person moves from a self-focused phase (pre-moral Level, Stages One and Two) to a propriety or other-oriented phase (conventional Level, Stages Three and Four), which reaches a logical culmination in "justice," that is, moral reasoning guided by shareable standards and duties. It is genealogically consistent, given the origin of this scheme in cognitive studies, that Kohlberg should accept Piaget's conception of subsuming particulars under general rules as his notion of moral judgment. Moral principles become directly analogous to logical rules in this Kantian kind of reasoning, organizing relations among elements in an orderly way. Moral judgment is then a practical application of a decision procedure which can be stated in a formal principle.[15]

It is important to be clear about the nature of this claim. Moral judgments are not simply cognitive operations; however, by demonstrating that there is a definable sequence of stages in moral development, Kohlberg hopes to show that moral development has a basic logical component such that moral reasoning can be described in cognitive-structural terms. If so, there should be a demonstrable correlation between maturity in affective aspects of

14. Kohlberg, "Stage and Sequence," p. 352.
15. See ibid., p. 375. It is possible to argue that science is today understood in a wider sense than the classic notion of subsuming facts under propositions: see Stephen Toulmin, *Human Understanding* (Princeton, New Jersey: Princeton University Press, 1972). However, both Kohlberg and Piaget construe valid knowledge in the classic meaning of science, as becomes clear below.

life, especially actual practical judgment, and cognitive levels of moral reasoning. This would be true if it were true that "empathy" or "affect" is structured according to the invariant sequence, as Kohlberg asserts.[16] Moral reasoning, like any cognitive operation, would then be educable by providing the proper problems for stimulation: Kohlberg tells us that problems or moral "dilemmas" just one stage in advance of the student's actual level of reasoning provide the optimal developmental stimulus.

As an example of this, consider Kohlberg's notion of structurally categorized motives for engaging in moral action. The test consists of the following "moral dilemma" to which the student must respond:

In Europe, a woman was near death from cancer. One drug might save her, a form of radium that a druggist in the same town had recently discovered. The druggist was charging $2,000, ten times what the drug cost him to make. The sick woman's husband, Heinz, went to everyone he knew to borrow the money, but he could only get together about half of what it cost. He told the druggist that his wife was dying and asked him to sell it cheaper or let him pay later. But the druggist said, "No." The husband got desperate and broke into the man's store to steal the drug for his wife. Should the husband have done that? Why?[17]

Notice that in the following list of answers there are no right or wrong responses. There are disagreements possible at each stage. A stage is defined by *principles* of reasoning, that is, by form, not content.

Stage 1. Action is motivated by avoidance of punishment and "conscience" is irrational fear of punishment.

PRO—If you let your wife die, you will get in trouble. You'll be blamed for not spending the money to save her and there'll be an investigation of you and the druggist for your wife's death.

CON—You shouldn't steal the drug because you'll be caught and sent to jail if you do. If you do get away, your conscience would bother you thinking how the police would catch up with you at any minute.

Stage 2. Action motivated by desire for reward or benefit. Possible guilt reactions are ignored and punishment viewed in a pragmatic manner. (Differentiates own fear, pleasure, or pain from punishment-consequences.)

---

16. Ibid., pp. 393ff., and Kohlberg, "From Is to Ought" pp. 188-89.
17. Kohlberg, "Stage and Sequence," p. 379.

PRO—If you do happen to get caught you could give the drug back and you wouldn't get much of a sentence. It wouldn't bother you much to serve a little jail term, if you have your wife when you get out.

CON—He may not get much of a jail term if he steals the drug, but his wife will probably die before he gets out so it won't do him much good. If his wife dies, he shouldn't blame himself, it wasn't his fault she has cancer.

Stage 3. Action motivated by anticipation of disapproval of others, actual or imagined-hypothetical (e.g., guilt). (Differentiation of disapproval from punishment, fear, and pain.)

PRO—No one will think you're bad if you steal the drug but your family will think you're an inhuman husband if you don't. If you let your wife die, you'll never be able to look anybody in the face again.

CON—It isn't just the druggist who will think you're a criminal, everyone else will too. After you steal it, you'll feel bad thinking how you've brought dishonor on your family and yourself; you won't be able to face anyone again.

Stage 4. Action motivated by anticipation of dishonor, i.e., institutionalized blame for failure of duty, and by guilt over concrete harm done to others. (Differentiates formal dishonor from informal disapproval. Differentiates guilt for bad consequences from disapproval.)

PRO—If you have any sense of honor, you won't let your wife die because you're afraid to do the only thing that will save her. You'll always feel guilty that you caused her death if you don't do your duty to her.

CON—You're desperate and you may not know you're doing wrong when you steal the drug. But you'll know you did wrong after you're punished and sent to jail. You'll always feel guilty for your dishonesty and lawbreaking.

Stage 5. Concern about maintaining respect of equals and of the community (assuming their respect is based on reason rather than emotions). Concern about own self-respect, i.e., to avoid judging self as irrational, inconsistent, nonpurposive. (Discriminates between institutionalized blame and community disrespect or self-disrespect.)

PRO—You'd lose other people's respect, not gain it, if you don't steal. If you let your wife die, it would be out of fear, not out of reasoning it out. So you'd just lose self-respect and probably the respect of others too.

CON—You would lose your standing and respect in the community and violate the law. You'd lose respect for yourself if you're carried away by emotion and forget the long-range point of view.

Stage 6. Concern about self-condemnation for violating one's own principles. (Differentiates between community respect and self-respect. Differentiates between self-respect for general achieving rationality and self-respect for maintaining moral principles.)

PRO—If you don't steal the drug and let your wife die, you'd always condemn yourself for it afterward. You wouldn't be blamed and you would have lived up to the outside rule of the law but you wouldn't have lived up to your own standards of conscience.

CON—If you stole the drug, you wouldn't be blamed by other people but you'd condemn yourself because you wouldn't have lived up to your own conscience and standards of honesty.[18]

The stage theory judges the *form* of the reasoning, not the content. The higher stages are judged more advanced because they are more formally adequate in that the rules governing the higher stages subsume the lower, each stage advancing closer to an ideal reciprocity of transaction.

The import of Kohlberg's theory becomes plain. The invariant sequence of stages, if empirically demonstrated, would set firm limits on the arbitrariness of genuine moral principles. At the same time, these valid principles would be universal and established independently of a substantive conception of human ends beyond maturation of natural, presumably genetic, potential. The moral principle of justice thus becomes a procedural norm of rational cooperation. Kohlberg's psychology is designed in part to complement empirically the moral claims of the social-contract doctrine as elaborated by Kant and Rawls. According to that view, justice is an obligation to contract which requires impartiality in administering the law and the right of individuals to equal treatment.[19]

The theory is an elaborate contemporary restatement of the liberal argument for the self-evidence of the moral scheme of the social contract. Kohlberg can then argue that moral education should proceed by focusing on the form, not the content, of moral

18. Ibid., pp. 381-82.

19. Piaget is explicit in subsuming this quality of reciprocity under the cognitive, finally logico-mathematical quality of "reversibility" characteristic of the "complete" structures of mathematics. Piaget's science is not an idealism, however. Instead, he aims at "functional and structural isomorphisms expressed as models," seeing thinking as an organismic mode of exchange and accommodation with the environment. See Piaget, *Biology and Knowledge: An Essay on the Relations between Organic Regulations and Cognitive Processes* (Chicago: University of Chicago Press, 1971), esp. pp. 62-65, 360-63.

See also Kohlberg and Mayer, "Development," p. 484. There Kohlberg cites the moral philosophies of Kant and Rawls as providing "a philosophical notion of adequate principles of justice which complements the epistemological argument from Piaget."

beliefs and action. From the perspective of the social contract, that is, Stage Five morality, all moral "contents" or ends are fundamentally arbitrary. *Obligation* is defined in terms of contract, as respect for mutual rights, especially the right to be treated as an end in oneself and never as a means to another's end.

Kohlberg proposes his conception of moral education as a solution to the First Amendment controversies about religious values in education. Religious education in itself he sees having only a "very limited influence" upon moral development. Its content is ultimately, to Kohlberg, arbitrary; thus it is as likely to retard as to advance moral maturation. Besides, because they are arbitrary, religious beliefs cannot be the core values of a liberal democratic regime founded on a social contract.

Here, then, is Kohlberg's appeal for liberal thinkers. He does not see recognition of individual rights as entailing a prohibition on a value-orientation in schools or public life. The legitimacy of a social contract rests on a kind of value-consensus, a shared belief which it is the schools' public obligation to teach. But those values are neither arbitrary nor substantive. They are procedural, yet universal in that they must be appealed to by majority or minority in support of their own beliefs. They have form but not content.

The problems as to the legitimacy of moral education in the public schools disappear, then, if the proper content of moral education is recognized to be the values of justice which themselves prohibit the imposition of beliefs of one group upon another.[20]

This "proper content" is the classic liberal formula for pluralism, for the bargaining, commercial society, and for interest-group politics restrained by the moral obligations of the social contract. Kohlberg's version of the "new science of politics" claims to reduce the arbitrariness of merely parochial values to a universal structure of reasoning which advances to closure within an intelligible world of moral ends.

While Kohlberg's theory is not the old psychological atomism, it remains firmly within the liberal philosophic paradigm. The moral legitimacy of the social-contract doctrine is correlated with the theoretical claim to adequacy of explanation. This claim to scientific status for his moral psychology is central and decisive for

20. Kohlberg, "Moral Education," p. 166.

Kohlberg's project. It is consistent with the reductive ethos of modern social science and liberal political philosophy. The theory tries to secure a kind of moral development by showing that ethics is an expression of an unchanging structure of human reasoning. Progressive thinkers such as Dewey saw moral development as heavily dependent upon active social-political involvement. Like the earlier proponents of classical virtue, they were forced to note the interdependency of the kind of moral development concretely possible and the state of contingent social and political relationships. Kohlberg's moral vision seems to him an improvement upon the Deweyan. It postulates an inherent, universal structure and can be developed with less dependence upon large-scale social conditions or active social experiment. Since Hobbes, analytic reasoning has attempted to gain control over contingency by narrowing its sights, displacing concern from the ends and meaning of action to its supposed underlying causes. In a similar way, Kohlberg follows the liberal hope of reducing the uncertainties and disorder of civic morality by concentrating on the mechanics of human relations. Kohlberg thinks that he has discovered an underlying logical pattern that can save deontological ethics from charges of arbitrariness. This is the claim of this new structuralist ethics.[21]

The project of a structuralist ethics is the latest and most conceptually sophisticated evolution of reductive epistemology in liberal thought. The theory's resolute concentration upon the essentially private ethics of civility already promises a cultural "fit" between Kohlberg's structuralist theory and the historical drift of American society toward seeing social life as a system susceptible to expert control. By contrast, the activist concerns of Dewey's progressivism, like the classical emphasis upon maintenance of a public civic culture, are not as compatible with policy science conceived of as technical administration.

Kohlberg has in fact borrowed most of the language and much of the direction of his theory not from Dewey but from Jean Piaget. Piaget has proclaimed structuralism as the ruling, indeed, archi-

---

21. The idea of a structuralist ethics as a meeting ground for interdisciplinary work in the human sciences is beginning to receive widespread attention: see Gunther Steng, "The Promise of Structuralist Ethics," *Hastings Center Report* 66 (December 1976): 32-40.

tectonic, method of science and successor to the old empiricism. With this Piaget is announcing another project of "unified science." The central insight of structuralist thinking is the notion that physical nature consists of structured wholes neither made up of atomic units nor given form by a pervasive essence or an emergent Gestalt. Rather, structuralist thinking conceives of a structure as simply a set of mutually determining relationships. This introduces a holism into scientific logic such that the idea of structure itself becomes the unit of intelligibility, replacing the atomic simples of earlier empiricism. The fundamental epistemological premise is "an ideal (perhaps a hope) of intrinsic intelligibility supported by the postulate that structures are self-sufficient and that, to grasp them, we do not have to make reference to all sorts of extraneous elements."[22]

The basis of intelligibility is the self-contained and precisely articulable notion of structure itself. While Piaget can point out that this means the abandonment of the atomistic logic of the old empiricism in social science, it does not mean abandonment of reductionism. On the contrary, structuralist method is an intensified effort at reduction. Meaning is now to be reduced to explicit, operationally defined rules that govern the transformation of structures. In the case of Piaget's developmental psychology, this means that the genesis of the personality takes place only accidentally, even though always, within a given cultural situation. At the deep level, the personality's maturation is measured and understood by means of the development of cognitive competences. The competences are defined as certain logical operations upon elements. Advance is then measured by the subject's ability to transcend the level of concrete operations, in which content is the focus, to that of formal operations such as mathematics, in which contents are, strictly speaking, interchangeable.

Piaget has proposed an evolutionary scheme of scientific progress based on his judgment that his genetic psychology has succeeded in explaining the development of intelligence in a way that neither phenomenological nor behavioristic inquiries have been able to do. Piaget applauds and supports the pragmatists' notion that thought proceeds from action; however, it is precisely the aim

22. Jean Piaget, *Structuralism* (New York: Harper and Row, 1970), pp. 9-10.

of thought to transcend the partial, ambiguous realm of what Kant called pragmatic anthropology so as to criticize and potentially reorganize it from the purified viewpoint of context-free, formal understanding. As in all modern scientific thought, the desired goal for theory is control over practical life. In Piaget's scheme, structuralist social science promises this by revealing beneath the refractory world of concrete persons and meanings the "epistemic subject" in its true home—the rule-governed play of operations upon signs.

> It might seem that the foregoing account makes the *subject* disappear to leave only the *"impersonal and general,"* but this is to forget that on the plane of knowledge (as, perhaps, on that of moral and esthetic values) the subject's activity calls for a continual "decentering" . . . as an uninterrupted process of coordinating and setting in reciprocal relations.[23]

The achievement of decentering is thus both cognitive and moral —or, rather, the two are forms of the same process.

This goal of knowledge also provides Piaget with his criterion for scientific progress. The "evolution of explanatory concepts" in history seems to exhibit a definite developmental sequence in which the concrete, lower-level functions are subsumed under more general and explicit rules of functioning of the higher stages. Piaget finds this displayed in the history of biology. There the "precausal" or "transcausal" teleological mode of thinking, which saw organisms as essential totalities, gave way to the linear causality typical of atomistic reductive explanation. That in turn has been supplanted by cyclic or feedback models of causality, which explain organisms as "relational totalities relying on autoregulatory mechanisms."[24]

The application of this vision to the human sciences is a thoroughgoing "naturalism." It comprehends human cultural life as ultimately the resultant of biologically based cognitive functions. The intricate webs of meaning and identity that humankind has spun through history, and through which we and Piaget think, are to be docoded—and decentered, in a radical sense—as "both reflections of mechanisms of autoregulation and differentiated organs for the regulation of exchanges with the environment."[25]

23. Ibid., p. 139.
24. Piaget, *Biology and Knowledge*, p. 131; cf. pp. 90-99.
25. Ibid., pp. 26ff.

Moral practice and moral thinking are also assimilated into the same scheme of development. Here both Piaget and Kohlberg reveal the deep ambiguity in the long-standing alliance between liberal politics and reductive science.

:: II

The ambiguity arises as soon as one asks what, in Piaget's and Kohlberg's schemes, morality is about. Practical moral life is interwoven with answers to that question, such as that morality is concerned with doing what is good or what is right. But what meaning can these terms have for a structuralist? The rational explanation of moral understanding is that practical discriminations are like concrete cognitive operations. They have only an imperfect grasp of the equivalence of contents-ordering by rules. The cognitive basis of moral reasoning is a developing ability to see the elements of that concrete thinking, the particular acts of persons, in abstraction from their experienced context so as to focus on the formal quality of reciprocity.

> By a moral principle we mean a mode of choosing which is universal, a rule of choosing which we want all people to adopt always in all situations. . . . A moral principle is a principle for resolving competing claims. . . . There is only one basis for resolving claims: justice or equality. Treat every man's claim impartially regardless of the man. A moral principle is not only a rule for action, but a reason for action. As a reason for action, justice is called respect for persons.[26]

The impartiality and universality criteria of Kantian ethics accord well with decentered operational thinking. However, all this, in Kant, is premised upon the worth of the person. From where, in the structuralist scheme, does that derive?

It is not evident that it derives from the scheme at all. Within the biological framework Piaget sketches for his work, moral norms find their intelligibility in the cognitive structures they exemplify. However, these have their basis in the successful adaptation of the human social system to the environmental ecosystem. Moral thinking, moral life, is thus an "adaptive organ," aiding

---

26. Kohlberg, "Education for Justice: A Modern Statement of the Platonic View," in Nancy F. Sizer and Theodore R. Sizer, eds., *Moral Education: Five Lectures* (Cambridge, Massachusetts: Harvard University Press, 1970), pp. 69-70.

the process of "equilibration" of man with the rest of the natural world. Now, continuing Piaget's historical analogy, we could say that a structuralist ethics substitutes for the utility of the earlier atomistic empiricism the functionality of its cybernetic success. However, Kant explicitly rejected the possibility of grounding human dignity in any such purely functional, utilitarian mode of thought.[27] Kantian ethics is not, as philosopher Henry Veatch has put it, a "transcendental deduction of the linguistic or ontological conditions of ethical norms." Human worth is a dictate of practical, not explanatory, reason, and from the point of view of a utilitarian theory such as structuralist biology it must remain, as Kant said it was, mysterious.[28] This loss of comprehension is the ineluctable price that must be paid for the reductive narrowing of thought about man. Piaget's structuralism reenacts the bifurcation of anthropological thinking which liberal philosophy has long failed to synthesize.

The ultimate criterion for a structuralist conception of moral and political systems must be adaptation, that is, survival, in some form. Like Piaget, Kohlberg seems to want to see his moral stages as self-developing wherever environmental conditions are suitable. Thus, since these universal stages are generated to meet the requirements of biological adaptation, reaching the higher phases becomes a measure of a society's as well as an individual's development. According to Kohlberg, cross-cultural applications of his moral-reasoning test confirm the liberal view that social and cultural evolution has progressed furthest in Western democratic countries. Most male adults in any society place in Stage Four, conformity to social propriety and authority. This is the case in the United States as well as in Taiwan, Turkey, and the Yucatán. However, American boys progressed faster and in greater numbers beyond Stage Four to Stage Five, the social-contract, legalistic orientation. Stage Five morality is the declared moral conception of the U.S. Constitution.[29] Significantly, and controversially,

27. See Immanuel Kant, *Anthropology from a Pragmatic Point of View*, translated by Mary J. Gregor (The Hague: Nijoff, 1974).

28. Henry Veatch makes this point in his critique of contemporary ethical philosophies such as John Searle's and H. Hare's: "For Kant, the only real, as opposed to phenomenal, knowledge about man comes from volition, that is, freedom itself." Henry B. Veatch, *For an Ontology of Morals: A Critique of Contemporary Ethical Theory* (Evanston, Illinois: Northwestern University Press, 1971), p. 94.

29. Kohlberg, "From Is to Ought," pp. 163-74.

Kohlberg found that development to the principled level was generally more common among middle-class than among working-class children.

From these results Kohlberg suggests the credibility of a "mild doctrine of social evolutionism" such as that proposed by the exponent of liberalism, L. T. Hobhouse.[30] The force of this "mild doctrine" is to support with putative empirical evidence the claim of the liberal Enlightenment that the idea of the social contract is the logical culmination of psychological and political maturation, for both the individual and the historical community—indeed, for the species. In Kohlberg's theory, cognitive psychology seems to ground the ethics of civility in a lawlike phenomenon of biological functioning. Note, however, that the key moral idea of the dignity of the subject (concrete, not general or abstract) appears in the scheme gratuitously, translated, so to speak, from the practical realm. The theory proceeds to cast the development of the implications of this idea as the unfolding of biologically given functions. But is Kohlberg's theory as "scientific" as he claims? If it is not—and there are now powerful objections raised against its claims—then do we not find ourselves again pressing the very limits of liberal anthropology?

To demonstrate the scientific character of his claims Kohlberg must be able to show that his theory actually can explain the motives and meanings of moral reasoning as variants of constant structural patterns. The structuralist claim is that a formula expressing relationships and their transformation can be defined over elements whose specific value or content can vary without thereby changing the structural relationships expressed by the formula. Now, by taking the Kantian ideal of generalization as his notion of morality Kohlberg has, one might say, heavily stacked his deck in advance. The moral ideal of impartiality, like its corollary of equal treatment under the law, seems to suggest that moral reasoning really is formally analogous to mathematic problem-solving: a matter of fitting formulas to the facts.

In Kohlberg's developmental scheme each higher stage of psychological development includes elements of earlier structures but transforms them in such a way that they can be integrated into the more developed structures so as to preserve the continuity and

---

30. Ibid., p. 178.

equilibrium of the whole. Thus reasoners at the higher stages can explain the reasoning characteristic of lower stages by reconstructing it, but reasoners at the lower stages cannot reconstruct reasoning at stages higher than their own. Kohlberg sees this as "naturally allied to the formalistic tradition in philosophical ethics from Kant to Rawls." This isomorphism of psychological and normative theory generates the claim that a psychologically more advanced stage is more morally adequate, by philosophic criteria.[31] He thus presents the rational reconstruction of moral development as not identical with but complementary to the rational reconstruction of liberal ethics.

In practice, Kohlberg's efforts at reconstruction of moral reasoning according to his scheme have generated more difficulties than the above formulation suggests. There is no precise formula for knowing which "facts" will count as "variables" unless the whole situation is interpreted. There is in those cases no standard of measurement that is not itself subject to discussion and further interpretation, because the process of discerning meanings in a situation can never be completely formalized as a decision procedure. Any interpretation put forward itself always represents a stand in regard to what Dewey called the matrix of interaction. This matrix is a constituent part of the practical context upon which the interpretation depends.

One major criticism of Kohlberg's work has been the charge that his results cannot be stated as generalized rules of the "if x, then y" form because the "scale of moral judgment" is unique and peculiar to each test. William Kurtines and Esther Greif, who advance this line of criticism, take Kohlberg to task for presenting interpretations of moral reasoning rather than a strictly explanatory account.[32] They have pointed out that after more than fifteen years of developing the moral-reasoning scale, Kohlberg has been unable to provide any reliability or predictability estimates for the validity of his tests. As Kohlberg's Heinz example discussed above indicates, the tests necessarily involve interpretation of the sub-

---

31. Lawrence Kohlberg, "The Claim to Moral Adequacy of a Highest Stage of Moral Judgment," *Journal of Philosophy* 70 (1973): 632-33.
32. William Kurtines and Esther B. Greif, "The Development of Moral Thought: Review and Evaluation of Kohlberg's Approach," *Psychological Bulletin* 81, 8 (August 1974): 453-70.

jects' styles of reasoning. Particularly in administering the tests cross-culturally or to various age, sex, or class groups in the United States, the interpretation of key terms such as *honor, duty, blame*, and *self-esteem* can be expected to vary widely and to make the development of a common scale of univocal meanings difficult if not impossible.

The bite of criticism from the "scientific" side is that Kohlberg must present his findings in publicly replicable form, with explicit rules for translating the responses of those tested into the consistent terminology of a scale of measurement. However, in the human sciences this goal is always problematical. Even were it attainable—and it is far from clear that it is—there is good reason to think that it would be of only small benefit for the kind of inquiry Kohlberg is conducting and the kind of practical difficulty he is confronting. Thomas Kuhn's widely known work on the history of the natural sciences and his much-discussed notions of normal and revolutionary science are helpful in clarifying these difficulties.[33] The real and powerful achievement of science has been the ability of scientists as a community to settle upon univocal standards of measurement and techniques of research, constituting what Kuhn calls paradigms. These common standards and procedures have enabled the natural sciences to make steady, incremental advances by subsuming events under lawlike patterns. Typically, in a period of "normal science" young scientists are trained in a paradigm and proceed to extend it into uncharted domains of experience.

There is, of course, irony here. The more imperially successful the paradigm in extending its domain, the more anomalous cases pile up. Eventually the anomalies may receive explanation through a new scheme of order and a new paradigm may be born. Displacement of an established paradigm by a new one Kuhn calls a revolution. It is a distinguishing mark of the natural as against the social sciences that they have been able to isolate events and transcribe them as patterns of lawlike regularity. However, as Kuhn points out, the concepts of the explanatory theory that makes sense of the mathematical statements cannot usually be translated

33. The now nearly classic work is Thomas Kuhn, *The Structure of Scientific Revolutions* (2nd ed., Chicago: University of Chicago Press, 1970), esp. pp. 401-5, 525.

into paradigms. Before the development of a firmly agreed-upon consensus on a paradigm, the world of investigation is marked by contention among a variety of incommensurable, competing paradigm candidates. Those who wish to see the coming of a paradigmatic age in the social sciences view all previous ages as sadly pre-paradigmatic. Piaget's hopes for structuralism should be seen in this light; he hopes that the method will at last advance knowledge of human psychology to the point of take-off into fully fledged paradigmatic science.

Kuhn, on the other hand, has called attention to precisely the aspects of scientific work that have remained in the background, at least among philosophic commentators on the history of the sciences. The development of agreement about the basic problems for research, about exemplary models of explanation, classic experiments: these facets of science are social activities. Even more importantly, the education of a scientific researcher is a process of coming to accept and finally to become part of a way of doing research that penetrates more deeply into the person of the student than do mere assumptions or beliefs. Kuhn has highlighted, in a way that recalls Charles Peirce, the fact that science is a social and cultural activity pursued in common, continued through shared activities and forms of cooperation. A large part of what Kuhn styles the "disciplinary matrix" of a normal science is actual know-how passed on from generation to generation of scientists, an apprenticeship that cannot be made totally explicit in rules of procedure. It is a kind of "personal knowledge," as Michael Polanyi has dubbed it, but it is essentially a shared knowledge. Normal science is a form of life. As scientific revolutions occur, more than concepts are changed. The cognitive, practical, even bodily skills of scientific research are being reformed.[34]

The distinction between the "disciplinary matrix" of a science and its formalized measuring system and explanatory theory provides an insight into why the social sciences remain pre- or, better, non-paradigmatic. The complicated skills passed on through scientific apprenticeship train the scientist to the difficult task of ignoring many of the everyday meanings and purposes of events. Scientists learn to view events within the specialized framework of scientific measurement. It is a task of relearning, of attending to

34. Ibid., p. 192.

the measurable "primary qualities" of things, in the seventeenth-century sense of that term. It means looking away from the human relevance of things in order to see them as detached, measurable "qualities" which can then be charted and interrelated by conceptual formulas. As Whitehead put it, the narrowness and artificiality of the concepts of science have proven to be precisely, as Bacon had hoped, the keys to power. Yet, the skills of the scientists, like the scientists themselves, are still guided by a matrix of cultural patterns and meanings, the scientific "sub-culture," and this is pervaded by the wider cultural world it inhabits.

When we extend these considerations to the conduct of the human sciences, the central difficulty immediately shows itself. The object of the human sciences is to gain insight into what human life is, specifically what makes it different from other aspects of the world, and so on. Human inquiry is embedded in the social matrix it seeks to understand. This suggests that there is a limit to the applicability of scientific techniques in human inquiry which does not obtain in natural science, because the ultimate object of human inquiry is exactly this underlying social matrix, the forms of life that sustain the inquirer even as they are his object. The realization of the embedded quality of our inquiries is simultaneously the realization of what it is to be human. It is the discovery that humanity is, as a species, living in a world of meaning, so that it is always necessary and possible to ask the question: What is human life? The answer is given by the way in which we in fact live out or try to live out our concrete situation.

Efforts to formalize this context, while they can and may be attempted for specific purposes, never achieve the power to compel assent in the way the paradigms of natural science do. The classical political economy of Adam Smith and Ricardo may serve as a case in point. Classical political economy proclaimed a formalized reduction of human culture to a measurable set of categories such as labor, capital, and exchange. One intellectual response to this was Marxism, which attacked those categories for what they omitted or misread in human affairs. The omissions here proved crucial. What political economy thought it could take for granted, the social matrix in which it operated, was shown by Marx and later Max Weber to have such critical importance that if a different "background," such as another society or historical period, were substituted for the background of nineteenth-century Britain that the political economists took for granted, the range of their "science" was severely narrowed.

The work of contemporary economic thinkers such as Fred Hirsch and Robert Heilbroner (discussed in Chapter One) contains a powerful argument that formalized statements about elements and rules in the human sciences are bought at high cost, utterly unlike anything found in the natural sciences. The "laws" of economics are statements about human activity which the policy-makers, as well as individual entrepreneurs, have often accepted as truths. Now, while molecules do not noticeably alter their behavior because a new theory has been published about them, conceptions of human behavior can and do change the way human beings act. Part of the cruel irony of the story about contemporary society which Hirsch has narrated is that by acting on certain notions of economic theory, modern governments have precipitated changes in the institutions of their societies which have fatally weakened the matrix of social practices, such as honesty and self-restraint, on which the apparent validity of those "laws" depends.[35]

Human investigation thus has an ineluctable moral, indeed, political, as well as a philosophical dimension. This is because it not only takes place within the cultural matrix but has direct and indirect effects upon the understanding of those living within the world it seeks to clarify. The objective of the human sciences is to deepen our understanding of what it is to live a human life. That understanding conditions the whole matrix of questions and themes within which the investigation proceeds. Because of the peculiarly intimate and complex bond between the subject and the object of study, all efforts to render the significance of human action can become either weapons of fanatical partisanship or mere apologies for the status quo. They may be subversive of deep elements of a culture. Indeed, theories of man may lead to a forgetfulness of the very question of what it is to be human, as Heidegger has reminded us. But the investigator's stance toward his subject is in part already formed by that subject. He takes up a position toward the question of what it is to be human regardless of conscious intention.

35. See Fred Hirsch, *Social Limits to Growth* (Cambridge, Massachusetts: Harvard University Press, 1976); also Robert Heilbroner, *Business Civilization in Decline* (New York: W.W. Norton, 1976).

There is thus an urgency, a risk, a responsibility embedded in the task of understanding human action which the disciplinary matrix of the natural sciences, pursuing quite different goals, is able to screen out without distorting the results of research. In human investigation, as economics powerfully illustrates, there is no way to attain complete clarity of theoretical language, because the epistemological question is actually derived from the practical or existential one. The epistemological question of the truth of a particular interpretation involves the quality of its penetration, its depth of insight. This depth reveals itself as a kind of practical questioning of self, at its deepest point forcing the knower to the realization that his knowing is actually a way of being. That means that his being is indeed ultimately a question, in fact the defining question for him.

But what, then, of the stage theory of moral development? The moral-reasoning tests seek to type the patterns of reasoning that persons use in forensically justifying a course of action. The stage theory functions to locate these types with reference to each other, describing the relationships as an ascending hierarchy of progressively more differentiated patterns of relating ideas subsumed under more inclusive principles. The stage theory further attempts to explain the observed changes in the types of reasoning exhibited by persons at different ages and levels of cognitive development as the logical unfolding, under proper stimulation, of a unified, developing structure of cognition.

An associate of Kohlberg, John Gibbs, has recently put forward a major revision of this structuralist account. Gibbs does not entirely accept the rigorous scientific critique of Kurtines and Greif and others, but he does argue that the principled level of Kohlberg's typology, Stages Five and Six, cannot be accounted for by using the criteria of the Piagetian stage theory.[36] Gibbs's reasoning is that the first four stages—through the conventional, social order-maintaining stage—confirm Piaget's supposition of directional cognitive growth. They show both "universality of form"

36. John Gibbs, "Kohlberg's Stages of Moral Judgment: A Constructive Critique," *Harvard Educational Review* 47, 1 (February 1977): 43-61; cf. Kohlberg, "Continuities in Childhood and Adult Moral Development Revisited," in R.B. Baltes and L.R. Goulet, eds., *Lifespan and Developmental Psychology* (New York: Academic Press, 1973).

and "unconsciousness of process." Children seem to advance in moral reasoning in much the way that Piaget conceives of them advancing conceptually, without their having to become consciously aware that their mode of thinking is changing or how it is changing. However, development of principled reasoning does not proceed with the same unconsciousness of process. As Gibbs puts it, the principled stages require "consciously taking on the anxiety of questioning," of moving from implicitly accepted moral criteria to consciously accepted ones.[37]

Second, Gibbs challenges Kohlberg's claim to have developed an integrated typology with a structure characterized by increasing differentiation and inclusion. The principled stages do not in fact subsume the lower levels. For instance, the law-and-order type of reasoning does not appear simply as a "special case" of a universal principle such as respect for persons. Instead, as with this example, the higher-level reasoning overrides the lower.[38] Thus at a key juncture Kohlberg's hierarchy appears discontinuous rather than integrated. Gibbs explains this by suggesting that Kohlberg is really using two incommensurable conceptions of moral reasoning. The lower stages, One through Four, are described and integrated by the "naturalistic" paradigm of structuralism, while the higher stages represent an "existential" understanding of moral reasoning. This point is critical. These two opposed conceptions of moral reasoning in fact restate the issue of the applicability of natural scientific, reductive explanation in social inquiry. On a deeper philosophic level they also shadow radically different conceptions of the self. This opposition poses the central difficulty of liberal culture: the relation of utilitarian to deontological modes of thinking.

The stage theory attempts, by reconstructing the logic used by people taking certain tests, to understand what it is to think morally. The distinction of types Gibbs has made between naturalistic and existential understandings can be rephrased in a way that links it to the battle of interpretations introduced by Hobbes's controversy with Aristoteleanism. It is the opposition between an analytical reconstruction of the structures of reasoning and an interpretive, self-reflective mode. Roughly, the distinguishing feature of formal reconstruction of the analytic type is explanation by

37. Ibid., p. 56   38. Ibid., p. 57.

means of a fixed frame of reference. Changes are mapped as relations among elements defined in terms of this frame of reference rather than in the language of either common experience or the specific language-context of the subject of investigation. But the logical discontinuity between the higher and lower stages of Kohlberg's scheme precludes a demonstration of one of Kohlberg's central claims, since it means that both the social contract and self-chosen principled orientations are not developed simply by making explicit the logical operations involved in lower-level concrete thinking. Therefore the attempted logical reconstruction does not succeed.

The difficulty with Kohlberg's characterization of moral reasoning as formal reconstruction rather than self-reflective interpretation appears to be a gain from a line of research pursued by a former associate of Kohlberg, Carol Gilligan. In a paper titled "In a Different Voice," Gilligan has put forth evidence that the moral-reasoning scale Kohlberg has used fails to take into account the moral developmental patterns her research finds typical of women in America.[39] Gilligan argues that the "feminine voice" needs to be heard in this debate because the "relational bias" of women's experience means that on Kohlberg's scale they generally test at Stage Three, the interpersonal-recognition orientation, rather than at Stage Four, the social-propriety ethic typical of most males. This outcome results from the fact that subordination of the interpersonal to the societal ethic is built into Kohlberg's scale, reflecting the Kantian ideal of moral reasoning that "thinks formally, proceeding from theory to fact" and defining the self apart from particulars of individual existence. Thus, on Kohlberg's scale the more advanced reasoning is always more general, impersonal, and decontextual.[40]

Gilligan argues that if one tries to understand women's moral experience in its own terms rather than through the decontextual Kantian categories, a different developmental direction appears. This "different voice" defines morality around the poles of selfishness versus responsibility, compassion versus autonomy. Adulthood, then, is defined in terms of nurture and care rather than

---

39. Carol Gilligan, "In a Different Voice," *Harvard Educational Review* 47, 4 (November 1977): 481-544.
40. Ibid., pp. 481-84.

strict adherence to principle. She summarizes her disagreement with Kohlberg's stage hierarchy as the contrast between the formal norm of respect for the rights of others and "the imperative to care."[41] Unlike the Kohlberg tests, Gilligan's tests involved dilemmas that were highly contextual. She argues that this was entirely appropriate, since for women morality is very closely tied to notions of self as intimately involved with others, whereas American male culture with its team ethic emphasizes displacement of personal loyalty and involvement in favor of "playing the game."

Notice that if we were to hold strictly to Kohlberg's conception of moral life, this ethic guided by an imperative to care would be evaluated as at Stage Three, an inferior level of functioning. Kohlberg describes the motivation for this kind of thinking and acting as "anticipation of disapproval of others, actual or imagined-hypoethical (e.g. guilt)."[42] To acquire a genuinely self-chosen *principle* of care for others such as Gandhi's nonviolence, an example Kohlberg often uses, one would have to progress through the decontextualizing process the stage theory outlines.

But how, at Stage Six morality, does one acquire a principle like nonviolence? Where does it come from? Certainly not from a purely formed, decontextual operation of the logical imperative. As Gilligan reminds us, Kant's ethics (which is not simply decontextual, proceeding from the mysterious core of freedom and rationality) arrives at the imperative of duty, not compassion. To pose the problem in terms of Gibbs's argument: in the existential process of "taking on the anxiety of questioning," from where does the new content of the self-chosen principles arise? It is as though, at the climactic point of the decontextualizing process, a whole other kind of development suddenly enters our vision. This other process, which must appear so mysterious from the structural point of view, is what Gilligan calls a contextual moral understanding. It is the notion of the self as a responsible, reflective agent-in-situation. From the formal, decontextual stance of Kantian and most liberal moral philosophy, this other view of moral development appears mysteriously subjective and arbitrary. It is, in fact, in order to avoid founding social and political life on an apparently arbitrary, voluntarist basis such as the one ascribed

41. Ibid., p. 511.
42. Kohlberg, "Stage and Sequence," p. 381.

to "existential" positions that liberals like Kohlberg and Rawls search so ingeniously for a securely rational, formal reconstruction of "the moral sense."

The purview of characteristically liberal moral understanding has been well described by Henry David Aiken. In Aiken's conception, morality is always a dialectical relation between communal convention and the "transcendent" aspect of individual freedom. The "ordinary language of morals" already contains, in Aiken's view, an inchoate ideal of "the moral agent as self-governing" in its everyday assignment of moral responsibility and in the giving and demanding of justifications for actions.[43] Ethics is seen as a second-order form of reasoning, a regulator and corrector of subjective, anarchic passions and desires which press for expression in the individual's life. Ethical reasoning and justification are always practically "ceremonious" in that they refer to the intersubjective realm of "communal convention." The limits of this kind of ethical thinking are reached, just as for Kohlberg the transition from conventional to principled reasoning begins, at the point when one asks why the communal ethical "game" is good. As Aiken sees it, Kant's answer to this question is to show that the sphere of moral reasoning, which is a self-defining and totally coherent realm, has an appeal to the individual, that it "moves the will" by its inherent coherence and rationality. But that is really to admit that a justification must become "subjective," become an insight about which one cares, if it is to answer the post-ethical question. This, in Aiken's scheme, is the post-ethical moment of transcendence and freedom that resolves the painful struggle between subjective desire and collective propriety. Thus, "decision is king"— and is beyond reason.[44]

As we have seen, this radically subjective characterization of the post-ethical movement is not the only possible interpretation of moral life. The famous "radical choice" situation of early Sartrean existentialism is an arresting problem, but not because the moral thinker makes up the options, for that would utterly trivialize the matter or make it merely neurotic. It is, rather, in William James's phrase, the forced nature of the situation which reveals that the

---

43. Henry David Aiken, *Reason and Conduct: New Bearings in Moral Philosophy* (New York: Knopf, 1962), pp. ix-x.
44. Ibid., pp. 80-87.

options have not issued out of mere will. The identity, the very self of the person is at stake precisely because of the person's involvement in the options. It is a moment of having to affirm and make one's own conflicting practical stances within, not outside, one's basic involvements. Once made, such affirmations will leave neither the identity of the person nor the affirmed form of life the same, but the person and the person's roles may, for all that, be recognizably continuous, with long-term involvements, while remaining open and not yet finished.

Gibbs's critique of Kohlberg, like Gilligan's, highlights the weakness of liberal moral philosophy. By revealing the different voice of women's experience in contemporary culture, Gilligan makes a strong case for rejecting Kohlberg's decontextual account as a reliable universal guide to the understanding of moral life. The difficulty with Kohlberg's theory is that the paradigms of social science and moral philosophy it embraces end by reducing moral reasoning to either an unchosen propriety or a finally inexplicable moment of "decision." The quasi-scientific and utilitarian naturalism of the structuralist idea is coupled to a virtually worldless voluntarism.

Politically, the liberal position has aimed to counteract the destructive consequences of zealotry and parochial partisanship. In the American case, liberalism has succeeded in directing passions into economic channels, but with results which now have forced its exponents to search for new measures to counteract the not-so-tame conflicts of interest. At this point, absolute trust in analytic reason renders liberalism unable to go beyond the barren epistemological alternative of arbitrary decision or a totally clear, exhaustive reductive account of human behavior. Subjectivity and objectivity, those split-off halves of concrete human existence, are the results of an epistemology that begins by rejecting our embeddedness in history, tradition, and nature. Thus, forgetting its roots in practical involvements and concerns, liberal theory loses sight of its limits and ends in the painful paradoxes of nihilism.

:: III

Moral life moves in an interpretive circle. Reflection necessarily begins with a pre-reflective sense of what is valuable and of concern for the self and the other selves who share that world. The aim of insight is to gain clarity about this world of shared meaning, the social matrix of meaning which is articulated in varying ways through the concrete behavior, desires, motives, and ideals that make up moral life. Reflection is not simply a cumulative growth process. It moves through contradictions and, often, unforeseeable changes. Understanding is itself an activity that we cannot totally objectify because in even trying to do so we stand within it, we are doing it. Its purpose is, rather, to open us to a lived awareness of what it is to be human. This understanding can be only partially articulated. Human finitude means that our lives, in time, are always partial articulations, yet, paradoxically, it is for that reason that they have not only opaqueness but direction and significance. Our embeddedness in a world and in time need not constitute arbitrary imprisonment. Our situatedness is in fact the only real ground for possibility, for our having an identity at all. Ironically, it is the recognition of this, the situation of moral reasoning, that can save moral and political philosophy from nihilism, the sense that all ethical norms are arbitrary. Nihilism is what modern consciousness fears most, but as Nietzsche and Heidegger have taught us, it is also what modern culture, at its core, seems unable to escape.

Kohlberg's structuralist scientific language and Kantian ethics converge in their identification of decontextualized general rules as the highest achievements of reason, but even within Kohlberg's own stage theory a coherent account of responsible moral reasoning requires a different dimension of reflection. This self-reflection necessarily draws its matter and its guiding principles from the actual patterns of life within which the reasoner lives. However, looking only through the lens of the cognitive-developmental theory, the content of this reflective thinking appears arbitrary and mysteriously arrived at. Admittedly, the hierarchical stage theory seeks only to set limits and to control specific forms of morality, to order and "purify" the concrete operations of moral thinking, but even here the universality and impartiality of the stage theory must be questioned. The conception of reasoning as subsuming particulars under univocal principles, so that morality culminates in fair exchange and reciprocal rights and duties, embodies a particular historical-cultural bias. The merits of this bias can be argued, but it remains a particular interpretation of the moral life that naively exalts its own premises as universal goals of development. A critique of Kohlberg's system must begin to re-cover an awareness of limitation that the stage theory lacks. The decisive limitation of Kohlberg's liberalism is its denial of its own selectivity. The pathology of liberal thought is just that ahistorical insistence on its own universality and superiority.

Seen from the practical point of view, as a mode of communica-tion that both embodies and affects our contemporary way of life, a scientific account of human affairs reveals itself as an inherently selective reading of our situation. The peculiar selectivity exhib-ited by early modern theorists such as Hobbes was, we know, congenial to such policy-makers of the day as the Court party in England.[45] The analytic conception of reason underlying the mod-ern science of politics coupled neatly with the atomistic individu-alism underlying the utilitarian notion of value, an idea that re-ceived immense new impetus with the triumph of industrial capitalism in the last century. The deontological strand of liberal-ism arose to counter the extreme utilitarian, finally nihilistic, im-plications of the reductive sciences of man. It tried to do this through its idea of a natural law resident in moral reasoning which was not reducible to simple calculation of interest. Kant gave classic expression to the problem that those two facets of liberal philosophy—the utilitarian and the deontological—while they share key premises, are finally radically disjoined and separate ways of thought.

Kohlberg's contribution to liberal theory is his attempt to re-state the deontological position within a mode of discourse that can also describe interest-motivated calculation as a less well-de-veloped form of one hierarchical system of reasoning. That, for Kohlberg's project, is the value of the structuralist method. The stage theory aims to show that utilitarian reasoning at the lower stages passes logically into progressively more decentered patterns of thinking about the self's relation to others, until ideal reciproc-ity emerges as the logical outcome. Structuralism's holistic logic thus presents moral reasoning as a growing, ordered system. The analytic bits of earlier empiricism are displaced in favor of a dy-namic interrelation among elements—the relation Piaget terms

45. See J.G.A. Pocock, *The Machiavellian Moment: Florentine Political Thought and the Atlantic Republican Tradition* (Princeton, New Jersey: Princeton University Press, 1975).

constructivity—structure and function coming into being at once. However, a deep continuity with the older analytic model lies in the structuralist insistence that these elements and rules can be defined outside any context, so that practical understanding of embedded moral teleology plays only a preliminary role, launching us into the purer ether of formal patterns.

Still, not even liberal society has ever been able in practice to ground its political life in the pure rationality of contract and reciprocal duties. The current concern over popular participation in politics, the discussions of leadership, patriotism, the "moral equivalents" of war, all glaringly light up latent dimensions of moral understanding that the stage theory sees only opaquely, if at all.

Those facts of our production-oriented society which have kept the competitive process from wrenching apart the social fabric, liberalism's prized norms of contractual morality, those too require a particular kind of moral order for their maintenance. The public role of the entrepreneur (later that of the professional) has been tacitly sustained by networks of mutual concern which have often gone unnoticed by liberal ideologues. The urge to dominate nature and circumstance, the celebrated traits of masculine society, turn out to rest in complicated ways upon a less visible world of care.

Kohlberg is not insensitive to this fact. He acknowledges that human life, even in a highly privatized modern capitalist society like the United States, depends on primary loyalties of men and women to each other and to those things they believe their lives to embody. He has attempted to flesh out his cognitive stage theory with an account of how these affective qualities of loyalty and love are related to the structures of cognition.[46] This account is worth noting not because it is entirely unfaithful to experience but because it reveals trenchantly the limited scope of the structuralist, indeed the liberal, vision. Recall that, for Kohlberg, the self is an organization of a primal motivation toward competence and self-actualization which develops through social interaction. The parent structure from which the socially organized forms of loyalty and love develop Kohlberg terms *imitation*. It precedes linguistic

---

46. See, especially, Kohlberg, "Stage and Sequence," sections xiv ff.

communication. Here he cites the early American social psychologist, T.M. Baldwin. Imitation, like empathy, is a fundamental given of human beings in the world, based upon the "intrinsic competence motivation." The complexities of attachment to persons, groups, social mores, and ideals can then be explained as varying modes of the same dynamic:

> Social motivation is motivation for shared stimulation, for shared activity, and shared competence and self esteem. Social dependency implies dependency upon another person as a source for such activity and for the self's competence or esteem. The basic nature of competence motivation, however, is the same whether self or the other is perceived as the primary agent producing the desired stimulation, activity, or competence, i.e. whether the goal is "independent mastery," social mastery (dominance) or social dependence.[47]

In this passage Kohlberg is polemically sharpening a contrast between his theory and a pure instinct theory, which would neglect the social context of the "drives of sex, aggression, and anxiety."

Particularly given this adversarial position, it is consistent and yet peculiar that he proceeds to generalize rapidly to the invariant conditions of forming attachments. He spends little time taking note of the myriad forms human attachments actually take. But what, then, is love? Kohlberg tells us that the invariant requirements are five. First, there must be a perceived similarity to the other; then a sympathy for and altruism toward the other, coupled with a reciprocal development of self-love. Fourth, attachment involves "a defined possessive bond," and, last, it "presupposes the desire for esteem in the eyes of the other or for reciprocal attachment."[48] Kohlberg summarizes his discussion by noting that "our account assumes that intense and stable attachment (love) is a mature end point of ego-development, not a primitive tendency."[49]

Contrast this logical skeleton of the "shared competence orientation" with the imperative embodied even for Kantian ethics in the moral struggle against selfishness that is the heritage of Christian culture. Or contrast Kohlberg's account of the "desire for esteem in the eyes of the other or reciprocal attachment" with the immense, often tragic, complexities of *eros* as interpreted by the Platonic heritage. Or, again, consider Sophocles' presentation of love and loyalty as realities so powerful as to be at once builders

47. Ibid., p. 460.   48. Ibid., pp. 461-62.   49. Ibid., p. 464.

and destroyers of families and cities. The tidy, cool organization of Kohlberg's account is breathtaking!

In a society and an age struggling with the emptiness of many traditional authorities and ways of life, yet profoundly disillusioned with the promise of endlessly rising affluence, this account of the affective springs of private and public life is dry indeed. The stage theory hardly speaks to individuals confronting the anxiety of nihilism. More clarity concerning our ways of thinking about moral principles is surely helpful, but it can in no way displace the character formation of a living culture, either by the schools or by the society at large. Finally, it is the *polis* which educates. The nature of the regime, the habits of the heart fostered in everyday life, these—as Tocqueville penetratingly saw—are the stuff of moral life. In the end, Kohlberg's approach is too narrow and perhaps too self-satisfied even to keep vivid an awareness of the scope of our problem. Such an approach in the hands of narrow, self-interested bureaucracies, private or public, could itself contribute to the moral confusion it seeks to resolve.[50]

By casting his theory as a scientific account of moral life, Kohlberg misconceives two issues. Practically, he misdirects attention, very rightly focused on the importance of education, away from reflection upon actual social conflicts and complexities toward formal rules and procedures. His approach also obscures the theoretical issues. By invoking a conception of reductive analysis in human investigation he obscures critical questions about the relation of his project to the social and cultural situation out of which it has arisen. The structuralist theory with its Kantian ethical resonances filters out the historical dimensions which are of necessity internal to investigation and advocacy in the human realm.

As the deepening crisis of liberal welfare politics in America forces us to reassess the notion of citizen participation in governance, and so of education for citizenship, the liberal ideal of character—the Lockean image of the calculating man of com-

50. This point is powerfully made by Ralph Potter in his unpublished paper "Justice and Beyond in Moral Education," Address at the Regional Conference on Moral Development of Youth, Wayzafa, Minnesota, June 1977. My understanding of Kohlberg has been greatly sharpened by Potter's paper, as well as by that of Edward Schwartz, "Traditional Values, Moral Education and Social Change," Address at the Conference on Moral and Political Education, Rutgers University, April 1978, and by the critical comments of Norma Haan.

merce—can no longer be taken for granted. Indeed, it is more and more often being questioned. However, liberalism has for so long dominated our discourse about public life that questions asked or alternatives posed have usually ended by becoming absorbed into the familiar paradigm of private wants played out in an indefinitely expanding market. Conscious articulation and cultivation of an alternative is crucial, and this project requires the realization that the privatized vision of life at liberalism's basis and its view of motivation as desire for power and gain are historically specific and therefore limited conceptions of life. Kohlberg's theory begins well but misses that decisive point.

A post-liberal public philosophy must articulate the relation between our present crisis of legitimacy and the limitations of liberal culture. To do this it has to bring to light those dimensions of human existence missing from the liberal account, and to do this in such a way as to bring into high relief the connections between our present problems and those aspects of life missing in or distorted by liberal culture. Morality is always a social or, in the classical sense, a political reality, and a moral philosophy must explicitly make this connection. If such a connection is missing or tangential, as is the case in contemporary American culture, a responsible moral philosophy must become persuasive about this connection. That means defining and discussing moral questions within the complex situation of social, especially economic, relations. It also requires us to do this with an understanding that admits the unfinished nature of the enterprise. Kohlberg's desire to give a respectable scientific basis to moral and political judgments, however, has led him to repeat the Hobbesian hopes for a "logic machine." Indeed, the formal system of this new structuralist ethics aims, like the earlier reductionism, to separate moral reasoning from dependence on contingent viewpoints and prudential judgments. The new notion of cognitive structure is another version of that purely general world of relations that is the glory of science, and that is precisely its decisive limitation when we naively try to use it as a lens for sharpening our insight into ourselves.

FIVE

A Renewal of Civic Philosophy

:: I

Contemporary American problems reveal the orthodox liberal conception of society and politics as considerably less than the self-sustaining whole it proclaims itself to be. Liberalism has boasted that it could uphold human dignity and respect for the individual while simultaneously encouraging each individual to adopt a self-seeking, instrumental stance toward others. It freed individuals from having to guide and restrain their behavior in common with others, replacing both traditional morality and discussion in common with hopes for self-regulating social machinery. Liberal thinkers rightfully decry the encroachment on individual life of the administrative state, and, though less often, the bureaucratic corporation and mass media. But they see no relationship between willful abnegation of an ethics of mutual concern, announced as freedom, and weakening of social solidarity outside those encroaching structures. Yet, as some thinkers sympathetic to the liberal vision have come to see, if personal dignity and self-determination are to survive the constraints and potentiality for social control found in modern society, it can only be through the political action of citizens joined in active solidarity.[1] That turnaround requires tapping a sense of purpose and possi-

---

1. This insight is developed with varying degrees of clarity in the recent works of social analysis discussed in Chapter One.

bility different from the ones liberalism has invoked. There is a circle here, though not a vicious one.

Conserving America's deepest founding values will require, ironically, a substantial change in the structure and direction of American society, and that will require development of a new civic consciousness. While a renewal of civic spirit seems possible only if there remain aspects of social and cultural life from which movements for social change can draw strength, political history suggests that those social and cultural potentials will fully come to light only dynamically, as part of the successful development of such movements. That there is an experimental and participational aspect to any renewal of civic politics seems inescapable. The articulation of the conceptual resources of the civic republican heritage is a necessary aspect of our effort to cope with our present.

The great tradition of modern social thought from Montesquieu and Rousseau onward has been a working out of the meaning of the transformation effected by seventeenth-century thinkers in the Western understanding of life. This tradition, which includes the American Federalists, has at the same time attempted to devise a functional replacement for the integrating conception of man as political being, the *zoon politikon* and *animal rationale* of the classical and medieval theorists. The development of this replacement has been a central preoccupation of modern culture as a whole, similar in stature to the efforts at devising a secular counterpart to the idea of authority transmitted by biblical religion.

Yet, the classical notion of citizenship from which so much modern social thought has drawn its strongest nourishment has been a singularly long-lived and, in purely pragmatic terms, amazingly successful ideal. Citizenship as a symbol has evolved a whole understanding of human nature, of the good life, of authority, of man's place in the world. And like all genuinely emblematic symbols, that of the citizen in the commonwealth has remained powerful in part because of its compactness. It has at times evoked stirring loyalties, harkening back to the idealized classic ages of Greece and Rome, yet enabling generations of medieval jurists, Renaissance humanists, American and French revolutionaries, Hegelians and Marxists to sum up their very diverse understandings of the ideal of a public life. Through these varied channels it continues to provide us with vital images.

Even on a cursory inspection the classical notion of citizenship strikingly sums up a vision of life that is also a moral ideal. The tradition of republican citizenship stretching from Plato and Aristotle to the makers of the American Revolution links power and authority within the state with the social, economic, psychological, and religious realms.[2] By contrast, modern discussions of citizenship that operate under largely liberal assumptions are far more abstract. The mechanisms of governance, the delineation of the institutions of the state as compared to those of society, the contractual relationship of citizens to each other, the ideas of authority and legitimacy all appear to float in a kind of Cartesian ether. Setting classical and modern views side by side, the troubling sense that there have been large losses as well as gains creeps upon us unavoidably. The principal loss is identifiable immediately. It is a loss of any relationship among political, social, economic, and psychological theorizing and the concreteness of citizenship as a way of life.

The contemporary starting point for understanding the classical conception of the citizen must be the recovery of a sense of civic life as a form of personal self-development. The kind of self-development with which the theorists of the civic life have been concerned is in many ways the antithesis of contemporary connotations of the notion of self-development in a "culture of narcissism."[3] Citizenship has traditionally been conceived of as a way of life that changes the person entering it. This process is essentially a collective experience. Indeed, the notion of *citizen* is unintelligible apart from that of *commonwealth*, and both terms derive their sense from the idea that we are by nature political beings.

2. See J.G.A. Pocock's *The Machiavellian Moment: Florentine Political Thought and the Atlantic Republican Tradition* (Princeton, New Jersey: Princeton University Press, 1975). For the transformation of that tradition during the course of the American Revolution and its aftermath, see Gordon S. Wood, *The Creation of the American Republic: 1776-1787* (Chapel Hill: University of North Carolina Press, 1969).

3. This term has been popularized by Christopher Lasch in his *The Culture of Narcissism: American Life in an Age of Diminishing Expectations* (New York: W.W. Norton, 1979). Richard Sennett has propounded an important interpretation of the same phenomenon as a defensive response to the failure of Western societies to maintain a vital public life during the social turmoil generated by industrialization: see Richard Sennett, *The Fall of Public Man: The Social Psychology of Capitalism* (New York: Knopf, 1977).

Self-fulfillment and even the working out of personal identity and a sense of orientation in the world depend upon a communal enterprise. This shared process is the civic life, and its root is involvement with others: other generations, other sorts of persons whose differences are significant because they contribute to the whole upon which our particular sense of self depends. Thus mutual interdependency is the foundational notion of citizenship. The basic psychological dynamic of the participants in this interdependent way of life is an imperative to respond and to care.

From the viewpoint of modern liberalism such a civic vision seems a distinct overvaluing of the political. Whatever loss may be incurred in finding public life to be only an impersonal mechanism of profit and loss is, for the liberal, offset by the room thereby created for a rich private life free of state tyranny. Indeed, the notions of mutual dependency and care do sound more like private than public values, as liberal culture makes that division. But—putting aside Tocqueville's revelations of the coercive effects of public conformity which liberal capitalist society seems condemned to generate—it is clear that no liberal regime actually operates without large doses of civic spirit.

Still, the cultivation of a more than instrumental citizenship is seen as a private matter. And, cut off from collective scrutiny and discussion as they are, the responses of individuals and groups to their social setting have often become as hostile, defensive, and self-serving as one might fear. Awareness of the interdependency of citizens and groups is basic to the civic vision because it enlightens and challenges these disparate parties about their mutual relations. The citizen comes to know who he is by understanding the web of social relationships surrounding him. This realization is not only cognitive, it requires experience, finding one's way about and thus coming to know, in practice, who one is.

However, it is important to see that the civic tradition does not simply romanticize public participation. The dangers of misguided, fanatical, and irresponsible civic involvement have been well documented, and some of the most eloquent warnings of those dangers have come from the classical theorists of citizenship. The point, rather, is that the notion of involved concern within an interdependent community provides the image for a collective enterprise in self-transformation. The civic ideal is thus alluring and disquieting, at once delicately fragile and morally consuming in the responsibility it demands.

As the questioning of the liberal assumptions of contemporary public policies for managing interests becomes progressively more fundamental, the self-confidence of the governing groups in America continues to weaken. The much-decried turning away from politics by many is surely related to these developments. However, the tremendous rise of interest in psychological and religious movements, the apparent national obsession with healing wounds, real or imagined, in the self are first of all social events. They undoubtedly reveal something of what the current American crisis of values is about. Instrumentalist, liberal politics is being abandoned not only because it is seen as ineffective, it is also being deserted because it is seen as corrupting and empty of a genuine sense of orientation. That political activity ought to be rooted in moral conscience, that politics is in an important way related to the search for a meaningful life—these themes, which were powerfully reenunciated in the movements of the sixties, have not disappeared. Instead, they seem to have become at least partially embedded in much apparent privatism. Part of the meaning of the current American retreat to privatism is a continuing search for what counts in life, a hunger for orientation that neither the dynamics of capitalist growth nor the liberal vision of politics provides.

For this reason, the resources of the civic republican tradition are especially well suited to speak to our situation. Those who read the American spirit as so dominantly individualistic that private comfort and competitive achievement define a monochrome of national traits are both dangerously distorting our past and threatening our future, because they are closing off a sense of that living civic tradition which has been and continues to be vital to national life.[4]

The language of civic republicanism addresses directly the craving of the human self for a life of inclusion in a community of mutual concern. The civic tradition addresses the public value of

4. The most influential presentation of that position is by the so-called neoconservatives, especially those gathered around the journal *The Public Interest.* For example, see Nathan Glazer and Irving Kristol, eds., *The American Commonwealth—1976* (New York: Basic Books, 1976).

exploring and developing those qualities of life that go beyond competitive success and economic well-being. It does this not by abstracting from social inequalities and economic needs but by addressing them as human, moral, personal realities rather than simply as the technical and distant issues of liberal understanding. In the imagination of great speakers for this tradition, as recently Martin Luther King spoke for it, social and economic relations become translated into the moral and personal meaning they have for members of the polity. Poverty and unemployment cease to be unfortunate side-effects of capitalist economic growth, to be neglected benignly or tidied up managerially. They appear in their full reality as institutionalized denials of dignity and social participation, glaring failures of communal responsibility. As such these issues emerge as painful spurs to challenge and change the shares of power and the institutions of collective coordination. The logic of King's republican understanding of politics led him to broaden the civil rights struggle to challenge institutions that perpetuate poverty. Finally, just before his assassination, he was advocating a coalition that would join opposition to the Indochina war and the military-industrial priorities to a broad struggle for economic and social democracy.

The great power of the civic vision, as contrasted with the liberal view, lies in its fundamental philosophic commitments. These entail the realization that the personal quest for a worthwhile life is bound up with the reality of interdependency and so with power. Large-scale social processes cannot remain merely technical issues but must be understood as part of the texture of personal living, just as personal life is woven into the patterns of collective organization.

Thus the fundamental language and symbols of the American civic tradition link private and public, personal and collective sensibilities in synoptic form. American patriotism is not a nationalism based upon immemorial ties of blood and soil, but neither is it in practice simply a kind of commercial contract. As observers from Tocqueville on have reported, the underlying conception that animates patriotism in America is a moral, even a religious, one: the notion of civic covenant.[5] Unlike the liberal

---

5. Robert N. Bellah, among others, has powerfully rearticulated this theme. See his *The Broken Covenant: American Civil Religion in Time of Trial* (New York:

idea of contract, which emphasizes mutual obligations within clearly defined limits, a civic covenant is a bond of fundamental trust founded upon common commitment to a moral understanding.

Covenant morality means that as citizens we make an unlimited promise to show care and concern to each other. It is the commitment to such a trust that is summed up in the mutual pledge of loyalty which concludes the American Declaration of Independence. Within the civic perspective, the business of politics at its highest is to fulfill these covenantal promises within the changing flow of events. In practice, which is almost never politics at its highest, the civic understanding provides the sense of conscience and idealism against which the institutions and the conduct of our collective life have to be judged. Again, Martin Luther King's relentless campaign for justice was a prime example of the practical efficacy of the civic imperative to care for the common good.

But what could the common good be? As a liberal would see it, the institutions of our society, the government, corporations, even the cities in which people live and work are all variations on the model of a business enterprise. Political, even social, vitality and progress are measured according to economic criteria. The public good, seen that way, becomes the utilitarian sum of individual satisfactions. A common interest can be presumed to lie only in ensuring advantageous conditions of general exchange—what is called, more realistically, a "good business climate." Beyond that interest in mutually advantageous exchanges, the civic language of a common good sounds to the liberal somehow darkly mystical or at least unnecessarily grandiose. Justice, as John Rawls makes clear, can be at most a matter of regulating these exchanges so that no one benefits unfairly. Why press further in confusing language, when it is likely to "overload" the political system, to encourage malcontents to assuage private wants, illegitimately, through public policy or mass movements?

To take this position is to fail to understand that the conception of the common good, with its long history in the civic tradition, is part of a language that articulates a way of living. In any practical context, language functions as more than the purely descriptive

---

Seabury Press, 1975). See also John Schaar, "The Case for Patriotism," *New American Review No. 17* (New York: Bantam Books, 1972), pp. 59-99.

vehicle which is the ideal of analytic science. A political philosophy is always more than a neutral description; it is also, and more importantly, a proposal and a vision. Political philosophies propose to evoke an experience of a kind of living. Indeed, it is the important peculiarity of liberal political theory that political language should be shorn of its evocative dimensions. That opinion is, seen in larger context, itself a proposal to think and experience life in a certain way. Now, all forms of life, especially those that have been consciously cultivated for generations, are rich with highly charged, compact phrases and gestures which serve to evoke a whole scheme of meaning.[6] In the civic tradition, *common good* is one of these phrases.

Thus it is not surprising that such an emblematic phrase would cause puzzlement when heard from within an alien scheme of meaning such as liberal utilitarianism. But if we grant to the civic tradition the possibility that its language points to a way of life which is meaningful in its own terms, then our imagination can rise to a new possibility. This new possibility is the idea of a civic life. To understand this requires at first, in Wittgenstein's phrase, coming "to feel our way around" in its characteristic language. Such an adventure may enable us to see the contemporary morass of liberal capitalist politics in a fresh way.

A virtue of the civic republican tradition is that its language provides an understanding of the social conditions upon which it depends. The chief of these conditions is an interpretation of psychic and moral development importantly different from the liberal account. The immediate merit of this alternative is that it offers an understanding of what liberal theory cannot provide: an explanation for the missing connections in its own interpretation of social life.

:: II

How, then, is a civic life possible? That is to ask, how can we conceive of individual fulfillment as realized through mutual

6. Herbert Fingarette describes these compact symbols in the context of personal psychodynamics as "cue phrases." The meanings they call up are as important as the information they convey. See Herbert Fingarette, *The Self in Transformation: Psychoanalysis, Philosophy and the Life of the Spirit* (New York: Harper and Row, 1963), pp. 23-26.

commitment to a common good? The answer the civic tradition provides is clear: civic life is possible because human nature is naturally disposed to find its fulfillment in what is called a life of virtue. This statement immediately calls up for us—partly as a kind of prophylaxis against a suspected tyranny—the proud ideal of freedom, the "core symbol" of liberalism. Leaving aside the confusions and controversies that continue to rage about the notion of freedom, in particular its relation to the other great liberal value of equality,[7] the civic conception of virtue becomes clearer when contrasted with liberal freedom.

In important respects, in fact, freedom is virtue's ambiguous child. For the republican tradition, civic virtue is the excellence of character proper to the citizen. It *is* freedom in a substantive sense, freedom understood as the capacity to attain one's good, where *goodness* describes full enjoyment of those capacities which characterize a flourishing human life. Since humans are by nature social beings, living well requires a shared life, and a shared life is possible only when the members of a community trust and respect one another. To participate in such a shared life is to show concern for and reciprocity to one's fellows, and to do so is simultaneously fulfilling for the individual. Thus the individual's true good must consist not in attaining a sum of satisfactions but in showing in himself, and sharing as a participant, an admirable and worthwhile form of life.

Modern liberalism isolates the act of free volition, the will as self-assertion, and emphasizes the individual struggling against constriction. The classical image of freedom as virtue, however, is quite different. It focuses upon the exhibition of form as the flowering of potential powers. From the Promethean standpoint of

7. Alexis de Tocqueville organized his monumental work on American society around what he took to be the opposition between liberty and equality. See his *Democracy in America*, translated by George Lawrence (Garden City, New York: Doubleday Anchor, 1969), esp. vol. II, pt. II, chs. 1-20 and IV, chs. 1-6. Compare Isaiah Berlin, *Four Essays on Liberty* (New York: Oxford University Press, 1969). Ronald Dworkin dissents from the notion that liberty and equality are opposed by arguing that it is possible to provide a coherent account of a right to equality but not of a presumed "right to liberty": see Ronald Dworkin, *Taking Rights Seriously* (Cambridge, Massachusetts: Harvard University Press, 1977), ch. 12. Charles Taylor provides a critical analysis of the nihilistic implications of the notion of radical freedom of the will as an absolute value in his *Hegel* (London: Cambridge University Press, 1975), pp. 546-69.

modern culture it is easy to mistake this ideal for mere static completion or passivity, but in fact it is neither static nor passive or, rather, the categories of civic language propose a way of seeing life that is different from the utilitarian. This language suggests that what makes life worth living is not simple pleasure but the peculiarly human satisfaction of feeling oneself to be a significant member of an ongoing way of life that appeals because of its deep resonances of beauty and meaning. (Curiously, modern advertising, that most ostensibly utilitarian of capitalist institutions, grasps this point profoundly, if narrowly. What else is most advertising but the rhetorical association of a commodity, such as a car or a cigarette, with a symbol of a commonly desired way of life or admired character ideal: the Beautiful People or, de gustibus, the Cowboy?)

The task of civic intelligence is to bring these inchoate appeals to clarity, to find and to weave a harmony among the various threads of significance embodied in family life, in the various skills and crafts, in religious and artistic traditions. In its most general formulation, the civic sense of virtue as freedom is captured in the idea of human dignity. Medieval natural-law theorists brought Christian theological commitments to bear on Greek and Roman notions of a common humanity in their statement that the fundamental natural end or purpose of political life is to provide dignity for all.

Notice that it is consistent in this context to speak of the political community as natural because it is a necessary condition for, indeed is an essential manifestation of, a dignified human life. This dignity is the most basic, general, even ontological aspect of the flourishing of human nature. Practically, it is the reality that Martin Luther King called the sense of "somebodyness." Dignity is thus the realization of freedom. It is the evidence of the full development of civic virtue.

The idea of "free institutions" (which bulks large in American political discourse), while a phrase much used in liberal thought, has its roots in the same civic conception of dignity and virtue. When Montesquieu and other early liberals looked for positive qualities in the republics of the ancient world, they saw above all free, as opposed to despotic, regimes. By this they meant that the structure and powers of the state derived from no force outside the citizens themselves. Neither occupying army nor dictator's mercenaries nor isolated elite maintained the practices of life, the laws, the defenses of those cities; rather, their strength came from the concerted spirit of their citizens.

It seemed to the early liberals living in an age of monarchy and the Old Regime amazing that the ancients could sustain, even for brief periods, the public spirit of Periclean Athens or Republican Rome, for it was evident from the descriptions and discussions of the classical theorists that maintenance of a self-governing polity required a generally high degree of identification, on the part of the citizen, of his own good with the well-being of the community.[8] Given the liberal assumptions of the early modern theorists, they had little trouble accounting for the "corruption" and decline of ancient republics into despotic empires. Indeed, as self-seeking competition weakened the bonds of commonwealth, those thinkers were proposing the liberal order as a way to engineer correctly what they took as the natural human gravitation toward competitive egoism. What seemed astonishing, and really hardly credible at all, was the notion of civic spirit, of civic acts as such.[9] Yet, the sheer weight of historical testimony forced them to accept its reality.

Holding to our intention to extend to the civic tradition a presumption of experiential validity, it is clear that citizenship is taken by republicanism as the natural fulfillment of human powers, not as an extreme feat of moral athleticism. However rare the truly excellent examples may be, citizenship remains the common vocation, and the proper object of moral education.

We may shed light on the matter by trying to describe a civic act, as opposed to a merely private one. In modern electoral politics, candidates frequently try to persuade citizens to cast their votes because their interests will be advanced by so doing. While the civic philosophers would agree with this reasoning, the "interests" to be advanced would be rather differently defined. Indeed,

8. See Baron de Montesquieu, *The Spirit of the Laws*, translated by Thomas Nugent (New York: Hafner, 1949), bk. III, chs. 3, 7; bk. IV, ch. 2. Compare Thomas L. Pangle, *Montesquieu's Philosophy of Liberalism* (Chicago: University of Chicago Press, 1973).

9. For example, see Adam Smith's deflation of traditional heroism as pride: Adam Smith, *The Theory of the Moral Sentiments* (New York: A. M. Kelley, 1966), pp. 405-9, 420-21. Tocqueville expresses similar sentiments: *Democracy in America*, translated by George Lawrence (Garden City, New York: Doubleday Anchor, 1969), p. 497.

the premise of public discussion of policy even in a liberal regime is not only to enlighten all interested parties as to what they stand to gain or lose in the event that a certain course of action is taken. When that is all or the greatest part of public debate, little "policy" results; instead there is a watering-down of choices to please everyone. Where the issue is simply a proposal to choose one kind of private enrichment over another, the arts of bargaining and political compromise are not inappropriate, tempered by a concern for fairness, like John Rawls's theory of justice, as a kind of rational and self-interested choice. But what about political decisions about making war, or the kinds of economic growth which should be pursued, or about use and care for the natural environment? Because these political decisions so affect the kinds of life that will prevail, public debate is critical for developing a shared understanding of the consequences of policy choices, of hidden costs and benefits to the whole community. Indeed, it is the general discussion of interdependency that brings a "public" into being. Public discussion aims to bring before the whole civic community an understanding of the "externalities" of policy choices—to use the language of liberal economics—precisely in terms of what pursuing these options will mean for the situation of various groups.

Voting to endorse a policy or candidate, were the choices really clear (which is another extremely critical matter), is a public, a civic act, because it carries with it responsibility for changing or maintaining the social, and often the natural, environment shared by all. Thus, to reduce such an act to a simple reflex of self-interest is fundamentally to misconceive the actual interdependence of citizens in a commonwealth. It is to imagine that the polity is a self-balancing mechanism—a familiar enough misassumption. But it is also to fail to take seriously the complicated web of interactions that ties together the lives of even the most private citizens. It is here that the liberal penchant for modeling political questions on economic choices in a marketplace shows its most dangerous and morally irresponsible side. Against the liberal claim that free institutions, in Montesquieu's sense, can be sustained merely by concentration upon an expanding market system, civic republican insight and historical experience strongly suggest that such a course is folly, because it rests on a misconception of politics and, finally, on too narrow an understanding of the reality of social life.

The strange utopian side of liberalism shows up clearly here. Confronted with the overwhelming fact of social interdependence, the liberal retreat to the mechanism of market choice is cloaked as humility! After all, one hears the argument, actually to make public decisions about the kinds of communities we should have, the kinds of lives people ought to lead, is moral arrogance and presumption. Let the ideal market of choices mediate. Then if consenting adults wish to commit capitalist or communalist acts, that is their private matter. But notice: this "value-neutral" position assumes that all humanly relevant goods can somehow be exchanged through the market, and that the moral qualities of respect and fairness can be developed in private life alone. Highly questionable assumptions indeed: not even the early modern liberal philosophers held such sanguine views.

To the early liberals the utopian element of classical republican morality was not the fact of interdependence and mutual responsibility but the expectation and requirement that citizens act in an appropriately responsible way in practice. For them, the key problem in the civic vision was the idea that self-interested motives could actually be transformed through a public culture to the extent that genuinely civic acts became widely practiced. Now, our present situation differs from theirs in one critical respect. We cannot fall back on the optimistic hope that an improved social mechanics will produce a functional equivalent of civic virtue by harnessing private egoism. Indeed, the viability of any self-governing institution is threatened by the failure of those dreams. We need to look closely at the civic tradition because, if democracy is to survive, we have no other option.

So, again, what conditions make civic life possible? Classical political philosophy understood the life of civic or moral virtue to stand in opposition to the life of self-interest which they called economic, meaning that the latter aimed at private satisfaction. Since economic life is concerned with wants that are in principle limitless, the motivation in dealings with others is always the expectation of gain. This is the marketing orientation familiar from utilitarian theory. By contrast, moral virtue represents a higher integration of the powers of the self. This integration was conceived as at once the goal and the effect of participation in civic life. Virtue, the *arete* ("excellence") of the Greek theorists, describes the disposition of a person whose conduct is guided by a shared value or principle rather than by private needs and desires.

This kind of excellence, moreover, is a personal ideal as well as a collective one, in that it describes a personality sufficiently integrated both to live up to commitments and to cooperate with others to achieve common values. In traditional language such an integration of the personality was described as *courage*, the ability to sum oneself up in word and action, and *temperance*, or self-control, an ordering of the person so that the higher values consciously affirmed can predominate over merely private impulses and desires.

The civic life has intrinsic value, then, because it is necessary for human maturation. The teleological conception of human nature which the civic tradition long maintained places the achievement of mature personhood within a context of interdependence and mutual concern. The great modern ideal of the autonomous self who is also respectful of others, as reflected in contractarian liberalism, is in reality a kind of echo of civic virtue. For the modern theorists of obligation, only autonomy is isolated from sociability, just as the modern theorists' state of nature locates man outside social relations. Given their assumption of the primacy of analytical reason, this conclusion appeared quite natural and obvious to the liberal thinkers. Again we see the tight connection among an understanding of politics, a theory of human nature, and a conception of reason. By contrast with liberalism, classical teleological reason situates achievement of an integrated self capable of self-reflection, and so of responsible action, within a continuity of life which is both social and natural.

What enabled classical thinkers to argue that a prudential reasoning, based upon a cultivated moral sense, could in fact be trusted to promote the good of the community? It was their vision of autonomy as always developing in tension with care for others in a particular shared situation. The whole classical notion of a common *paideia*, or moral-civic cultivation, rested on the assertion that growth and transformation of the self toward responsible mutual concern is the realistic concern of public life. Aristotle argued, and the civic tradition since then has agreed, that the first and final concern of politics, like that of the family though in a more universal way, is mutual moral cultivation.[10] It is a precarious and difficult undertaking, but, to Aristotle, not wholly utopi-

---

10. In this connection see Aristotle, *Nicomachean Ethics* bk. X, ch. 9.

an, because it is rooted in what was to him an obvious observation about human life.

A natural impulse is thus one reason why men desire to live a social life even when there is no need of mutual succor; but they are also drawn together by a common interest in proportion as each attains a share in the good life through the union of all in a form of political association. The good life is the chief end, both for the community as a whole and each of us individually. But men also come together, and form and maintain political associations, merely for the sake of life, for perhaps there is some element of the good even in the simplest act of living, so long as the evils of existence do not preponderate too heavily.[11]

The notion at the end, that even survival gets its significance from its implicit aim at fuller realization of human powers, is the characteristic of the teleological approach.

Notice that Aristotle's position does not totally reject the economic or marketing orientation toward mere "life," nor does it depict virtue as a mere external counterbalance to private needs. His is not a pure ethics of obligation, remorselessly struggling to control an implacable nature. On the contrary, the teleology of desire implicit in this passage from the *Politics* suggests that the life of virtue is good because of the qualitatively better fulfillment it opens for the individual. The meaning of good as the achievement of natural potential includes the idea that self-conscious reason is as genuine an expression of nature as sensual wants, even more so in the sense that the sociable and reasonable desires awaken uniquely human powers. Thus, the natural impulse to a shared life is not generated by a surplus of energies arising from analytically more primitive sensual needs. Aristotle's theory is in this way very different from Abraham Maslow's "hierarchy of needs."[12] The teleology of human life reconciles the disparate desires of appetite and reason, lust and love, by giving each its due in the full achievement of personhood.

11. *The Politics of Aristotle*, translated by Ernest Barker (New York: Oxford University Press, 1962), bk. III, ch. 5, p. 111. See also the useful discussion of contrasts between Aristotle's notion of a politics of virtue and the modern notion of obligation in Stephen G. Salkever's "Virtue, Obligation and Politics," *American Political Science Review* 68, 1 (March 1974): 78-92.

12. See Abraham Maslow, *Motivation and Personality* (2nd ed., New York: Harper and Row, 1970). Michael Macoby has provided a critique of this theory and its contemporary vogue from a perspective influenced in important ways by classical philosophy: *The Gamesman: The New Corporate Leaders* (New York: Simon and Schuster, 1976).

But the achievement of maturity, or moral virtue, consists in a genuine transformation of motives, not simply their combination. And this takes place only through a certain kind of educative social interaction. Civic moral education is, then, natural in that it fulfills humanity's distinctive need to be at once self-reflective and yet interdependent members of a community. Classical philosophy saw this human ideal as a reflection of its conception of the cosmos as a teleologically ordered relationship among different kinds of beings; yet, the peculiarly human form of life requires active artifice for its continuation. We must take care to nurture ourselves and our environment, including our progeny and each other. And that task is only possible through the development and maintenance of a full moral education, a *paideia* that includes political culture. That is a difficult and complex task. A civic culture is necessarily defined by its two poles: it is aiming at a universal sympathy, an ideal enunciated by the Stoics and given powerful expression in Christian natural-law teaching; yet, civic culture is grounded and rooted in the historical circumstances of its place of origin and the particular conditions of life in which it comes to grow.

:: III

The tension between particular circumstances and the *telos* of a universal community reflects in another form the root polarities of individual autonomy and mutual care. It also poses the formidable cognitive problem of how to conceive of the relationship of practical politics and political theory. For the classical tradition, as for the Middle Ages, the civic life was considered to draw its ultimate referents from the realm of *theoria*, or disinterested contemplation of the universal principles of nature or God. The "higher reaches of human nature" were achieved not outside human society but in the qualitatively higher realm of philosophical sagehood, the egoless mirroring of the cosmos. Theoretical knowledge in this ancient sense provided a feeling for man's ends and place in nature, and situated the shifting events of politics within a universal perspective that showed the finitude of political endeavor.

But *theory* did not possess its modern meaning of explaining how things work; it thus lacked any technical application. Instead, moral and political life were conceived of as requiring another sort of knowledge which could only be acquired through guided experience. This knowledge Aristotle called *phronesis*, or prudence.[13] Prudential knowledge is always situated and guided by qualitative analogies rather than abstract principles. The working out of *paideia* so that particular viewpoints and loyalties are given their proper places and are integrated into a wider framework of loyalty is at once a universal ideal and a highly particular—and valuable—achievement.

Modern liberalism began with an effort to circumvent the precarious nature of traditional prudence with a science of social engineering. Today the problems of that effort at political science make reappropriation of the classical insights increasingly desirable and perhaps even necessary. Chief among these insights is the dependence of a republican political life upon a vital political culture that continues the prudential tradition. If it is not to die, tradition must be recast with each generation.

The chief effort of civic education is to combat corruption—that is, in the civic view, to forestall despotic rule by which some group within the polity would substitute its particular conception of good for that of the whole. A despotism of "economic" men, of special interests, is what the tradition feared most, but it also warned of the dangers of a rule of the best and wisest untempered by the need of such groups to share power and thus aid in the civic development of the less good and wise.[14] Corruption, then, is domination, as the good of the polity is justice, but both are continually shifting balances within the particular circumstances of the society. The common good and its corruption are always discriminations in the situation, arrived at through discussion already founded in the sense of justice transmitted by the civic *paideia*.

Statesmanship must, then, by its very nature remain a prudential art. The living reality of the civic vision is the repeated effort

13. See Aristotle, *Ethics* bk. I, ch. 3, bk. VI, ch. 5, and bk. X, ch. 9, on the relation of prudence to cultivated experience in the moral sciences. Plato is often asserted to have maintained that theoretical knowledge of first principles was in fact necessary for the conduct of practical affairs, a position Aristotle criticized in *Ethics* bk. I. However, bearing in mind the difference between ancient and modern meanings of theory and practice, as well as the emphasis Plato placed upon linking practice and reflection—especially in *The Republic* and *The Statesman*—we should beware of reading their disagreement in terms of modern usages of these words.

14. See Aristotle, *Politics* bk. III, ch. 10.

to institutionalize a moral ideal. But the ideal is understood not through a deduction of abstract concepts but within the kind of interpretive circle that describes all moral life. Political prudence is an informed understanding of what contributes to the genuine growth of responsible common life. That reflection takes its root in the implicit sense of goodness and right which is shared and developed in civic life.[15] The attempt to formulate and fix this understanding, as in theories of social and economic progress or in Kohlberg's theory of moral development, runs the heavy risk of omitting or disparaging just those concrete loyalties which provide a standing place for reflection and criticism. As with the moral education of the individual, the liberal penchant for a universal scheme of "development" in the end misses the critical problem of our time: the economic and administrative processes that threaten to sever the bonds of involved understanding which make possible the development of a rooted and responsible sense of self.

It is therefore important to understand the relationship of prudential reasoning to the classical teleology of human life. For that tradition, the criterion of value is the full realization of a meaningful life as a member of a just community. There is a form of consequentialist reasoning in this position, in that acts are judged good or bad not according to their motivations or formal qualities alone but as they advance this full self-realization. However, self-realization is defined not by subjective needs but by the ontological notion that humanity is inherently social and linguistic and so tends toward a responsible shared life.

In the classical conception, the *telos*, or end, is the display of the full capabilities of humanity, and this immanent tendency is thought to structure the relations among the parts of the developing whole. Thus, while analytic reason is given a significant place, it is conceived of as essentially a reconstructive process. One can gain a detailed knowledge of a compound, by reducing it to its parts, only after first grasping its whole and overall tendency. In direct opposition to the purely analytic method, teleological reasoning declares that truly to know a thing is to see it not in its simplest terms but in its fullest development, which means within the widest set of its interconnections.

15. See Aristotle, *Ethics* bk. I, ch. 3, bk. X, chs. 8, 9.

Thus, while the modern individualistic notion of the state of nature has regarded generation of social ties as an instrumental process, the classical view begins from the *telos* of social life. Outside a linguistic community of shared practices, there would be biological *homo sapiens* as logical abstraction, but there could not be human beings. This is the meaning of the Greek and medieval dictum that the political community is ontologically *prior* to the individual. The *polis* is, literally, that which makes man, as human being, possible. It is therefore, as an association of justice and fellowship, the fullest expression of human nature.

The tradition of modern social thought reaching from Hegel through Marx, Durkheim, Dewey, Parsons, and others can be seen as a prolonged effort to refocus this teleological insight against the distorting efforts of the reductive social science initiated by Hobbes.[16] Aristotle referred to his way of coming to understand this human *telos* as induction, a process of gradual discernment of the common form derived from experience of many analogous cases. The tempestuous history of controversy over what is needed for induction to take place defines much of Western epistemology; however, Aristotle, like Plato, seems oddly confident that such a progress is quite natural. He does not seem to wonder in amazement that the "mind" can know "the world," but takes it as unproblematical that cognition is some sort of participation of human beings in the environment that sustains them.

Even more perplexing to moderns formed by centuries of epistemological debate is the ancients' evident assumption that there is a connection between a right cognitive grasp of the human *telos* and an individual's moral character, as well as his socially cultivated experience. That idea reappeared in Hegelian philosophy, whence it was disseminated through Marx and the American pragmatists. Yet, it has rarely been considered of importance in "rigorous" philosophy or the "scientific" study of society. An interpretive conception of social inquiry and philosophical understanding helps clear up the perplexity. It can also make sense of the ancient teaching about the superiority of the contemplative to the active life.

16. This is the position of Roberto M. Unger: see the discussion in his *Law in Modern Society: Toward a Criticism of Social Theory* (New York: Free Press, 1976), esp. pp. 1-46.

From the modern point of view, the weak point in the classical notion that a knowledge of human ends must undergird and guide prudential reasoning is that this putative knowledge of ends is asserted to be available only to the well-ordered character; that is, the argument is circular. There are no democratic procedures of verification, open to all disinterested outside observers, by which to test the "common-sense" claim that "man is an animal so constituted that he is truly himself only when he shares life in a *polis.*" Political—and so, for classical thinkers, genuine—anthropological knowledge rests upon a claim to an already interpreted experience.[17]

Political authority in classical political thought ultimately rests not on any objectively testable "science" but upon a claim to a kind of experience. This experience is one that transforms the person who is shaped by it, so that the original trust in authority is redeemed by a kind of self-justifying fulfillment of its claims. But that means that knowledge of human ends cannot be had outside the experience of coming to realize them. The great task of the true statesman, said Plato, is to communicate this process and its value to others who have not yet undergone it. Socrates was the incarnation of this communication for Plato, though in a wider sense the whole tradition of *paideia* must play this critical practical role.

The contemplative life, if we can take Socrates as its embodiment, is, then, a detachment from action in its self-serving sense, a purification from private wants so as to respond to the common good and, indeed, to the world wider than human concerns. The contemplative life thus transcends the interdependent life of the *polis*, but only to make the theorist empty of any purely private goal. There is much here to suggest instructive comparison between this central concern of classical philosophy and the spiritual traditions of the world religions.[18] The ideal of contemplative detachment as the highest fulfillment set distinct limits to the

17. Again, see Aristotle, *Ethics* bk. 1, chs. 4-5; also Eric Voegelin, "Reason: The Classic Experience," in *Anamnesis*, translated by Gerhart Niemeyer (Notre Dame, Indiana: University of Notre Dame Press, 1978), for an explication of this claim.

18. Karl Jaspers developed this in his portrait of Socrates as a great "paradigmatic religious personality" alongside Jesus, Confucius, and the Buddha: *The Great Philosophers*, edited by Hannah Arendt (New York: Harcourt, Brace and World, 1962). See also Herbert Fingarette's portrayal of sagehood as detached engagement in *Self in Transformation.*

claims and demands of politics while it introduced a higher norm of authority into politics.

For civic republicans, then, moral authority has been embodied in a common understanding of justice as a proportionate sharing in the common good. While liberal theorists have viewed justice as a contract of reciprocity motivated by equality in fear and need, the civic tradition has always maintained that justice finds its *telos* and so its orientation beyond itself in *philia*, or fellowship.[19] Because men in fact pursue a multitude of goods and can make various claims as to what is their due, principles of justice must remain general. At the same time, however, the tradition maintains that all members of a differentiated community must be enabled by common agreement and concerted public effort to take full part in the good life, that is, citizenship. It is this concern for participation which has given the civic tradition its recurrently radical edge.

Equality is a part of the complex value of justice. Because the *telos* of justice is fellowship, a polity must be so ordered that all citizens share the grounds for uncoerced participation. Neither equality of result nor of opportunity per se, this "common sense" of justice for centuries led civic republicans to identify political justice with a widespread distribution of the necessities of life and rough equality of wealth. Office and honor were to be awarded on the basis of advancement of this vision of the common good.[20] Reciprocity is thus a part of justice but ultimately has no meaning without a conception of what the good polity should be like, of what each citizen requires to share the good life of virtue.

In the republican vision the ideal of justice is characterized as proportional, not arithmetical—meaning that distribution of the possibilities for sharing the good life must seek to treat all citizens with equal concern but must recognize their different needs and contributions to the overall community. Civic virtue sets as a kind of minimum standard of competence for political participation

19. Aristotle, *Ethics* bk. IX.

20. Quentin Skinner has argued that this conception of justice was the dominant notion in Renaissance humanist political thinking and that it provided a point of reference for social criticism. It was not new to the Renaissance, however; it was in fact an inheritance from medieval Christian political theory. See Quentin Skinner, *The Foundations of Modern Political Thought*, vol. I: *The Renaissance* (London: Cambridge University Press, 1978).

the ability to observe the common rules and laws, to understand how these laws are arrived at and changed by reference to the notion of the common good. Moreover, discernment of the general good is the guiding norm for discussions of justice. That this discernment always depends on shared understandings derived from a tradition of cultivated experience requires that the civic community continually struggle to articulate anew the concrete meaning of justice for the situation. Republican thinkers long acknowledged that this was a precarious and difficult task.

Republics were admitted to be fragile and always liable to corruption into a dictatorship of particular groups and activities over others. Furthermore, civic life was known to be an interdependent life in which the individual's moral development and happiness depended directly upon the virtue and wisdom of his fellow citizens' lives and vice versa. Yet, by being aware of the complexity and difficulty of concretely realizing the ideal of the just polity through imperfect institutions in unpredictable circumstances, the formulators of the republican tradition were also drawing limits to what politics could claim to achieve; hence, their high valuation of civic life did not preclude their openness to the ultimate loyalties expressed in philosophy and religion. The danger of despotism they saw as always present: talk of tradition can be used to cloak vicious oppression as well as to sustain virtue. But since they held no vision of an ultimate achievement of a totally just society, the major republican thinkers did not see as either good or realistic the mobilization of total societies in the name of future utopias.[21] Republican statesmanship is always a matter of achieving a complicated and delicate balance.

All this explains the high hopes of the progenitors of liberalism. They sought, rather immoderately, at last to overcome the limitations and fragility of the traditional civic culture. The new project was in part a response to the great difficulty early modern thinkers faced in bringing the new forces of commerce, warfare, and centralized government within the republican conception of moral order. The actual relations of interdependence among Euro-

21. Christian millenarian hopes did play an important and complicated role in the modern development of republicanism, particularly in the English and American radical republican tradition which so much influenced the founding generation of the American republic. For overviews, see Pocock, *Machiavellian Moment,* and Wood, *Creation of the American Republic.*

pean men grew ever more complex and indirect after the sixteenth century, gravely weakening the self-confidence of the traditional understanding of the individual. It was more and more difficult for a person to know who he was in terms of his "calling," which was interpreted by both Christian and civic humanist vocabularies in terms of ideal social interrelationships.

The enormous crisis of orientation and meaning that swept Europe in the sixteenth and seventeenth centuries testifies with terrifying eloquence to a great depth of confusion about where the individual was in the world and what made life worth living. Instead of the older confidence of knowing oneself through one's social relations, however fraught with moral precariousness that may have been, the new age was one in which the individual came to see himself as inhabiting a strange world. It consisted of private passions and concern for self-image no longer bound to a coherent set of social relations, the amour propre of which Rousseau would later be the great theorist. J.G.A. Pocock captures the situation well:

> He could explain this realm, in the sense that he could identify the forces of change that were producing it . . . but he could not explain himself by locating himself as a real and rational being within it. The worlds of history and value therefore extruded one another, and what would later be described as the alienation of man from his history had begun to be felt; but, far from seeing himself as a mere product of historical forces, the civic and propertied individual was endowed with an ethic that clearly and massively depicted him as a citizen of classical virtue, but exacted the price of obliging him to regard all the changes transforming the world of government, commerce and war as corruption. . . . Hence the age's intense and nervous neoclassicism.[22]

The search for a new understanding of these problems—anomalies, from the traditional republican perspective—led enterprising thinkers into the complex developments of modern political theory and culture. That liberal utilitarian modes of thinking should have dominated these developments is not surprising.

The utility-language of liberalism, once armed with the model of the self-balancing political economy of growth, could separate the inner quest for meaning from the public questions of administrative order, military power, and commercial expansion. The

---

22. Pocock, *Machiavellian Moment*, p. 466.

unique liberal answer to the classical problem of the just polity was the premise of moral neutrality of wants plus free market exchange among equals. Individuals could look to their inner gyroscopes as best they might. They might find personal solace in the notion of vocation or of devotion to family, but also by pursuing personal, corporate, and national aggrandizement. The primacy of material motives, especially fear and greed, led to a politics in which justice was best ensured by governmental umpiring of the economic games.

Because of the primacy of growth over justice, of the material over the spiritual, the idea of historical progress has played a crucial role in liberal culture as the replacement for the civic language of the common good. To its credit, Marxism has emphasized the moral quality of interdependent fellowship as the *telos* of historical progress in a way that liberal capitalism has not; yet, Marxists and liberals alike have consistently talked of the achievement of a just society as being dependent upon growth of the society's capacity to fulfill economic wants. This conception has provided sanction for the brutalities of "primitive accumulation" in both its capitalist and socialist forms, a sacrifice of presently living persons, most often peasants, for the sake of future abundance—on balance, a delivery from want that has been bloody indeed.

The great liberating aspect of the civic tradition for our present circumstances is its freedom from thrall to the idea of progress. A civic politics begins with the demand for justice as the condition for genuine growth. The test and measure of that growth is the realization of fellowship, replacing the hostility and antagonisms of social groups with an interrelationship of equal dignity. But the path toward that realization, always a difficult one, is made extremely complicated by the tremendous complexity of modern industrial society. Here the mutual dependence of all groups is more intricately woven than in any previous society, yet, it is denied by the curious rhetoric of individualism—a situation that perpetuates a corporate dominance of American life the more pervasive because it is so denied. Our liberal conception of politics, however, makes the tracing out of these factual relationships of unequal participation seem unnecessary. Economic advancement, tempered by an eye cast toward playing fairly—in a word, progress —must work inscrutably toward a better tomorrow. That is the dream turned nightmare from which we are struggling to awake.

A recovery of democratic politics in America must start with re-awakening a living sense of the social and historical relationships within which we stand. A recovery of citizenship would be at the same time a crucial reinvigoration of a sense of personal responsibility. The paradox of citizenship is that civic virtue entails conflict in a way that liberal civility does not, yet, the conflict inevitably triggered by any challenge to the threatening despotism, soft or hard, is in fact a sign of vitality in our republic.[23]

There is a second kind of conflict which the recovery of democratic citizenship entails. That is the painful struggle which must go on in the body politic and within ourselves as we become aware, at personal cost, of our general complicity in unjust social arrangements that provide advantages for some at the expense of dignity for others. The struggle for democratic politics is always a struggle for a more inclusive community, and that will require changing our sense of who we are both in public and in subtly private ways. In this sense the civic vision is a personal moral challenge as much as a critical perspective on the social status quo. Peace, as King reminded us, is not the absence of tension but the presence of justice.

The major contribution we can hope for from a cultural and intellectual reinvigoration of civic republicanism is that it will bring to the emerging movements for grassroots democracy the historical vision and wisdom of such a long and rich tradition. Chief among these insights is the understanding that citizenship is rooted in a moral tradition. The civic heritage shares the under-

23. Lawrence Goodwyn has provided a re-creation of the context within which, just before the turn of the century, the Populist movement struggled for a democratic political-economic order against the forces of capitalist monopoly. Their defeat, like the later decline of Socialism, was partially balanced by the power of their example in providing a moral challenge to the dominance of corporate power. See Lawrence Gooodwyn, *Democratic Promise: The Populist Movement in America* (New York: Oxford University Press, 1976). The Progressive movement, including the pragmatic philosophy with which it was closely aligned, continued to exert diminishing influence until after World War II. At that point the now familiar anti-ideological politics of interest became itself the dominant political ideology. See also Robert H. Wiebe, *The Search for Order, 1877-1920* (New York: Hill and Wang, 1968).

In contrast to Goodwyn, Richard Hofstadter celebrated that waning of the reforming impulse as he documented it. See Richard Hofstadter, *The Age of Reform: From Bryan to FDR* (New York: Knopf, 1963); also *The American Political Tradition and the Men Who Made It* (New York: Knopf, 1973).

standing that practical reasoning moves in a circle, growing by the efforts of citizens formed by the civic *paideia* to extend and realize the ideal of a more human and just commonwealth. This requires a creative, indeed, an experimental reinterpretation of the meaning of their primary commitments for the contemporary situation.

In America the civic tradition has numerous roots, many of them religious, as is appropriate in a diverse society and for a political vision focused on integrating diversity. Yet, the central symbols of the citizen and the commonwealth—the moral imperative to live according to the principles of justice and mutual support grounded in civil covenant—are held in common. It is the sharing of these ideals, rather than blood, soil, or economic growth, that holds out hope for a renewed struggle toward a just community that embodies the sense of dignity, of "somebodyness" in a nation worthy of the respect of all. And this too is appropriate, for the quality of political fellowship is determined by what is shared.

This, then, is the hope civic republican ideals hold out to us. The difficult task is to articulate successfully this possibility, to bring the resources of that tradition into the present national and international arenas so as to provide a new political vision for a confused and divided public. The lurking suspicion that undermines our confidence in any tradition is that our capitalist and bureaucratic modern society has, like a cancer, grown beyond the point at which its corruption could be healed by self-regeneration. The great intellectual challenge is to develop conceptual means to reinterpret the formidable problems that prevent realization of an authentic citizenship. And the first step in that direction must be to assess, with the present crisis in view, the resources the American civic experience has previously brought to its struggles. By those reflections it may become possible to tap a still-living civic energy with which to generate a new political and social vision for the American present.

SIX

Commerce and the Democratic Republic:
An Uneasy Tension

:: I

The civic republican tradition contains disagreement and ambiguity, but its principles and the direction of its moral aspiration are clear. Civic republicanism has manifested its vitality as its aspiration toward an inclusive community providing dignity and justice for all has encountered the limits of actual institutions. For the tradition, the civic ideals of justice and dignity entail moral equality of all individuals, based on a recognition that all share the same human ends.[1] Human fulfillment takes many forms, but the common attribute is that concern and care for the dignity of self and others which the tradition calls virtue. For the civic republican vision, equality is a fundamental value of political life, but its foundation is not, as for utilitarian liberalism, a studied agnosticism about the nature of a good life. Rather, it is based upon the common aim of the basic goods of dignity, justice, and community through which human beings become equally worthy of respect and concern.

Because of the importance it gives to practical, prudential reasoning, the republican tradition has emphasized ideals of charac-

---

1. Wilson Carey McWilliams makes this point well, citing Aristotle on the equality of citizens in a *polis*, particularly the importance that their most important desires be equal, that is, that they aspire to the life of citizenship and not tyranny. See Wilson Carey McWilliams, "On Equality as the Moral Foundation of Community," in Robert H. Horwitz, ed., *Moral Foundations of the American Republic* (Charlottesville: University of Virginia Press, 1976), esp. pp. 185-89.

ter, models of conduct, and exemplary institutions. As the classical theorists of the tradition taught, the form and the end immanent in a style of life give significance and worth to living. The moral and political discourse of republicanism is built around qualitative language, in particular the qualitative contrast between virtue and corruption. This mode of discourse emphasizes what utilitarian language denies: that qualities are intrinsic to forms of life, that there are important differences of kind among various ways of living, that it distorts and trivializes life to treat all claims to quality as directly comparable on some supposedly neutral and objective scale of satisfaction.

Liberal utilitarianism treats quality as a subjective experience, a satisfaction an individual "has" or "derives" from an exchange with the outside world. Since in this scheme qualitative judgments are entirely subjective and individual, social practices are imagined to be instruments for providing individual satisfactions. For the utilitarian there is no standard of worth except the satisfaction of subjective needs and, since these differ among individuals, there is no hope of assessing the worth of any social practice except by taking the sum of the individual experiences it generates. It is thus consistent for utilitarians to maintain that value judgments are nonrational and cannot be defended on intrinsic grounds. The term *value* already suggests this: it derives from economics, in which discipline utilitarian philosophy has been most completely embodied.

An intrinsic claim of quality, on the other hand, states that an activity is important because there is some prized good which exists within and is not separable from that activity. Life is clearly such a good, and so is friendship and, for civic thinkers, so are justice and civic community. For example, collective deliberation on matters of common concern is good intrinsically, not just instrumentally. As long as the participants can share in the discussion without coercion, it is in the deliberative process itself that the participants come to understand each other and, through a sharing of viewpoints, expand and deepen their sense of worth and efficacy in a way impossible in any private experience.

Satisfactions have meaning for those who experience them; they are not mere sensations. Indeed, satisfaction of individual desires is shaped through the social forms by which individuals orient themselves, whether or not they are conscious of this. The great defect of liberalism is its almost willful blindness to this fact. The limitation of conservative thinking of Edmund Burke's stripe is that it notes only the passive side of the individual's relation to the community. It is thus a perfect mirror-image of liberalism, and it is equally incomplete. The civic tradition sees that individuality grows in a social matrix but also stresses that this process can be cultivated by the participants themselves. Unlike the liberal, the civic thinker realizes he is always within and shaped by a tradition of moral orientation. Yet, unlike the conservative, the civic thinker sees that he has a responsibility to shape this tradition by actively responding to new situations with a style and sensitivity shaped by his *paideia*. The critical difference in understanding that puts the conservative and the liberal on one side and the civic republican on the other is that the latter takes seriously and critically his involvement in the forms of life he shares.

The assumptions undergirding liberal theories of politics, human nature, and social investigation have, as we have seen, given rise to both the liberal and conservative variants of modern political theory. In American political thinking the liberal utilitarian strand has predominated, so that utilitarian assumptions, like the capitalist exchange system which embodies those assumptions, have often distorted articulations of republican movements—or, at least, they have made it difficult for the civic tradition to find its voice. A major step, if not the starting point, in the contemporary effort to reformulate a civic public philosophy in America must be development of a conception of politics that builds from the understanding of life as both shared tradition and responsible, critical initiative. Concretely, this means finding a way to transcend conceptually a purely utilitarian understanding of politics and a way to challenge the domination of social relationships by bureaucratic management and the workings of capitalist economics. The elucidation of this project would be at the same time a recovery of the notion of practical reason.

For civic republican thinkers, political understanding has its basis in the social cultivation of practical prudence. Indeed, civic ideals make sense only in a context in which human beings live more than instrumental lives. This is to say that there is an intrinsic relationship between cognitive understanding and practical involvement, but that relationship is not one in which social location determines awareness in any simple sense. Rather, the insight of the tradition of practical reason discussed in the last chapter is precisely that human beings live within as well as use language and forms of social life, that they can both understand and take up a stance toward their situation and, by so doing, help to organize and structure it. Persons are not simply counters in a systemic map or game, moved from without, but are moral agents in that they can question both themselves and their situations and take responsibility for the stances they adopt. Understanding requires a kind of enactment, and this further entails an ineluctably social and, finally, political dimension.

Insight thus requires a disposition toward a certain kind of ethical relationship toward others, a notion of society as aiming at a consensual and shared realm characterized by reciprocity. This conception implies a political practice opposite to the strategic and instrumental conception. An understanding of practical reason reveals that recovery of the civic republican tradition is actually a process of coming to understand in a new way what is important and possible in our own historical situation. The civic tradition is important for us because it articulates an understanding that the interdependency of the members of a society is a moral and political relationship. The tradition speaks to our predicament of great factual interdependency organized by an economic and administrative ethos which conceals, denies, or suppresses the moral and political nature of those relationships.

Our need is to extend the spirit of republican democratic life into the sphere of the major economic and administrative institutions. And the heritage of the civic tradition is in part responsible for our being able to see the situation this way. Thus developing effective strategies to transform our predicament so as more fully to actualize civic life has the kind of fruitful circularity that characterizes engaged practical reasoning. Any view of our past is already formed by a diagnosis of our present situation; yet, historical inquiry can help correct and deepen our present understanding.

:: II

It has been common in American thinking to see the nation's growth as a majestic expansion of a unified liberal political culture. Louis Hartz's well-known work on American political thought proposed such a conception in the mid-1950s, and it resonated powerfully with the national mood of those Cold War years.[2] According to that vision, America has always been an essentially Lockean society, dedicated to the advancement of individual interests. Lacking a feudal past of aristocratic privilege and peasant misery, America was also spared the bitterness of European-style social antagonism. Thus Hartz interpreted the American Revolution as conducted in spiritual equanimity, the assertion of a native liberalism against a British version of the Old Regime. Aside from efforts by antebellum Southerners to conceive an ideology of caste privilege and paternalism, Americans never developed real class oppositions or ideologies; hence the failure of socialism to root here and, Hartz argued, the mistake of Progressive historians who sought to find in social conflict a significant dynamic in the United States.

While the mainstream of post-war orthodoxy, represented by Hartz's view of America as an almost purely liberal society, tended to banish social conflict from United States history, it also celebrated the dynamic, expanding character of the society. Indeed, the deepest motif of liberal culture and the liberal conception of politics is the notion of dynamic expansion. In the idealized portrait of liberal society that was reasserted during the post-war years, the great superiority of liberalism over all earlier as well as contemporary nonliberal philosophies was said to lie in the tremendous capacity of liberal society to free the potentials for economic development slumbering through the night of centuries of feudalism. The superiority of "the American way of life" was alleged to lie in an unrivaled capacity to arouse and then organize the energies of individuals, energies aroused in the hope of fulfilling individuals' material needs. The result of liberated energies, harnessed through work and commerce, was abundance, and this the proponents of liberalism declared to be the true goal of civilization and the definer of progress. So the history of the liberal tradition in America became identical with national success defined as economic growth, and the venerable liberal ideal of personal freedom in the sense of security of person and ability to enter into contracts

2. See Louis Hartz, *The Liberal Tradition in America: An Interpretation of American Political Thought since the Revolution* (New York: Harcourt, Brace, World, 1955). A similar argument forms the substance of Daniel Boorstin's *The Genius of American Politics* (Chicago: University of Chicago Press, 1953).

for personal advantage became identified with successful expansion of the American economy.

Thus, the peculiar genius of America was said to lie in its ability to transform potential social antagonisms into mutual enrichment. The instrument of this social alchemy was the competitive market, aided by the vast natural endowments of North America and the "cultural capital" of an Anglo-Saxon nation naturally given to enterprise and the tradition of limited government. There was about that vision of the 1950s some quality of a caricature of liberal philosophy, but it was essentially faithful to the liberal spirit in its celebration of economic dynamism as the goal and result of a new kind of society.

Thus utilitarian liberalism finds itself in principle committed to a program of economic expansion: hence its close ties with commercial capitalism and the vision of material abundance. Liberal historians such as Louis Hartz and Daniel Boorstin have tried to justify America's present commitment to capitalistic growth as, over the long run, the most effective and humane means of fulfilling the promise of a modern liberal society to "deliver the goods" and so to provide the greatest happiness for the greatest number. This implies that human needs and satisfaction can always be dealt with as individual preferences that have a minimal impact on the preferences and fulfillments of others. For this reason, the repeated turns to government to regulate and sometimes restructure or even plan distribution of resources and kinds of production, which have been especially pronounced since the New Deal, put strains on the apparent coherence of this liberal scheme.

But there has long been an optimistic quality about mainstream liberal thinking, one still present after the trauma of the Great Depression and, indeed, not without voice today. However, in the American context there has also been a contrapuntal theme even among proponents of the instrumental vision of economic society. James Madison's early optimism about the ability of the liberal system of Constitutional checks and balances to disperse and regulate the struggle of interests was forcefully challenged by Alexander Hamilton. Hamilton argued that the inevitable result of unrestrained commercial development was—and he advocated this— the development of large economic organizations, sharp inequalities of wealth, and international competition for markets.[3] In such

3. See Gerald Stourzh, *Alexander Hamilton and the Idea of Republican Government* (Palo Alto, California: Stanford University Press, 1970), pp. 158-62.

a case, Hamilton thought, the state necessarily became a Leviathan, acting to uphold some and to flatten others, and controlling all.

This Hamiltonian understanding of liberal capitalism and the modern state emphasized that competitive action is strategic, aiming at besting other competitors. Hamilton saw that once social relations are lived as being instrumental to competitive success, as they are in liberal society, the public realm becomes the scene of a power struggle. The benign vision of competitive society offered by liberal thinkers such as Hartz plays down the strategic aspects of utilitarianism and greatly deemphasizes conflict and domination. Hartz largely dismissed Hamilton and his party as Whigs and would-be aristocrats radically out of synchrony with mainstream liberal thought and practice.[4] And of course the Hamiltonian conception does raise fundamental questions about the effectiveness of the institutions of market or constitutional government in transforming the struggle for dominance into a dynamic equilibrium. Hartz has loaded into his notion of liberal society more than the individualist, utilitarian, capitalist core of philosophic liberalism can carry. It is as though Hartz, fearing that the suffocating organic ties extolled by Conservative thinkers of Burkean stamp were the sole alternative to liberal individualism, felt compelled to ascribe any sense of moral solidarity among Americans to some kind of magically sublimated self-interest.[5] At the same time his interpretation rendered him oblivious to the connection Hamilton saw between market capitalism, administrative social control, and international military struggle.

That unawareness, of course, was widespread in Cold War America. While some liberal intellectuals were celebrating the liberal consensus and others had declared an end of ideology in American politics, however, uneasiness with the individualistic, growth-oriented direction of American society did arouse still others to

4. Hartz, *Liberal Tradition*, pp. 15ff.

5. It might seem as though Hartz was following Alexis de Tocqueville's famous discussion of "self-interest rightly understood." However, a close reading of Tocqueville shows that this is not the case. Tocqueville's point is that while Americans often interpret their acts of public involvement as self-interested, and while they may in fact begin as such, the importance of civic life lies in its transformative effect. It is an educative process in which self-interested motives become enlarged into genuinely altruistic ones. See Alexis de Tocqueville, *Democracy in America*, translated by George Lawrence (Garden City, New York: Doubleday Anchor, 1969), II, ch. 5.

question the adequacy of the liberal notion of the good life to the nation's own ideals. The political and cultural turmoil of the 1960s began with an awakening of moral idealism spurred by the nation's failure to achieve its ideal of human dignity, and it expressed itself in the political emergence of groups marginal in post-war society. The movement for the civil rights of Black Americans embodied in its leadership and rhetoric civic themes and criticisms of a complacent society which had been silent for at least a decade. The student movement of those days recalled ideals in the American tradition not readily assimilable to the liberal vision. After announcing that the United States was at a point of moral and political stalemate—dominated by a corporate Leviathan, its citizens withdrawn from public life—the new movement proposed a counter-image of the good society: participatory democracy.

In a participatory democracy, the political life would be based in several root principles: that decision-making of basic social consequences be carried on by public groups; that politics be seen positively, as the art of collectively creating an acceptable pattern of social relations; that politics has the function of bringing people out of isolation and into community, this being a necessary, though not sufficient means of finding meaning in personal life.[6]

Particularly significant in this statement is the concern that politics be seen as a positive, indeed, necessary activity conceived of not as the advancement of preformed, private interests but as a shared process of social construction. The notion that public action was positive affirmed the New Deal's brand of Liberalism as well as the direct-action politics which that era made a common feature of political life.

The practical concerns which led to this turn toward an explicitly positive, participatory, and egalitarian notion of politics stemmed from a negative appraisal of post-war society, especially the "permeating and victimizing fact of human degradation," the Cold War orientation toward military needs, the apparent cynicism and narrowness of political leadership.[7] In appealing for a mass social movement of reform the students, the Civil Rights

6. From the *Port Huron Statement* of the Students for a Democratic Society, quoted by Kirkpatrick Sale, *SDS* (New York: Vintage Books, 1973), p. 52.
7. Ibid., p. 72.

activists, and other fledgling movement leaders found themselves invoking ideals they sensed to be part of their tradition but which clashed with the self-interested utilitarian language of the dominant interpreters of American politics.

Some American intellectuals were able to respond to this clash by rediscovering an important dimension of American experience which post-war preoccupations had virtually relegated to silence. In various fields, but significantly in historical study, new conceptions of the national experience were stirring. A distinction between the liberal strands and a civic or republican constellation of thought in American democracy became apparent. This conceptual change has evolved along with a new configuring of American history and as a crucial part of that development.[8] The rediscovery of a civic republican strand in the American tradition has thus proceeded hand-in-hand with new enunciations of civic activism as a political concept, and this intellectual development has occurred in interrelation with the political and moral aspirations of the reform movements themselves.

During the 1960s American historians were constructing a more complex understanding of national development, one which gave special attention to the political and religious cultural context out of which American society, and in particular its political tradition, emerged. Perry Miller's work on early New England provided a groundwork by giving a far broader and generally more sympathetic understanding of the Puritan impact on national culture. The discovery that the Americans who made the Revolution and launched the new republic were not the straightforward Lockeans beloved of liberal legend suggested reassessments of many assumptions.

Indeed, the effort to reconstruct the intellectual work of early America revealed a strong concern with individual character, but a concern centered on the idea of virtue as the subordination of

8. This development provides a vivid illustration of the procedure in human inquiry called interpretive or hermeneutical. Jürgen Habermas has described this approach in his *Knowledge and Human Interests* (Boston: Beacon Press, 1971), pp. 309-10, as follows: "The world of traditional meaning discloses itself to the interpreter only to the extent that his own world becomes clarified at the same time. The subject of understanding establishes communication between both worlds. He comprehends the substantive content of tradition by *applying* tradition to himself and his situation."

private wants to the common good, a preoccupation with self-development rather than self-advancement. The liberal theme of "pursuit of property" was certainly there, but it appeared in conjunction with a strongly egalitarian concern with the social conditions that must obtain in order for citizens to become full participants in republican government. Perhaps most surprising of all, the new historiography revealed that Jeffersonians and Federalists shared these concerns to a high degree, and that the liberal conception of government as an instrument for advancing interests emerged only gradually and in tension with an older idea of republican politics as active community initiative.[9]

The new historiography revealed a more complex picture of the American founding, one full of tensions and conflicts. The inequalities generated by the pursuit of self-interest and an expanding market grew along with and often in opposition to the republican concern with civic initiative and the equal dignity of citizens. The rediscovery that Americans of the Revolutionary period thought of themselves as the inheritors of both the covenantal tradition of radical Protestantism and the republicanism of the Commonwealthmen of the seventeenth-century English Revolution challenged the view of Hartz and Boorstin that Americans were acting from a native individualistic notion of liberty.[10] The civic republican tradition to which the colonial patriots were heir countered the individualistic emphasis of Hobbes and Locke with a social conception of human nature derived from classical, Christian, and Renaissance sources.

Enlightenment liberals generally thought of individuals as morally preformed by their largely private needs and wants, so that

9. The development of these themes is discussed in some detail by Robert E. Shalhope, "Towards a Republican Synthesis: The Emergence of an Understanding of Republicanism in American Historiography," *William and Mary Quarterly*, 3rd series, 29 (1972): 49-50. See also Jack Green, *The Reinterpretation of the American Revolution* (New York: Harper and Row, 1968).

10. Bernard Bailyn's work has been a powerful catalyst in launching this direction in interpretation: see his *Ideological Origins of the American Revolution* (Cambridge, Massachusetts: Belknap Press, 1967) and *Origins of American Politics* (New York: Knopf, 1968). See also Pauline Maier, *From Resistance to Revolution* (New York: Knopf, 1972). The importance of religious sentiments in the American revolutionary experience has been explored by Perry Miller, *Errand into the Wilderness* (Cambridge, Massachusetts: Harvard University Press, 1975) and Alan Heimert, *Religion and the American Mind: The Great Awakening to the Revolution* (Cambridge, Massachusetts: Harvard University Press, 1966).

government was a matter of regulations—the view the Federalists used to structure the new Constitution, though not without strong opposition. The "Real Whig" republicans, on the other hand, saw civic participation and the moral equality making it possible as active achievements of a particular kind of social and political life. Their term for this kind of active social life, in which politics was a positive culturing of individuals, was the traditional one of civic virtue. It was the goal of republican statecraft. The untrammeled pursuit of self-interest, on the other hand, they saw as drawing men away from their full development as ethical persons and undermining the civic spirit on which liberty depended. The anti-egalitarian tendencies of self-interest, which they associated with "empire," were called corruption.

The conflict of interpretations between the new historiography and the liberal one rediscovered, as was expressed in the struggle for independence, a conception of politics which was not an instrumental politics of interest, indeed, not a liberal vision of politics at all.[11] Rather, in that republican view politics was a positive art, a necessary expression and completion of social life. But neither could this view be called conservative in the modern philosophic sense. The patriots' republicanism contained little enthusiasm for social passivity. The language of civic virtue versus corruption, of republic versus empire, suggests a highly active and engaged notion of the good society. In fact, allied with the strong resonances those terms held for members of the dissenting religious bodies so important in America, that republican moral-political language fired a revolution. Thus the recovery of the civic republican understanding of politics, so powerful through the early years of the republic, has enabled to emerge historical continuities that the liberal orthodoxy could not see.

Moreover, recent historiography has shown how historically rare and difficult an achievement a genuine public philosophy really is. The kind of public philosophy the revolutionary era

11. Liberalism's overshadowing of the republican tradition in the development of the new nation is presented, though in perhaps too simple a scenario, by Gordon S. Wood, *The Creation of the American Republic: 1763-1787* (Chapel Hill: University of North Carolina Press, 1969). The complex interrelations between republicanism and philosophic liberalism are interestingly explored in the collection by Robert H. Horwitz, ed., *Moral Foundations of the American Republic* (Charlottesville: University of Virginia Press, 1976).

generated in America was a distinctive collective achievement, directly involved with and dependent upon the moral culture of citizenship. Subsequent American history, like earlier European experience, has shown that civic life is not possible simply any time, under any circumstances, and that an effective public philosophy is tied to the destiny of republican political life in the full sense. But for this very reason, the difficulties Americans have experienced in realizing a civic life in a liberal, commercial society are instructive. The recurring problem has been the struggle to bring the economic and social conditions for equity and citizenship within an effective and democratic public sphere.

Seen in that perspective, the history of republicanism in the United States after the founding efflorescence can be divided into two phases. The first phase, extending roughly to the Civil War, was an effort to balance the effects of commercial society by means of citizen association and initiative. That era marked the classic democratic movement in American development. Following the destruction of the slave society in the South, the dynamism of capitalist expansion called forth movements for reform as efforts either to check and control or, in the socialist movement, to supplant the private, corporate economy. That phase culminated in the New Deal and the militarily oriented welfare state that developed after World War II. Today, the relative slowing of the postwar economic dynamism, along with dissatisfaction with some of the reform efforts, have at least potentially reopened the entire question of the relationship between democratic life and American institutions, both corporate and governmental. However, before confronting that complicated situation directly, the practical and conceptual difficulties that caused the early civic public philosophy to become overshadowed by liberalism must be examined.

:: III

Thomas Paine is an emblematic figure of the American search for a way to maintain the moral climate of republicanism within social conditions generated by a capitalist economy. In this, Paine resembles Jefferson and his Republican party, to whom Paine felt a kinship. To thrive, civic ideals require a carefully wrought accommodation between political institutions and social relationships. The whole of the republican tradition had emphasized this.

Yet the events that gave the opening for republican hopes in the American struggle for independence also made it seem possible to achieve civil goals by the individualistic means of the market economy.

In the dark days of the Revolution, in 1779, the first burst of patriotic enthusiasm had waned. The Spirit of '76, the vision of a united and virtuous people rising to throw off the yoke of tyrannical corruption, was disintegrating under the weight of contrary realities too patent to be denied. The war dragged on, but fervor seemed to be giving way to venality. The Continental Army was constantly shrinking from desertion. The Continental Congress considered, then rejected as futile, the idea of appealing to the states for financial support for the patriot cause. The states balked at direct taxation. The result was the issuance of vast quantities of currency, the notorious Continentals, to fund the war effort. The result was catastrophic inflation of several hundred percent a year. Profiteering on war contracts appeared openly. Instead of the "Christian cooperative commonwealth" Samuel Adams had seen at the beginning of the struggle for independence, it struck thoughtful leaders that the destructive effects of the very moral corruption Britain had come to personify were all too apparent in the new republic. A ferocious economic individualism was wrenching apart the civic covenant still being bonded by patriot blood.

In the spring of 1779 Tom Paine—the most widely read pamphleteer of the Revolution, whose *Common Sense* had swelled patriot ranks with its exaltation of republicanism and denunciation of monarchy—found himself directly confronted by this crisis. Paine's response moved him from advocacy of the traditions of a communal economy to a common front with proponents of economic expansion. Tom Paine's quandary spoke for the experience of many good-willed republicans in the Revolution and was to have a dramatic impact on the shape of the new nation which emerged from the war, as it would upon the political vision that would continue to shape the nation's future.

The spring of 1779 found Paine in Philadelphia, America's largest commercial city and capital of Pennsylvania, one of the most internally divided of the new states. Paine was a leading figure among the fervently anti-Tory artisans of the city and, through his pamphleteering, on good terms with the leaders of many state delegations to the Congress. He was therefore in a good position to grasp the scope of the economic turmoil the war had brought to the city. Before the war Philadelphia had been the nearest approximation in the colonies to a commercial city on the European model, exercising a preeminence through its role as chief port and entrepôt for the most populous and prosperous of the colonies. The key figures of Philadelphia's life were then the merchants, many of them Quakers, who carried on the import-export trade and the diverse community of artisans who provided the varied kinds of skilled labor and technology that this trade required. Benjamin Franklin, the most spectacularly successful of the artisans, summed up in his person their aspirations and, to a large extent, their values: a pride in their worldly calling linked to a sense of social and political responsibility. The effect of the war had been at once to split Pennsylvanian society into loyalists and patriots and to foster an extraordinary economic boom for merchants, who now benefited from the sudden need for munitions, foodstuffs, clothing. Farmers, too, felt a jump in demand and artisans found contracts to build ships and make boots, rifles, and the other requirements of war.

However, the prosperity was uneven. The debts of Congress and the states were paid in paper money. The new French alliance enabled merchants such as Robert Morris to buy goods and then resell them to the French for gold. As some profited enormously, the pre-war relationships between the city and the Pennsylvania hinterland broke down; farmers sold directly to French supply agents, bypassing the Philadelphia markets, while the grain that did get marketed there rose dramatically in price. Similar dislocations affected most staple commodities, including the artisans' new materials. By May 1779, Philadelphia was a scene of spreading want and widespread agitation, mobilized by the popular militia to control prices and protect citizens' livelihood. The agitation was fueled by a heated battle in the Congress over charges of embezzlement leveled against a merchant, Silas Deane, who had been commissioned to purchase munitions from France. Paine involved himself hotly in that controversy. He joined the side of Samuel Adams, who attacked Deane in traditional republican language as a corrupt and avaricious merchant who was undermining civic virtue at a time of public crisis.

Paine's alignment with Adams and other defenders of a "Christian cooperative commonwealth," against the corruption of "monopolists" profiting hugely from public contracts while their fellow citizens suffered privation and death, embodied the Old Whig republicanism that was the common heritage of the whole Revolutionary generation.[12] His reaction to the Philadelphia artisans' demands that the economic chaos be brought under public control was also consistent with that political culture. In May Paine joined other Philadelphia leaders previously active in the struggle for independence in setting up a City Committee of Trade. This Committee had no official legal standing but relied on widespread citizen support and compliance to carry out its decisions. In this the price-control movement was simply continuing the extremely successful pattern, developed during the independence movement, of organizing the moral power of the community outside formal governmental channels. Similar committees had gradually taken over control of affairs from Royal and Loyalist officials in many parts of the colonies a few years previously. And, as previously, the popular militia, often also involved in the committees, stood ready to give teeth to the new committee's acts.[13] The committee movement embodied popular civic spirit in practice, and one of its dramatic effects had been a much wider inclusion of artisan groups in Philadelphia politics than had been the case before the Revolution.

As few merchants joined the new City Committee, the price-control movement for the first time divided artisans and merchants. Paine found himself the opponent of Robert Morris. That summer the price-control movement spread to other Pennsylvania towns and then to other states as well. In Albany two merchants convicted by the local committee of overcharging for the controlled staple, rum, were forced to confess their crimes publicly. Merchants' spokesmen such as Pelatiah Webster protested:

Freedom of trade, or unrestrained liberty of the subject to hold or dispose of his property as he pleases is absolutely necessary to the prosperity of every community. . . . Gain is the soul of industry. . . . It is a sad omen to

12. See Bailyn, *American Revolution*, and Wood, *Creation of the American Republic*, as well as Maier, *From Resistance to Revolution*.
13. Paul Ryerson has provided an in-depth look at the committee movement in revolutionary Philadelphia in his *The Revolution Is Now Beginning: The Radical Committees of Philadelphia, 1765-1776* (Philadelphia: University of Pennsylvania Press, 1978).

find among the first effects of independence, greater restraints and abridge-
ments of natural liberty, than ever we felt under the government we have
lately renounced and shaken off.[14]

To which the Philadelphia Committee shot back, invoking the
conceptions of citizenship, commonweal, and justice central to the
civic tradition:

The social compact or state of civil society, by which men are united and
incorporated, requires that every right or power claimed or exercised by
any man or set of men should be in subordination to the common good,
and that whatever is incompatible therewith, must, by some rule or regulation be brought into subjection thereto. . . . If the freedom of trade is to
be [absolute] then must all and every species of engrossing be sanctioned
thereby, because [the merchants'] idea of a free trade is for every man to do
what he pleases; a right which . . . is repugnant to the very principles on
which society and civil government are founded.[15]

The idea of free trade was not altogether new to American thinking
at that time, but this polarization of economic individualism as a
moral system independent of, even opposed to, the notion of civic
community was new. In Paine's *Common Sense* (1775) the civi-
lizing effects of commerce were contrasted with the arbitrariness of
royal government, but at that time he saw commerce as a servant
of the commonwealth. In 1779 his support of the Committee suggests that he still saw the classical moral ideal of the common
good as overriding the rights of property.

Through the summer of 1779 the conflict wore on, but the price
controls did not relieve the plight of Philadelphia's citizens. Farmers sold produce elsewhere or in unregulated markets. The city's
merchants withheld imported goods against a rise in prices. Scar-
cities continued and inflation raged on. Short of releasing full-
scale internal economic warfare, the committee could do little to
control these events. During the midst of the Continental struggle
against Britain, Paine and other Committee leaders felt impelled
to urge popular restraints, while assailing and threatening merchants suspected of hoarding. Crowd actions more than once
turned violent as the summer gave way to harvest time. The climax
came in a bloody attack in October by a militia group on the

14. Quoted by Eric Foner in his *Tom Paine and Revolutionary America* (New
York: Oxford University Press, 1976), p. 170.
15. Ibid., pp. 169-70.

house of James Wilson, merchant and outspoken opponent of the Committee. The "Fort Wilson Riot" ended bitterly, though with little actual bloodshed. Significantly, Paine and other artisan leaders did not support the crowd action. It was evident to them that municipal action alone could not control economic events that were clearly Continental, even international, in scope. Efforts to institute a Continental control network of committees never got beyond an ineffectual convention early the next year. Finally, in March 1980 the Congress enacted Robert Morris's counterplan to deal with the inflationary crisis through currency devaluation. The effort to apply traditional remedies to the new war-fueled American economy had collapsed.

By March 1780 Tom Paine emerged as an advocate of Morris's devaluation plan and against any further attempts at direct control of markets. Paine, like many other Patriots, now saw the expansion of Continental commerce as a mainstay of republican government. He joined Morris in promoting a national bank through which to link the commercial groups newly grown powerful more tightly to the national government. Paine was later to write that "in all my publications . . . I have been an advocate for commerce."[16] That was true. Implicit in *Common Sense* was the notion that a commercial society, once free of despotic royal controls, would grow toward a naturally harmonious and bountiful future. Paine thus complemented Adam Smith's defense of an economic order "emancipated" from governmental and social control in the very year Smith published his *Wealth of Nations*. What is remarkable is that Paine in 1779 did not see that his own view of "natural" society as founded on property and exchange was at variance with the traditional conception of republicanism he also espoused. However, once Paine became convinced of the political impossibility of asserting public control over the economy—without, that is, further splintering the divided Patriot cause—he drew the conclusion that a firm foundation for liberty had to be built on the basis of property and free trade.

That conclusion brought the great radical of the Revolution into temporary alliance with Morris and other future Federalists. Men such as Alexander Hamilton saw the dawn of the American republic as closely connected with the emancipation of commercial

16. Quoted by Foner, *Tom Paine*, p. 160.

relations from their traditional subordination to social and political order. The unique quality of American political language, embracing both individualism and the civil covenant, stems from the historical experience and reflection of the revolutionary generation. The American republic came into being just as the notion of the free-enterprise economy was reaching maturity as a moral and political ideal in its own right, and the ideas of Locke and Adam Smith came readily to hand to explain developments that the older republican language of virtue and corruption apparently could not encompass.

The key transition in understanding begun by Hobbes and Locke about a century earlier reached theoretical completion and popular acceptance in the final decades of the eighteenth century. In fact, the revolutionary experience had the ironic effect of "modernizing" the Americans. It rushed them into new worlds of economic expansionism and the centralized state even as they struggled, in the terms of their political understanding, against the very corruption of which "empire" and "commerce" were the archetypes. The Americans' civic republicanism had been transmitted to them through the Country Party in Britain, a lineage descending from the English Radical Whigs of the seventeenth century. The Country opposition to the Court linkage between commerce and imperial expansion provided the American Patriots with their highly charged images of both tyranny and corruption. the Old Whig tradition unanimously condemned the pursuit of "interests" (canonized by Hobbes, who was after all a Court theorist, as the sole forces of politics) in classical terms as releasing "a chaos of appetites productive of dependence and loss of personal autonomy."[17]

But Old Whig theory and American revolutionary republicanism were already on the defensive against the ruthless new forces of the centralized administrative state and the pursuit of economic gain in commerce. All this the republicans struggled to understand in moral terms. The great intellectual jump of early modern liberalism was precisely to abandon the moral interpretation in favor of a new one which conceived of the polity no longer as a differentiated community but as a mechanism, a collection of instruments for advancing interests.

---

17. J.G.A. Pocock, *The Machiavellian Moment: Florentine Political Thought and the Atlantic Republican Tradition* (Princeton, New Jersey: Princeton University Press, 1975), p. 486. Pocock's full discussion is enlightening.

Since Paine had arrived in America only in 1774, it is not improbable that his republicanism was in this sense already unorthodox, halfway "advanced" toward the Federalist rejection of traditional civic virtue. Still, by 1779 the earlier hope that civic virtue would triumph in the new nation had dissipated. And if the corruption of commerce might only be controlled, not cured, what then? Paine and others sought, and indeed thought they had found, a new basis for a self-governing polity. Civic republicans had conceived of politics as a relation of individuals sharing a common moral order, embodied in certain authoritative and participatory institutions. The pre-revolutionary committees and crowd activities embodied this philosophy well.

In the new conception, the order of "government," as they came to call it, was distinct from the other and especially from the economic relations of the society. Government was a purely instrumental realm, entered into for the express purpose of advancing or defending the pursuit of interests in those other, private spheres of life.[18] Tome Paine had already exposed the skeleton of these ideas in *Common Sense*, where he wrote that "Society is produced by our wants, and government by our wickedness. . . . Society is in every state a blessing, but government, even in its best state, but a necessary evil."[19] If we recall the classical assertion that man outside the self-governing association of a political community could not be a fully rational or sharing creature, the vast change in conception is immediately visible.

Contrasting this passage from *Common Sense* with the Philadelphia Committee document of 1779 quoted earlier, it is clear that we are moving between different realms of discourse. The Committee explicitly defines the common good as the sovereign value and aim of society from which all particular rights and powers derive. Economic interests justly persist as long as they do not become "incompatible" with the common good. Trade cannot, therefore, be an absolute right, for that would mean every man doing what he pleases, "a right which . . . is repugnant to the very principles on which society and civil government are founded." What is significant here is that the Committee is implicitly denying the Lockean doctrine that human rights are founded on an absolute

---

18. See Wood, *Creation of the American Republic*, especially pp. 500-506.

19. Philip S. Foner, ed., *The Complete Writings of Thomas Paine* (2 vols., New York: Citadel Press, 1945), I, pp. 4-5.

claim to the fruits of one's labor. Instead, the Committee recalls the earlier teaching that the institution of private property is only a means to the higher end of civic community. The individual derives his dignity from his claim to share in the good life rather than from a claim to the fruits of his labor wrested from nature.[20] Though Paine supported the Committee's actions, his must have been a complicated loyalty. His own language and thought is at points closer to that of the merchants' spokesman, Pelatiah Webster, than to the Committee's.

The Federalist resolution of this contradiction between the interest politics of an economic society and the civic politics of the Radical Whig tradition was their idea of a republic capable of indefinite expansion. The Constitution of 1787 embodied a novel compromise between the two social and political visions. The idea of commerce was tied by the tradition to empire and so to corruption and loss of virtuous citizenship. The Federalists were able to change this perception by substituting the view of society as a homogeneous system of exchange relationships for traditional notions of society as a corporate body.

Long before the 1780s, the commercial fluidity of American social life, particularly outside New England, had been given cultural form in early liberalism. This was a conception of life which recognized the public realm as purely instrumental and sought deeper satisfaction in the domestic and private scene.[21] The Federalists institutionalized this culture of privatism by erecting their elaborate system of governmental institutions in abstraction from any particular arrangement of social elements. That was an historical novelty. Unlike Britain's famed Mixed Constitution, the American system recognized no qualitatively different social orders, no permanent social relationships. It enabled new elements to emerge into the political arena from the dynamic whirlpool of a utilitarian capitalist economy. The extraordinary achievement of the new

20. This is a central point, to be developed at more length later. See Louis Dumont, *From Mandeville to Marx: The Genesis and Triumph of Economic Ideology* (Chicago: University of Chicago Press, 1977), especially pp. 49-51.

21. Sam Bass Warner has given a perceptive and concrete portrayal of the meaning of this pervasive privatism in his study of its effects on the development of American urban life after Paine's crisis of 1779. See Sam Bass Warner, *The Private City: Philadelphia in Three Periods of Its Growth* (Philadelphia: University of Pennsylvania Press, 1969), esp. pp. 23-45.

Federalism was the creation of an instrumental structure at once stable and expansive. The key to the success of the system seemed to be the very lack of a unifying public purpose in American political life.[22]

Yet, even at the time of the nation's founding Alexander Hamilton explicitly questioned James Madison's benign vision of the republic as a peaceful balance of interests. Commerce, Hamilton argued, meant empire; that is, commerce creates specialization and division of labor and, with that subordination, a pattern that is necessarily repeated on the level of international affairs in the form of military competition.[23] There was thus, in the long run, a contradictory relationship between republicanism and commerce. From the present point of vantage, Hamilton's iron logic seems only too well confirmed. This era of physical limits, complex, international division of labor, the continuance of poverty amid wealth, and international competition has proven to be Hamiltonian rather than Madisonian. And that overwhelming fact raises the question as to whether the optimistic liberalism of the Federalists is still useful and appropriate for the preservation of republican liberty, whatever might be said for their mutual relationship in the past.

In fact, the era prior to the Civil War, long celebrated as days of America's democratic innocence, was characterized by a tense if still viable compromise between "republic" and commercial "empire."

Thomas Jefferson, like traditional republicans, viewed with deep mistrust the new economic and social developments that attended the coming of commercial capitalism. His famous attacks on commerce and cities in his *Notes concerning the State of Virginia* summed up that position, one which would animate American radical democrats for another hundred years.[24] Their problem, like Paine's in 1779, was that the capitalist pattern of exchange seemed both pervasive in the new nation and generally benign in

---

22. See Benjamin Barber's critical essay, "The Compromised Republic," in Robert H. Horwitz, ed., *Moral Foundations of the American Republic* (Charlottesville: University of Virginia Press, 1976), pp. 19-38.

23. See Stourzh, *Hamilton*, esp. the first chapter.

24. See the discussion of Jefferson's "Query XIX" from his *Notes on the State of Virginia*, in Leo Marx, *The Machine in the Garden: Technology and the Pastoral Ideal in America* (New York: Oxford University Press, 1964), pp. 116-44, esp. pp. 124-25.

its effects. In *The Rights of Man,* published in Britain during the 1790s, Paine advocated a massive system of government welfare measures, public works, and control of the society, but neither he nor the Jeffersonians saw a need for such measures in America.[25] A largely agrarian capitalism, provided Western expansion remained possible, seemed to the Republicans a viable basis for civic life.

Jeffersonian democracy was thus a compromise program that tried to provide one key requirement for civic culture: basic dignity for all citizens would be guaranteed by their freehold of a productive farm. However, the compromise was hobbled from the start. There was the fundamental contradiction of slavery, which threatened the freehold system and produced intense regional conflicts during the period after Jackson. There was the planned clearance and destruction of the Native Americans. Touring the United States during the Jackson administration, Alexis de Tocqueville saw these as fundamental flaws in the nation's republican structure. To them must be added the fact that the freehold system was tied to a national market in which large-scale industry and credit would inevitably develop, though in an age before Marx this fact was not so obvious.

The democratic ideal of the nineteenth century was collective to the degree that it saw justice as demanding conscious promotion of the economic basis of the agrarian yeomanry. That meant collective action to regulate the operations of the national and local economy so that large-scale speculation and monopoly did not corrupt republic into empire. Here the spirit of the Revolutionary committees remained alive, and Tocqueville was struck by the vitality and ubiquity of this collective participation, especially in the intense life of voluntary associations. However, Tocqueville also saw the precarious quality of the moral balance that Jeffersonian republicanism was trying to sustain. The balance between civic community and economic individualism was and must be exceedingly precarious, because it is based upon fundamental opposition, an opposition of two divergent social and moral visions of life.

Tocqueville's assessment of the long-term success of republican life in the United States was cautious. He had imbibed republican ideals from reading Montesquieu and Rousseau, and he could not

25. See Eric Foner, *Tom Paine,* pp. 220-33.

celebrate the new capitalist social order even in the manner of Montesquieu's praise of England as a "commercial republic," for Rousseau's pessimistic conclusion that modern civil society was incompatible with civic virtue had made a strong impact on Tocqueville. Yet, the new social and economic order of liberal capitalism appeared to him an historical inevitability. With it came, he clearly saw, the new moral order of individual self-interest, which he labeled "equality." This great process of historical change, apparently irresistible, filled Tocqueville with what he described as "religious dread." And he knew from the experiences of his own aristocratic family and his active political involvements the ironic and contradictory results of the French revolutionaries' great efforts to impose an order of civic virtue on a society morally splintered by despotism. Tocqueville shared with Paine and Jefferson the conviction that the great task was "to educate democracy; to put if possible, new life into its beliefs; to purify its mores; to control its actions; gradually to substitute understanding of statecraft for present inexperience and knowledge of its true interests for blind instincts."[26] The chief means to this end Tocqueville saw as the ongoing life of public spirit and participation. In this he was at one with Paine and Jefferson and, indeed, with the entire civic republican tradition.[27]

Tocqueville, writing in the 1830s, was thus not as optimistic as the Americans of the founding generation about the chances that civic association would contain and "purify" the social dynamics of liberal capitalism. Indeed, Tocqueville saw that the preservation of liberty—understood in Montesquieu's sense, as security of person and property[28]—was threatened by the onward sweep of equality of condition fostered by small-scale capitalism. Utilitarian capitalism as an ethic and way of life was not, for Tocqueville, a likely basis even for the liberal value of liberty, a point at which he separated himself from his master Montesquieu. Liberty and equality are opposed and in tension, Tocqueville argued, and economic self-interest will overwhelm liberty unless it is tempered by civic association. Even the values of a liberal regime require a measure

26. Alexis de Tocqueville, *Democracy*, "Author's Introduction," p. 12.

27. See Hannah Arendt's vigorous reassertion of this theme in the concluding chapter of her *On Revolution* (New York: Viking Press, 1963).

28. See Baron de Montesquieu, *Spirit of the Laws*, I.2, p. 4, and XII.2, p. 183. This notion of liberty as security is liberal in origin, deriving from John Locke.

of civic virtue for their survival: hence the crucial importance of civic participation.

The relative equality of condition typical of the United States at that time stood in strong contrast to the European systems of hierarchical order, which Tocqueville refers to as "aristocratic societies." In those nations, preeminently traditional, men and women were bound tightly together in customary relations of dependency, so that there was little perception of society as a whole but there was an intricate understanding of particular relations within it. The moral norms differed qualitatively for nobles and commons, yet to each they said: maintain and fulfill the duties of your station.

The novelty of the new democratic order was its dramatic enlargement of social reference points. Now the citizen was told to pursue whatever he could; each was to have the same chance as the next fellow. And with the collapse of qualitative differences among types of persons came a radical alteration in the sense of what was worth pursuing. The central value for the new society became the pursuit of wealth, which meant, particularly in America, a sense of material well-being. This revolutionized the forms of social striving and their motivation. Instead of the competition for status typical of aristocratic "honor," a competition restricted to the few, the new society opened out a general and untrammeled competition for wealth, so that poverty became a sign of sloth, not of misfortune. But while the old aristocratic competition for prestige had been checked by the noblesse oblige attaching to status, the new egalitarian spirit of enterprise in itself turned citizens toward the private rather than the public realm.

It was there that Tocqueville saw the incipient danger to liberty, even the specter of despotism:

As social equality spreads there are more and more people who, though neither rich nor powerful enough to have much hold over others, have gained or kept enough wealth and enough understanding to look after their own needs. Such folk owe no man anything and hardly expect anything from anybody. They form the habit of thinking of themselves in isolation and imagine that their whole destiny is in their own hands. . . . Each man is forever thrown back on himself alone, and there is danger that he may be shut up in the solitude of his own heart.[29]

---

29. Tocqueville, *Democracy*, II, ch. 3, p. 508.

This picture is the now familiar one of the atomized mass society. Such isolated citizens, Tocqueville observed, are both self-interested and threatened in a society they cannot influence and scarcely understand. They come to depend on anonymous "public opinion" for their ideas, and they drift in a curious way toward the condition of subjects of despotic regimes. So long as their desires for comfort are satisfied, the price others must pay for these things—how the society comes to provide them—is a matter of small consequence.

> Each one of them, withdrawn into himself, is almost unaware of the fate of the rest. Mankind, for him, consists in his children and his personal friends. As for the rest of his fellow citizens, they are near enough, but he does not notice them. He touches them but feels nothing. He exists in and for himself, and though he still may have a family, one can at least say that he has not got a fatherland.[30]

Resembling the subjects of a despotism, except that these are well-fed, such citizens become like "tenants" or casual laborers, indifferent to where they dwell. Servility is balanced only by individual license and rage.[31] Such citizens have lost their republic. Through manipulated public opinion and bribes, a would-be despot would have little difficulty in imposing his yoke.

The only possible counterbalance to this deadly process, the one hope for even individual civil liberty, is a vigorous civic life. Tocqueville did not envision an American Rome or even an American Athens. What he hoped for and thought he saw signs of was a more modest public spirit which, like Jefferson's and Paine's, could keep off despotic encroachment by would-be tyrants. He saw in the highly decentralized American government a great asset in this endeavor.

Tocqueville glimpsed the possibilities for "an industrial aristocracy" in the new mill town of Pittsburgh, but his America did not have powerful coordinating institutions on a national scale beyond the modest and unobtrusive federal government. Without a highly centralized bureaucracy, national news media, or massive concentrations of private wealth, he could realistically hope that participation in local government, juries, and civic organizations

---

30. Ibid., II, IV, ch. 6, pp. 692-93.
31. See ibid., I, ch.5, pp. 93-94; also I, I, ch. 2, p. 47.

could expand and educate the character of privately engaged small proprietors in an expanding nation.

American religion, which Tocqueville saw as universally shared, unquestioned Christianity of a Protestant cast, he expected to be a powerful ally of civic life. Not because American religion promoted a powerful civic vision—on the contrary, American religion was oriented almost exclusively to private morality and matters of the heart. But it taught a moral restraint to self-interest and encouraged compassion and trust in one's neighbor. It performed a vital civic role without being explicitly involved in political life. Religion, as Tocqueville summarized, was considered as the guardian of mores, and mores were regarded as the guarantee of the laws and pledge for the maintenance of freedom itself. Again, the point is the same. In the social conditions of a fluid, dynamic capitalist society without a centralized state, despotism might be kept at bay and an order of liberty flourish, provided a measure of civic virtue could be maintained. That task would fall partly to religion as educator of private virtue, as a support for public participation both within and without formal government, but the brunt of the task had to be sustained by active civic life.

Conceptually, Tocqueville thus advanced a new version of the republican argument for the intrinsic good of active citizenship. The liberal would warn us against the totalitarian dangers of republican virtue—"positive freedom," as Isaiah Berlin called it in his famous argument to this effect. Tocqueville could counter by showing that in a competitive, individualistic society the only reliable support for the "negative freedom" of personal liberty and security from interference is, paradoxically, a measure of "positive freedom."[32] Only an actively associated people can maintain free institutions. To the Conservative who fears the dangers of "mass democracy," Tocqueville's argument is to agree that modern market societies generate mass conditions through their competitive dynamic, but that the only alternative to despotism is genuine public participation.

America was indeed the first "new nation" to Tocqueville. Its predominant ethos he saw as egalitarian and commercial, by which he meant something very close to liberal utilitarian. If his prog-

---

32. See Isaiah Berlin, "Two Concepts of Liberty" [1958], in *Four Essays on Liberty* (London: Oxford University Press, 1969).

nosis for the nation was guardedly pessimistic (or cautiously optimistic), this was because of the tremendous difficulty he saw in
finding a social and moral basis for civic life in the capitalist type
of society. In the end, Tocqueville probably accepted the liberal
view that man was "naturally" self-interested. And that meant
that while he could see the reality of civic culture in American
mores and felt impelled to argue for its value, his Rousseauan
understanding made it difficult for him to conceive of civic virtue
as triumphing in an interest-driven society.[33] Thus arose the pessimism that hangs over so much of Tocqueville's work. His contribution to a contemporary public philosophy is complex—at
once suggestive and cautionary. The same can be said for the
experience of nineteenth-century American democracy.

33. Tocqueville's pessimism was much greater regarding chances for free institutions in France. This was based on his analysis of French society as so deeply
atomized by the despotism of the Old Regime that civic cooperation was simply
impossible. See Tocqueville's *The Old Regime and the French Revolution*, translated by Stuart Gilbert (Garden City, New York: Doubleday Anchor, 1955). France
after 1789 continually split into ferocious struggles among competing class and
ideological interest parties, quite unlike the social and economic "consensus"
Tocqueville saw established in the United States after Jefferson's presidency. He
noted, however, the great threat the slave system posed to American civil tranquil-
lity. See his *Reflections*, edited by J. P. Mayer and A. P. Kerr (Garden City, New York:
Doubleday Anchor, 1971). They are especially enlightening because they were not
intended for publication and therefore include discussions of his participation in the
revolution of 1848.
   But see Robert H. Wiebe, *The Segmented Society: An Historical Search for the
Meaning of America* (New York: Oxford University Press, 1975).

SEVEN

Toward a Public Philosophy:
Articulating a Democratic Economy

:: I

A public philosophy develops out of the insight that the quality
of personal life is grounded in social relationships, an insight that
is embodied in the political art of integrating the various kinds of
self-concern into an awareness of mutual interdependency. Despite
its discontinuous development, the civic republican tradition has
been a major vehicle through which this insight has been transmitted in American experience, and it may once again provide a
new articulation of the understanding underlying a self-governing
society, as the antagonism of self-interest, fed by inequity, pushes
a badly shredded civility to the breaking point.[1] Our best hope for
an alternative to authoritarian tyranny is to develop an awareness
of our interdependency out of which to forge the movements and
institutions which can give new political and social form to our
sense of common concern. Public philosophy, like a meaningful
public life, must be a continuing process of reappropriation and
experiment, of reinvigorating the tradition by creating anew.

Americans of the revolutionary, founding generation were able
to envision a public life, however imperfectly, within economic and

---

1. Public philosophy in this sense is more than the vector-sum of contests
among competing interests. To this extent Walter Lippmann's famous formulation of a public philosophy as a "code of civility" that transcends human choice is
correct: see Walter Lippmann, *The Public Philosophy* (Boston: Little, Brown,
1955). However, serious reflection upon the historically rooted nature of all cultural forms makes a univocal articulation of this "code" dubious.

social conditions that did not seem completely antagonistic to their hopes. They consciously sought, and found, religious and cultural traditions that could buttress and reinforce the social and moral bases of a self-governing society. They feared excessive wealth, excessive poverty, and lack of independence in one's occupation. They thought self-employment to be the best guarantee of the sturdy virtues of citizenship that would then lead to civic cooperation in the local community, particularly when nurtured by the religious and moral ideal of the covenant. These conditions, described so well by Alexis de Tocqueville, persisted throughout much of the nineteenth century.

Our present situation, with its massive concentrations of economic power, great inequality of wealth, and the near-disappearance of the self-employed farmer, merchant, and artisan, seems so far from the social conditions of early republican America as to have no connection with it. But if the guiding purpose of republican society is to create citizens who can then cooperate to produce a democratic culture, it is both realistic and vital to consider how we may gain the same ends under the conditions of the present world political economy.

A renewed citizenship must build upon our still-living traditions of voluntarism and cooperation wherever they may be found, but it cannot take the older forms and resources for granted. Contemporary citizenship requires at once a moral culture and an institutional basis appropriate to the interdependent, occupationally segmented national society we have come to be. And because professionalism and occupational identification have become so crucial to contemporary society and personal identity, a renewed civic culture must be institutionalized in the workplace as well as in the community at large if it is powerfully to influence public mores. Indeed, it is clear that if we are to recover the social and personal commitment to free institutions that is the lifeblood of a democratic society, we must bring a public and democratic ethos into the sphere of economic life. To view economic institutions as private perhaps made sense when most Americans spent their lives on family farms or in family firms, but today, when most American men and a rapidly increasing proportion of American women spend much of their lives in large economic structures that are for most purposes public—except that the profits they make go to an impersonal collection of institutional and individual private stockholders—it becomes imperative to bring the forms of citizenship and of civic association into a more central position in the economic sphere.

The theme of a reconstructed republican spirit must be to subordinate the flows of economic capital, now overwhelmingly collective in their generation, to a process of disposition more equitable and effectively democratic than the present American political economy. Democratizing and realigning economic relationships at national as well as regional levels according to a civic conception of justice means aggressively developing alternatives to the dominance of private capital over public life. Such a transformation, requiring nothing less than a renegotiation of the public covenant against powerful particular interests, will be the long-term test of the viability of the republic. Yet, though immensely difficult, this project also opens the heartening possibility of transforming the nation's international stance toward a more republican sense of equity.

However, if the ethos and mores remain heavily individualistic and competitive, then Americans will continue to define the goals of economic organization in essentially private terms. Conceiving of economic justice as a mere balance of self-interests has often focused reform efforts on obtaining for disavantaged groups greater relative advantage within an inequitable system; certainly, that has been better than nothing. But, as many contemporary analysts warn, American hegemony in international politics and trade, the economic and technological cornucopia which has been the premise of that method of accommodation, is rapidly running dry.[2] In these conditions, the option of a genuinely cooperative economic democracy becomes a particularly unlikely choice from the basis of self-interested calculation. Thus the interrelation between public institutions and mores has today become particularly salient, which is why Tocqueville's analysis retains its importance.

2. See Lester C. Thurow, *The Zero-Sum Society: Distribution and the Possibilities for Economic Change* (New York: Basic Books, 1980). Thurow notes the high concentration of wealth in the top quintile of the population: the top quintile by *wealth* owns 80 percent of all assets, while these households receive just 44 percent of the national income. In other words, inequality of ownership—and thus control of resources—is far sharper than the more widely discussed inequality of income distribution, despite the alleged "leveling" tendencies of the welfare state (see pp. 167-68).

Our contemporary situation highlights the relevance to both national and international affairs of a civic republican politics that insists on the primacy of interdependency over self-interest. If one key blockage to revitalizing public life is the privatism so deeply embedded in liberal culture, then no new democratic advance and, probably, no more equitable international order will be possible without widespread expansion of public understanding, not only in the cognitive but in the full practical sense of understanding. Therein lies the importance of renewed civic practice as well as public philosophy.

:: II

To address the problem of the relation of private interests to collective responsibility is to arrive at the central tension in the American moral order. As an acute analyst from the republican tradition Tocqueville is again a highly instructive guide. He summed up that focal point of controversy in the American moral order in the concept of individualism. Unlike egoism, which had choked social life for millennia, individualism was "a calm and considered feeling" rather than a mere passion, but one based no less upon a "misguided judgment" about the true relation of the individual to society.[3] Egoism flourished in aristocratic ages, to be sure, but then the social hierarchy bound each individual, as a member of a status group, to those above it by deference, "someone whose protection he needs," and to those below, "someone whose help he may require." Thus, each status group, or estate, "being clearly and permanently limited, forms, in a sense, a little fatherland for all its members, to which they are attached by more obvious and more precious ties than those linking them to the fatherland itself."[4] But it would be a huge mistake to read these last statements as contrasts between the American egalitarian order and the Old Regime. The Old Regime was a despotism, Tocqueville tells us, destroying all forms of social solidarity for the purpose of greater centralized control. The effect of centuries of tight-

---

3. Alexis de Tocqueville, *Democracy in America*, translated by George Lawrence (Garden City, New York: Doubleday Anchor, 1969), vol. II, pt. II, ch. 1, pp. 505-6.
4. Ibid., II, II, ch. 2, p. 507.

ening royal absolutism was to force each small group in French society into competition for royal favor, perpetuating what Tocqueville called a "group individualism" that prepared the practical climate in which individualism as a moral conviction could find acceptance.[5]

Thus centralized political power produced a moral situation curiously similar to the competitive individualism of liberal capitalism. Recalling that Hobbes both first postulated self-interest as the basic human motive and was a supporter of Court versus Country interests in England, this conclusion is not surprising. Tocqueville presents the collapse of the Old Regime in France as the result of a long-term process of atomization, an isolation of citizens from their fellows so effective that revolutionary efforts to generate a new republican solidarity and civil liberty seemed doomed to result in more centralized despotism. The destruction of the French monarchy was the inevitable consequence of the monarchy's too successful policy of severing the hierarchical links of reciprocal duties which constituted the traditional social order: "Though the nation came to seem a homogeneous whole, its parts no longer held together. Nothing had been left that could obstruct the central government, but by the same token, nothing could shore it up."[6] Tocqueville's anxiety for modern society was that the individualism engendered by the market, if unchecked by the cohesive power of civic association, would reproduce the social and cultural conditions of an atomized despotism. That situation would then cry out for centralized control to prevent the war of all against all which it resembles.

The incompatibility Tocqueville saw between equality of conditions and political liberty is, then, not quite what it first appears to be. Taken together, Tocqueville's studies of France and America reveal a more encompassing understanding than that shown by those who would use Tocqueville simply to warn us against the alleged dangers of social and economic leveling.[7] First of all, what is it that threatens liberty, that is, civil rights and personal security, in modern societies? Tocqueville's formulation of the answer as

5. Tocqueville, *The Old Regime and the French Revolution,* translated by Stuart Gilbert (Garden City, New York: Doubleday Anchor, 1955), p. 96.

6. Ibid., p. 137.

7. For example, see Robert Nisbet's discussion of Tocqueville in *The Twilight of Authority* (New York: Basic Books, 1975).

the unitary concept of "equality of conditions" is equivocal. Surely the threat to liberty does not stem from mores which urge treatment of all citizens with equal dignity and respect. That sense of equality is both the great positive value of the liberal tradition and the tradition's legacy from civic political philosophy. The difficulty with liberalism is that it provides no coherent support, theoretically or practically, for that moral ideal.

The destructive aspect of Tocqueville's "equality of conditions" is just the opposite. As he sees it, equality dissolves the moral bonds of superior and inferior which traditionally oriented and restrained social relations. The result is a utilitarian stance of each citizen toward the other. They do not and cannot trust each other, because they understand themselves as self-interested individuals, so each must envy and secretly regard the other watchfully, eager for the chance to go one better than his neighbor. In such a situation, the mutual care from which civic culture grows is truncated and suffocated. The impersonal mechanism of the market is, for such decayed citizens, preferable to common deliberation about their common welfare, and so too is the administration of a bureaucratic despotism.

What stands revealed here is the compatibility of individualism's utilitarian moral outlook with the centralized structures of power that dominate modern American society. The modern business corporation, which grew up after the Civil War, drastically altered Tocqueville's America. It is internally much like Montesquieu's aristocratic type of society, with its internal competition for status and wealth. And these concentrated structures of economic power in fact promote a vigorous individualism while generating a steeply graded inequality of condition.

The strongest manifestations of American civic ideals since Tocqueville's time have often been Jeffersonian in inspiration. With the Populists as perhaps the most remarkable case, the reforming movements in America have usually seen egalitarianism as wedded to civic republican forms of association.[8]

Yet, the American future was to be Hamiltonian in character. Americans first encountered enveloping centralized power in the

8. See Lawrence Goodwyn's discussion of interrelations between Jeffersonian impulses and European ideals of socialism and cooperation, especially the links between the Knights of Labor and the Farmers' Alliance in *Democratic Promise: The Populist Movement in America* (New York: Oxford University Press, 1976).

Civil War governments, both North and South, and during the Gilded Age at last fell under its thumb. It came not so much directly as state power as through the vast new trusts and corporations which have, though against recurrent revolts and opposition, established a largely effective dominance over national life. All this was accomplished by utilizing competitive self-interest, but it was not the work of overzealous Jeffersonian democrats. The crisis of American civic culture has been generated far less by rampant democracy than by the atomization that accompanied the erection of private economic tyrannies.

As Tocqueville saw, the chief threat to freedom within the liberal order comes from the constricted moral culture of individualism. But it does not arise from egalitarianism in any global sense. Tocqueville himself knew that maintenance of private liberty depends on active citizenship and that in turn upon public virtue, a shared moral order. That order, the civic tradition teaches with nearly one voice, demands and expresses an egalitarian ideal, an equal concern and respect among citizens. The corrupting force is utilitarian individualism, but that has no necessary connection with equality in the civic sense. On the contrary, utilitarian social forms, in particular the market, generate moral and psychological pressures in a directly anti-egalitarian direction.

The self-interested individualism of liberal capitalism which Tocqueville saw in America has subterranean linkages to the individualism he observed with horror in France. Both undermine civil liberties because both destroy the basis of liberty, a sense of the dignity of persons. Personal dignity is possible only within a community whose laws and institutions encourage its members to treat each other with concern and respect. And that requires a real sense of the equal dignity of persons. Finally, all this depends upon the character and disposition of these citizens, that is, upon their virtue. Civic association in mutual trust is the absolutely necessary condition for the dignity of individual or group and the destructive aspect of self-interested individualism is that it undermines the sustaining web of civic trust.

But the culprit is not equality of conditions. On the contrary, it is the lack of a vital moral culture of equal dignity and respect. As John Stuart Mill observed about Tocqueville's *Democracy*: "Nearly all these moral and social influences [that contribute to self-interested individualism] are shown to be in full operation in aristocratic England."[9] The crucial factor, Mill went on to say, was the spread of commercial capitalism and its attendant values.

Tocqueville confusingly conflated equality with self-interested individualism because the two seemed to emerge together with the rise of liberal society, and he looked upon both phenomena as inescapable results of vast historical forces beyond human control. By doing this he failed to see the crucial distinction between the two senses of equality within liberalism itself, and so came dangerously close to targeting all the egalitarian sentiments of democracy as the great enemies of freedom and dignity. What Tocqueville in fact saw as missing in the France of the Old Regime and threatened in commercial America was a moral order that could support individual dignity.

The tradition of civic philosophy answers the question of how to respond to the challenge of competitive individualism with the vision of a political life that begins not with self-interest but with the moral culture of justice, dignity, and fellowship. The value the individual has in the civic vision receives a ghostly restatement in the liberal doctrine of equal rights, but the civic conception emphasizes that such a moral order is only possible through a life that enables individuals to know themselves in regard to the social interdependence in which they live and to respond actively to and share in shaping that wider community. That kind of moral understanding is the basis of civic virtue, and such a life is the civic meaning of politics. The preservation of liberty, which is the preservation of individualism in its positive meaning of personal dignity, thus turns on the preservation of public life, and that is necessarily a cooperative work.

In Tocqueville's vision, as in the thinking of many liberals as well, there is often a running together of two very different, even opposed, meanings of individualism. Tocqueville was certainly right to see that individualism and equality go hand-in-hand. Again Rousseau is the thinker who drew the distinction most sharply: the bourgeois and the citizen, the self-interested and the altruistic, the Economic and Civic Man of the tradition. Tocqueville himself is part of an important lineage of French thought on these questions that stretches from Montesquieu and Rousseau to

---

9. John Stuart Mill, *Essays on Politics and Culture*, edited by Gertrude Himmelstein (Garden City, New York: Doubleday Anchor, 1963), p. 262.

Emile Durkheim. For Durkheim both sociology and socialism became vehicles for articulating the central republican theme: that persons become fully human, individuals in a true sense, only as citizens.

Perhaps more clearly than Tocqueville, Durkheim saw the moral threat to individual dignity posed by competitive individualism. Durkheim's answer was a conception of republican politics as the representative expression of all aspects of a society, but a society whose moral center was the dignity and worth of the individual person. It seems fair to see Tocqueville as struggling toward such a vision. What made the articulation very difficult for Tocqueville, as indeed for such American thinkers as Jefferson and Lincoln, was the ambiguity of the meanings of *equality* and *the individual.* Influenced as he was by the assumptions of the liberal theory of man, Tocqueville—like J.S. Mill, with whom he shared so much— had difficulty in conceiving of a meaning of individualism that was not naturally self-interested and an equality that did not derive from *ressentiment.* Thus his search for the democratic equivalents of civic virtue ended in a combination of restraint fostered by an unquestioned religious authority and the education of self-interest "rightly understood."

Yet, Tocqueville's insight was profound. By focusing on the relation of self-interested individualism to the moral ideal of personal worth as a social and political problem, he was deeply faithful to the civic tradition. His American contemporaries were perhaps not at all as simplemindedly utilitarian as Tocqueville sketched them; certainly the waves of moral passion against slavery count as evidence for a vigorous public morality. However, he correctly located the long-term problem of American society as how to sustain an active public culture against a powerful drive toward privatism, and he saw clearly that on the outcome of this conflict would hang the fate of American freedom.

:: III

In ways that American founders such as Jefferson and Adams would have understood, Tocqueville argued that the heart of American democracy was active civic association. He observed that through active involvement in common concerns the citizen could overcome the sense of relative isolation and powerlessness resulting from the insecurity of life in an increasingly commercial society. Associations, along with decentralized administration, were to mediate between the individual and the centralized state, providing forums in which opinion could be publicly and intelligently shaped by reference to principles transcending simple self-interest and the subtle habits, learned and passed on, of public initiative and responsibility. Associational life Tocqueville believed to be the best bulwark against the condition he feared most: a society of mutually antagonistic groups and individuals who would easily fall prey to a despot. Intermediate structures might check, pressure, and restrain the tendencies of centralized government to assume more and more administrative control.

What Tocqueville sought, then, was a modern functional equivalent of the differentiated unity of the classical ideal of the *polis*. He thought social differentiation inescapable, since division of labor creates differences among groups in the goals they seek to attain. But he urged that democratic politics must seek to coordinate—and adjust—these differentiations in the interests of equity and the liberty of all. Without those specific loyalties to community and function identified by older religious tradition as the "sense of calling," Tocqueville feared that the individual lost his sense of involvement and worth and, literally, his identity as a citizen. On the other hand, without a sense of belonging to a larger community governed by common laws, which political life provided, local and occupational groups were always prone to an exclusive narrowness antithetical to the universal ideals championed by modern democracy at its best.

If Tocqueville was correct, a vital democracy requires a complex effort to achieve a political community through balancing the relationships among the administrative organization of the state, the private citizen, and the associations that come between individual and state. Tocqueville argued that were the individual to stand alone the centralized state would quickly reduce him to its thrall. The crucial balance must be provided by intermediate structures of social participation such as local government, juries, and civic associations through which individuals can do for themselves collectively what they could not do alone. Association does something more fundamental than accomplish the liberal goal of providing the greatest happiness for the greatest number: it brings into being a political situation qualitatively different from that of individuals confronted by an apparatus of state control. By association, individuals can become citizens and thereby acquire a sense of personal connection and significance unavailable to the depoliticized, purely private person. Through mutual deliberation and joint initiative guided by the public framework of law and search for equity, moral relationships of trust and mutual aid are built up which come to transform the individual into a citizen.

Politics in the genuinely associational sense is, then, more than pursuit of self-interest, since it involves sharing responsibility for acts that create a quality of life different from the mere sum of individual satisfactions. Consequently, Tocqueville could hope that civic participation might make the individual an active, politically aware subject rather than a passive object of state control. For Tocqueville, lack of participation, no matter what its material effects, was humanly degrading and ultimately a manifestation of despotism. In this he was rearticulating the traditional civic-republican notion that human dignity requires the freedom that flourishes only in a context of active civic community. The uneven experience of democratic culture in America since Tocqueville's time has not contradicted this part of his message, though it is an insight American society has never fully absorbed.

In Tocqueville's America, as indeed for most Americans throughout the nineteenth century, the basic unit of association and the practical foundation of both individual dignity and participation was the local community. There a civic culture of individual initiative was nurtured through personal ties inculcated by custom and a widely shared, largely Protestant and Christian religious ethos. Concern for economic betterment was strong but it operated largely within the context of a still functional covenantal concern for the welfare of one's neighbor.

In the town the competitive individualism stirred by commerce was balanced and humanized through the restraining influences of a fundamentally egalitarian ethic of community responsibility. These autonomous small-scale communities were dominated by an active middle class, the classic citizens of a free republic, whose members held similar economic and social positions and whose ranks the less affluent segments of the population aspired, often successfully, to enter. Most men were self-employed and many who worked for another were saving capital to launch themselves on their own. Westward expansion, as Tocqueville noted, reproduced all across the continent this pattern of a decentralized, egalitarian democracy. American citizenship was anchored in the ethos and institutions of the face-to-face community of the town. Its weakness in practice came from the limited moral vision such communities often fostered.

Yet Tocqueville carefully distinguished two forms of socioeconomic organization that differed profoundly from this form of civilization, which he considered basic to American democracy, and that threatened the very possibility of its continued existence. One was the slave society of the South, which not only treated blacks inhumanly but—as Tocqueville, in ways quite similar to Jefferson, noted—degraded whites as well, reducing them to something considerably less than autonomous responsible citizens. The second ominous social form was the industrial factory system that was becoming evident in the Northeast, which concentrated great numbers of poor and dependent workers in the burgeoning mill towns. There, Tocqueville feared, a new form of aristocracy was arising which made owners and managers into petty despots and reduced workers to a condition incompatible with full democratic citizenship. Ironically, the traumatic civil war which destroyed the slave civilization enormously furthered the growth of the industrial structures that so profoundly threatened the original American pattern of decentralized democratic communities.

By the end of the nineteenth century the new economic conditions had fatally unbalanced the community pattern of American life. Assisted by a federal government favoring commercial expansion, new technologies—particularly in transport, communications, and manufacturing—pulled the many quasi-autonomous local societies into a vast national market. The development of this increasingly centralized and economically integrated society created a new class of industrial magnates and the new economic form called the corporation, and it required growth of the structures of central government, thereby steadily sapping the ability of local associations to deal with local problems. Under these conditions the very meaning of the traditional idea of American citizenship was called into question.

One response was to adapt to the new structures of centralized economic power by adopting a career whose rewards are wealth and power rather than any calling that provides status and meaning within a community of complementary callings. This shift, already becoming evident by the mid-nineteenth century, has progressed enormously in the twentieth. Virtually all Americans now depend directly or indirectly for their livelihood, information, and, often, ideas and opinions on great centralized organizations, and they identify themselves more by professional prestige and privilege than by community ties. Increasing uniformity of national life has developed concomitantly with the rise of a national pattern of unequal social segmentation that has replaced the more immediately perceived differentiations of the local community.[10]

Thus individual hopes for betterment have come to focus upon rising through a status ladder of occupations and so, increasingly, upon the progress of the national economy as a whole. Westward migration and the founding of new settlements that could give ever greater numbers of citizens the status of yeoman-farmer have given way to expectations of rising income, higher occupational status, and suburban living, with the expansion of the national economic system having replaced the frontier as the locus of opportunity. In modern American experience, constraints and social discipline such as tax-paying, company loyalties, and professional solidarity have been increasingly justified because they are instrumental to individual security and advancement. Some measure of equality of opportunity seemed the appropriate and "American" way to democratize this new national society, but the focus has been on private economic betterment, not the quality of shared public life.

These tendencies, which bear an all too close resemblance to Tocqueville's description of his fear that an exclusive concern with material betterment would lead America away from free citizenship and toward a form of what he called "soft despotism," have not gone unopposed. Some forms of opposition, like the efforts of the late-nineteenth-century Populists to defend the integ-

10. This description relies on the work of Robert H. Wiebe and Thomas Bender: see Robert Wiebe, *The Search for Order: 1877-1920* (New York: Hill and Wang, 1968); and *The Segmented Society: An Historical Preface to the Meaning of America* (New York: Oxford University Press, 1975); and Thomas Bender, *Community and Social Change in America* (New Brunswick, New Jersey: Rutgers University Press, 1978). The ambiguous nature of the Progressive movement is important in this connection. Progressives, usually middle-class in origin, both advocated a greater "rationalization" of American life through expert managerial planning and sought to reawaken in some new way the old spirit of community and place, which industrial capitalism was destroying.

rity of the local community or the struggle by the Socialist movement of Eugene Debs to redefine the national society, have failed, though even in failure they have given examples of a citizenry that will not passively accept its fate. Other efforts to control the most exploitative tendencies of industrial capitalism—for example, the enactment of health and safety laws, and the regulation of working hours and minimum wages—have been more successful. Significantly, the growth of labor unions has brought some sense of citizenship rights into the workplace. The tendencies toward despotism inherent in profit-oriented bureaucratic corporations have been muted at the bargaining table, where wages, hours, and working conditions as well as grievance procedures have become subject to quasi-political negotiation. With minor exceptions, this has not given workers any role in the direction of the system that employs them, but it has given them some sense of active participation in the conditions of their employment and some protection against the tendency of employers to treat their workers as mere objects of control.

Significant social movements such as the Civil Rights movement and the movement to oppose the Vietnam War have continued to appear even in our recent history. Such movements have mobilized large coalitions of people, who were motivated by a combination of self-interest and a great deal of disinterested civic concern, to a degree of participation in the political process not common in day-to-day political life. That such movements can still make a difference in our society, even though not as quickly or as completely as some would desire, is evidence that the civic republican spirit is still an effective force in American life.

Yet, although the spirit of republican citizenship and the social conditions that support it are by no means gone from American life, there are clear danger signals visible today. The conception of the individual as an "economic animal" maximizing self-interest is certainly not new in our history, but it is less and less tempered by the covenant conception nurtured in local communities and mores. Now, shorn of many of the nurturant values of traditional civic association, the ethos of self-advancement has been able to work itself out with fewer constraints. The result has been a widespread definition of personal worth almost exclusively in terms of competitive success, measured by status and advancement in large organizations embedded in the national economy. In this atmosphere the ideals of loyalty and service based on personal trust and commitment have faltered. Even when the national economy was rapidly expanding and the hope of significant self-advancement was realistic the social consequences were often what we have recently heard described as "moral malaise." Inability to commit oneself to or believe in anything that transcends one's own private interests leads to a weakening of commitment in family and community and to the self-absorption that is sometimes called narcissism.

But difficulties arising from too exclusive a concern with self-betterment have of late been enormously compounded by the gradually dawning knowledge that the cornucopia of plenty is not inexhaustible. Material goods were never shared equitably in America, but while the economy was growing everyone could look forward to an increase in prosperity. But if wealth is not going to grow or is going to grow much more slowly, and our values have become focused on self-interest, then we are on the verge of the classic war of all against all, as each interest-group strives to get to the well first, before it dries up.

We have for a long time turned, not unwisely, to government to regulate the quest for economic aggrandizement. The ideology of radical individualism, with its notion that pursuit of self-interest is the best incentive for a free society, has always required an umpire who will guarantee at least minimal conditions of fairness in the race for material goods. Government has been that umpire and has become increasingly active in that role in recent decades. While privileged individuals and groups have often in principle viewed the role of government as intrusive and even destructive, they have in fact often used its power for their advantage. On the other hand, underprivileged groups have only recently found in government a protector against the worst consequences of coming out less than successful in our competitive economy. The welfare state, with all its inadequacies, has brought not only social stability to a turbulent capitalism but even a measure of justice to people who have been deprived and handicapped by poverty and prejudice.

Our present danger does not come from government as such, or from the entrepreneurial spirit either, for that matter. The danger to our democratic institutions comes, rather, from the declining effectiveness of just those intervening structures, the civic associations of all sorts that serve to mediate between individual and state. It is those intermediate structures that nurture citizenship and provide the best defense against despotism, soft or hard. Without them the state, even when acting benevolently, may encourage a dependence and lack of civic concern that play into the hands of nascent authoritarianism. Particularly when the economic pie is growing slowly and erratically and the privileged are talking about "social discipline" while the deprive feel existent inequalities more keenly since they lack the hope of significant betterment, there is danger that the state may be called upon to solve our problems in the interest of the dominant economic groups even without our traditional sanction of democratic consent.

In the meantime, public cynicism is growing about the peculiarly American politics of liberalism. That tradition of politics, beginning in the New Deal, has both sanctioned the pursuit of economic self-interest in the context of free enterprise and sought to temper it by a degree of income redistribution and expert bureaucratic fine-tuning by the federal government. However, the failures of bureaucratic captialism to meet the problems of inflation, slow growth, and anxiety about energy have engendered widespread public disillusionment in government and business corporations alike. One form of this disillusionment is a growing cynicism and a push to "look out for number one," together with a deepening fear of one's fellow citizens. Such sentiments as these, as classic republican theorists warn, are the preconditions of despotism.

Another response to the failures of the recent pattern of American political and economic life is to look to the possibility of the revival of our democratic civic culture and the social structures, above all the intermediate associations, that nurture it. There are those who view the present necessity to rethink the idea that continuous economic development is the answer to all our problems as an opportunity to recover aspects of our public life that could never be fully absorbed into that pattern. They view the present challenge not with dismay but as a stimulus to become our true selves as a democratic society.

On both the right and the left of the political spectrum there is much talk of intermediate structures. Some use the language of participatory public life simply as a means to attack the growth of "big government" without assessing the social benefits conferred by government and presently provided by no other structure in our society. For such critics the ideal intermediate structure is the business corporation, which they feel should be freed from "government interference." Others who talk about intermediate structures view business corporations as themselves massive structures of bureaucratic power, largely unresponsive to citizen needs and certainly not a forum for civic participation and democratic culture. Or they see business corporations as themselves in need of drastic reform before they can function as truly democratic intermediate structures.[11] At any rate, however important it is to nurture religious, ethnic, neighborhood, and other forms of civic association, the lack of a linkage between these and economic institutions is the key to our present difficulties, and a new way of linking our economic life with our democratic culture is the key to their solution.

This is not the place for programmatic discussion of how to transform our economy into a more democratic and responsible one, but such a development will clearly require a series of experiments with new forms of autonomous or semi-autonomous public enterprise as well as reformed versions of private enterprise if we are to pursue with circumspection the aim of a more democratic economy. Indeed, democratization of our economic institutions, by whatever name it is called, is a key to the revitalization of our mores and our public life. The reconstruction of democratic culture in America, made possible by the crisis in confidence that has overtaken our present system of bureaucratic capitalism, must develop the conditions for a new, shared public authority through a movement for the reform of economic life in the direction variously called *economic democracy, social control of the economy,* or *democratic socialism.*[12] The process must invite the enclaves of neigh-

11. For example, see Gar Alperovitz and Staughton Lynd, *Strategy and Program: Two Essays toward a New American Socialism* (Boston: Beacon Press, 1973). An argument for mediating structures which deemphasizes the nature and structure of the larger political economy is made by Peter L. Berger and Richard J. Neuhaus in *To Empower People: The Role of Mediating Structures in Public Policy* (Washington, D.C.: American Enterprise Institute, 1977).

12. The terminology, still in a highly formative stage, is certainly not the crucial point. However, the widespread American taboo against use of the word *socialism* has for decades truncated discussion of economic possibilities of other than a liberal capitalist form. A revived public philosophy would be very useful in

borly cooperation out from their present defensive position on the periphery of our public life, to join in a larger effort to transform the mainstream institutions into vehicles and expressions of citizenly fellowship. This politics would be a process of mutual education at the same time that it attempts to restructure institutions. It would aim to decentralize where that makes sense, to include in participation through new forms of cooperative enterprise many of those who have been left out, to provide a broadly representative collegial leadership from which executive management can take its cue, and to empower citizens by providing experience in civic life. All this is quite different from a strategy that would "upgrade" the disadvantaged to share the private vision of competitive advancement often promoted by corporate ideology. Rather, the effects of this new movement, already visible in some areas, would be to revitalize the principle of civic association, to strengthen the intermediate structures that make it possible for the individual citizen to maintain his independence and to make his voice heard, and so to reinforce the vitality of our free institutions generally. Moving into the world of tight resources without such a process of civic development would only precipitate a Hobbesian struggle between groups to see who can profit at the expense of whom, a struggle already too evident not only in our present domestic politics but in an increasingly unstable world situation as well.

But a major shift in the organization of our economic life, with all it would entail in our society, cannot be expected as a result of mere technocratic or organizational manipulation or even a new round of interest-group bargaining. So great a change, overcoming not only entrenched power but entrenched ways of thinking, will require a new ordering of the ecology of social relationships.

---

moving us beyond this blockage in national consciousness. The three terms are, respectively, put forward by several significant thinkers on these topics. For *economic democracy* see Tom Hayden, *The American Future: New Visions beyond Old Frontiers* (Boston: South End Press, 1980). Barry Commoner introduced *social control of the economy* in *The Politics of Energy* (New York: Knopf, 1979). Michael Harrington is a long-time proponent of *democratic socialism* in America. See his *Decade of Decision: The Crisis of the American System* (New York: Simon and Schuster, 1980), and see also Martin Chernoy and Derek Shearer, *Economic Democracy: The Challenge of the 1980's* (White Plains, New York: M. E. Sharpe, 1980).

:: IV

Our situation is a difficult one. Liberal culture today finds itself at a grim impasse where its underlying logic of technique and control seems to have overwhelmed the earlier ethos of emancipation. But we have seen repeatedly in earlier analyses that the liberal framework is not all-inclusive or all-pervasive and that contemporary practice and thought in some important aspects point toward different kinds of relationships within society and with nature. Those aspects of contemporary American society do not stand fully formed in opposition to the destructive features of bureaucratic organization and instrumental rationality, however. They will require careful nurture and development if they are to prevail, and that is impossible without both utilizing and importantly transforming the institutional structures of our society. Without a renewal of a public philosophy that enterprise will be even more difficult and unlikely to succeed.

Particularly now, as renewed international competition, both military and economic, is shaping the context for political debate, it is critical that there be more developed articulations of the civic insight. For example, revitalizing and "reindustrializing" the American economy could come to mean real efforts at bringing economics and participatory politics together in dramatic ways, but in the absence of an understanding of their interconnection it will very likely only push them further apart. A reformulated republican consciousness could likewise make a difference in the formation of policies aiming at a more equitable world economic order.

The effort to renew the tradition of civic public philosophy in America can profit from John Dewey's observation that moral theory is "all one with moral insight, and moral insight is the recognition of the relationships at hand."[13] This is a way of describing the basis of public philosophy in practical reason. In fact, given the disarray in which we find ourselves as a nation, a serious public philosophy can hardly help being critical and disturbing as it brings hidden or half-ignored facets of our collective condition to light. But even in this its premise is that it speaks within a

13. John Dewey, "Moral Theory and Practice," in *Early Works of John Dewey* (Carbondale: Southern Illinois University Press, 1972), vol. 3, p. 94.

consensus that affirms the equal right of each person to a moral existence and thus to taking part in the common discussion about how we should live together.

The premise of a responsible public philosophy is thus a social and moral relationship with the members of the society within which one speaks. In one expression this is the republican understanding of mutual interdependency. However, this idea carries the implication that development of a public philosophy through dialogue and consensus among citizens is an historically rare and difficult collective achievement. It is directly involved with and dependent upon the moral culture of the polity. Its fate is tied to that of republican political life and so to the American moral imagination, an insight that gives cause, if not for optimism, then at least for a measure of hope and courage.

Index

Moore, G. E., 96
moral ambiguity, 70
moral authority, 175
moral character, 110-11, 153, 173-74, 181-82
moral consensus, 15-16, 58-60
moral context, economic life's, 37-38
moral development: cognitive stage theories of, 121-48; women's different patterns of, 145-46; in everyday life, 153
moral dignity, 92-97
moral dilemmas, cognitive stage theory tests of, 128-30
moral ecology, 76-77, 81-82, 105-106, 109, 115f, 121
moral education, 130-31, 170f
moral imagination: challenge of, 89, 227; failure of, 118-54
moral insight, 226
moral intuition, 107-109, 112, 119-20
morality, 74-76, 84-89, 94-95, 103-106, 107*n*, 109-17, 135-48, 154
moral knowledge, 68-69
moral life, 126, 153-54
moral norms, lack of shared, 42
moral order, 39, 211-16
moral philosophy, 72-73, 94-97, 106-17, 154
moral principle, 130, 135
moral reasoning, 74-75, 84-88, 95, 110-15, 121-54
moral sciences, 64-69
moral theory, 99-104, 115-16, 119-20
moral tradition, citizenship as rooted in, 54, 179-80
moral values. *See* values
moral virtue, 87*n*, 170
Morris, Robert, 194f, 197
mutuality. *See* common good, the

narcissism, culture of, 157, 222
Native Americans, 202
naturalism, structuralism and, 134-35, 144, 148
natural rights, 62, 70, 72-73
nature (human). *See* human nature
nature (nonhuman), 60-61, 62. *See also* science
neo-conservatives, 25, 159*n*
Neuhaus, Richard J., 224*n*
new consciousness, 17
New Deal, 3, 24f, 186, 188, 192
New Left, 17
night-watchman state, 100f
nihilism, 148f, 153, 163*n*
Nisbet, Robert, 27*n*, 50, 212*n*
nonviolence principle, 146
Nozick, Robert, 14, 33, 94-97, 99-104

obligation, concepts of, 86, 131
optimism, 3, 23
organizations, centralization of, 219-20

paideia, 170f, 174, 180, 183
Paine, Thomas, 192-203
paradigms, 139-41
Parsons, Talcott, 73*n*, 173
participatory democracy, 188
passions, the. *See* human nature
patriotism, American, 160-61
pessimism, 1-2, 4, 52-53
Philadelphia Committee, 196, 199-200
philosophical traditions. *See* civic republicanism; classical tradition; liberalism; *etc.*
philosophy, in American universities, 95-96, 97*n*
phronesis, 66, 106*n*, 111*n*, 171. *See also* prudential reasoning

Designer: Steve Renick
Compositor: Sue Somit/Sallie Wells
Text: Compset 500 Baskerville
Display: Compset 500 Bembo
Printer: Braun-Brumfield, Inc.
Binder: Braun-Brumfield, Inc.